The Constitutional
Foundations of
Intellectual Property

The Constitutional Foundations of Intellectual Property

A Natural Rights Perspective

Randolph J. May

Seth L. Cooper

Carolina Academic Press

Durham, North Carolina

Library of Congress Cataloging-in-Publication Data

May, Randolph J., author.
 The constitutional foundations of intellectual property : a natural rights perspective / Randolph J. May and Seth L. Cooper.
    pages cm
 Includes bibliographical references and index.
 ISBN 978-1-61163-709-0 (alk. paper)
  1. Intellectual property--United States--Philosophy. 2. Constitutional history--United States.. 3. Natural law--United States--Influence. I. Cooper, Seth L., author. II. Title.

 KF2980.M393 2015
 346.7304'8--dc23

                              2015020193

CAROLINA ACADEMIC PRESS
700 Kent Street
Durham, North Carolina 27701
Telephone (919) 489-7486
Fax (919) 493-5668
www.cap-press.com

Printed in the United States of America

Randolph J. May

For my children, Joshua and Brooke, and my grandchildren,
Samantha, Ciaran, Benjamin, and Francis

Seth L. Cooper

For my wife, Gretchen

Contents

Preface   xiii

Introduction   3

An Account of Copyright and Patent Rights Rooted
    in Natural Rights Principles   3
Copyright and Patent Rights in the Framework of
    American Constitutionalism   6
Drawing upon Key Historical Figures, Authorities, and Events   7
A Sketch of the Book's Chapters   9

Chapter 1 · The Constitutional Foundations of Intellectual Property   15

Introduction   15
Government's Purpose: Protecting Natural Rights to
    Life, Liberty, and Property   16
The Natural Rights Basis of Locke's Political Philosophy   18
Locke on the Origin and Broad Meaning of Property   20
Locke in Relation to Other Transmitters of
    Natural Rights Concepts   21
Jeffersonian and Madisonian Adaptations of Lockean
    Natural Rights Concepts   23
Intellectual Property: Safeguarding the Fruits of One's Labor
    in Civil Society   26
Intellectual Property as Constitutional Law   27
Conclusion   28
Sources   28

Chapter 2 · Reasserting the Property Rights Source of
    Intellectual Property   31

Introduction   31

Intellectual and Physical Property Are Both Encompassed Within
Classical Liberalism's Broader Understanding of Property   33
Classical Liberalism's Narrower Understanding of Property   34
Blackstone on Property's Origins in the Laws of Nature
and Laws of Society   35
Intellectual and Physical Property Share the Same Institutional
Role in Defining and Limiting Governmental Power   37
Despite Differences, Intellectual and Physical Property
Share the Same Source   38
A Property Rights Approach to Intellectual Property Reform   39
Conclusion   41
Sources   41

Chapter 3 · Literary Property: Copyright's Constitutional History
and Its Meaning for Today   43

Introduction   43
Webster's State Copyright Quest   44
Virginia's Copyright Law: Webster and Madison
Joined in Alliance   47
Protecting Literary Property: Copyright During the
Articles of Confederation   48
Copyright at the 1787 Constitutional Convention   49
Copyright and Constitutional Ratification   50
Conclusion   51
Sources   51

Chapter 4 · The Constitution's Approach to Copyright and Patent:
Anti-Monopoly, Pro-Intellectual Property Rights   53

Principled Differences Between Government Monopolies
and Individual IP Rights   54
The British Backdrop to American Anti-Monopolistic
Understanding   56
The Anti-Monopolistic Spur to the American Revolution   58
Anti-Monopoly, Pro-IP Rights: The Constitution's Approach
to Copyright and Patent   59
The Constitution's Structural Safeguards Against Monopolies   60
Literary Property and Liberty of the Press: Copyright and
the Free Press Clause   61
Conclusion   64
Sources   64

Chapter 5 · The "Reason and Nature" of Intellectual Property:
    Copyright and Patent in *The Federalist Papers*   67

The Federalist and Its Constitutional Legacy   69
Federalist No. 43 on Congressional Power, Copyright, and Patent   71
Federalist No. 43: Natural Right as the Reasoned Basis for IP Rights   72
    Confusion Surrounding British Common Law Copyright   72
    Explaining Madison's Reference to Common Law Rights
      of Authors   74
Madison's Appeal to the Reason and Nature of IP Rights   76
"Utility to the Union" in *The Federalist*   77
    The Utility to the Union of a Congressional Power
      to Protect IP Rights   77
    The Public Good: Rights of Liberty and Property in
      the Interests of All, According to the Rules of Justice   79
Social Utility Under *The Federalist*'s Natural Rights Framework   81
Conclusion   82
Sources   83

Chapter 6 · Constitutional Foundations of Copyright and Patent
    in the First Congress   85

Introduction   85
The First Congress's Constitutional Precedent-Setting Role   87
Constitutional Credentials of the First Congress's Membership   89
The First Congress as Authority on Constitutional Meaning   89
Copyright and Patent in the Context of the First Congress's
    Critical Agenda   91
Legislation in the First Congress as the Culmination of
    Concerted, Long-Term Efforts   92
First Congress's Record Confirms IP's Fit in the American
    Constitutional Order   93
Basic Principles Prevail over Particulars in Considering
    the First Congress's Precedents   95
The First Presidential Administration's Impact on IP Policy
    in the First Congress   96
The First Congress's Consistency on Copyright and Free Speech   97
Conclusion   100
Sources   100

Chapter 7 · Life, Liberty, and the Protection of Intellectual Property: Understanding IP in Light of Jeffersonian Principles   103

Jefferson's Private Letters on Intellectual Property   105
Jefferson's Exaggerated Opposition to IP and Peripheral Influence
  on Constitutional IP Policy   106
IP Rights in Light of Jefferson's Philosophy of
  Constitutional Government   110
IP in Light of Jefferson's Philosophy of Public Administration   115
Conclusion   117
Sources   118

Chapter 8 · Intellectual Property Rights Under the Constitution's Rule of Law   119

The Rule of Law in the American Constitutional Order   122
IP's Consonance with American Constitutionalism and
  the Rule of Law   127
Rule of Law Implications of IP as a Constitutionally Protected
  Property Right   128
  Due Process of Law   128
  Equal Protection of the Laws   129
  No Takings for Public Use Without Just Compensation   130
  Vested Rights   131
Conclusion   132
Sources   133

Chapter 9 · Reaffirming the Foundations of Intellectual Property Rights: Copyright and Patent in the Antebellum Era   135

The Natural Rights Basis for Private Property in
  the Antebellum Era   138
Antebellum Legal Treatises Reflect Property Rights
  Understanding of IP   143
Antebellum Copyright Jurisprudence Reinforces a
  Property Rights Understanding of IP   145
Antebellum Patent Jurisprudence Reinforces the
  Property Rights Understanding of IP   149
Antebellum Legislation Bolsters Copyright Protections   153
Antebellum Legislation Bolsters Patent Rights Protections   157
Jacksonians Recognized the Constitution's Distinction
  Between Monopolies and IP Rights   159

Conclusion 161
Sources 161

Chapter 10 · Adding Fuel to the Fire of Genius: Abraham Lincoln,
    Free Labor, and the Logic of Intellectual Property 163
The Importance of the Civil War and Reconstruction to an
    Understanding of America's Constitutional Order 166
The Free Labor Logic of Intellectual Property Rights 168
Lincoln and Free Labor 169
Lincoln the Pro-Entrepreneur, Pro-IP Whig 170
Lincoln the Pro-IP Republican 171
Property in Men as an Inversion of Liberty and Self-Ownership 174
"Freedom National" as a Policy Program for Liberty and Property 176
Rolling Back *Dred Scott*'s Rule on Intellectual Property Rights 178
Intellectual Property Rights Under Reconstruction 179
Implications of the Civil War Amendments for
    Intellectual Property Rights 183
Conclusion 183
Sources 184

Bibliographical Essay 187

About the Authors 205

Index 207

Preface

We both consider ourselves lifelong students of the Constitution and its history. But not only students. In the realms in which we toil at the Free State Foundation, a think tank devoted to promoting free market, limited government, and rule of law principles, we strive to defend constitutional rights. And we seek to educate others as to why it is important to defend those rights.

In that regard, a central aim of this book is to defend intellectual property rights and to explain the reason why they are worth vigorously defending. In one sense, of course, intellectual property ("IP") rights should be defended simply by virtue of the fact that, indeed, they *are* rights explicitly secured by the Constitution. Article 1, Section 8, of the Constitution grants Congress the power "To promote the Progress of Science and useful Arts, by securing for limited Times to Authors and Inventors the exclusive Right to their respective Writings and Discoveries." As the reader will discover throughout the chapters in this book, Congress has exercised the power granted by the Constitution many times by adopting successive copyright and patent laws. Indeed, shortly after the Constitution's ratification, the First Congress adopted laws in 1790 to secure and protect both copyrights and patents.

But aside from defending IP rights simply because they are *in and secured by* the Constitution, many of the chapters in the book explicate *why* our Founders thought IP rights sufficiently important that our foundational governing charter should grant Congress the express power to secure them. This book will make amply clear—if the book's title has not done so already—that the Constitution's framers, or at least key ones, considered property rights, including intellectual property rights, to be rooted in the idea of natural rights. As we explain more fully in the Introduction which immediately follows, by "natural right" we mean an inherent right of human nature, that is, a right that belongs to all individuals simply because they are human beings.

Here it is enough to say that the Declaration of Independence, asserting as it does that certain "self-evident" truths are consonant with "the Laws of Nature and of Nature's God," embodies the natural rights approach we embrace in this book. In our view, when the Founders adopted the Constitution in Philadelphia in 1787, and when the American people through their state conventions ratified it, a natural rights perspective was woven into at least part of the fabric of our constitutional inheritance. And, as will be seen, a commitment to the protection of property rights, including intellectual property rights, is fully consistent with—indeed, required by—a proper understanding of our constitutional order and the obligations of civil society established by such order. Absent acting to secure IP rights, the government would fail in its principal objective of securing what the Declaration of Independence calls our "unalienable Rights," among them "Life, Liberty, and Pursuit of Happiness."

In an important sense, this volume is, in part, an intellectual history of the idea that intellectual property rights are at their core inalienable, natural rights deserving of recognition and protection. This intellectual history stretches from John Locke in the seventeenth century to Abraham Lincoln and Reconstruction in the nineteenth—which, by the way, leaves room for further work to carry the endeavor forward. John Locke, the prominent seventeenth century English philosopher, was a major influence on the thinking of our Founders. As Locke explained in a famous passage in his landmark *Second Treatise of Government*:

> [E]very man has a property in his own person: this no body has any right to but himself. The labour of his body, and the work of his hands, we may say, are properly his. Whatsoever then he removes out of the state that nature hath provided, and left it in, he hath mixed his labour with, and joined to it something that is his own, and thereby makes it his property.

Stated plainly, Locke understood each person to possess a natural right to the fruits of his or her own labor which the civil society established by government was obligated to protect.

Now flash forward all the way to Abraham Lincoln's time. While Lincoln was fonder of quoting America's Founders than he was of Locke, it is difficult to miss the Lockean philosophical bent in Lincoln's own words, for example, when he said, "each individual is naturally entitled to do as he pleases with himself and the fruit of his labor." It is a short leap from this expression of the idea of a natural right to ownership in the property arising from an individual's own labor to Lincoln's sentiment praising patent laws on the basis that they add "the fuel of interest to the fire of genius." Or, to the same effect, in the more colloquial Lincoln: "I always thought the man that made the corn should eat the corn."

We would like to think that a book such as this one, exploring as it does the foundations of important rights secured by the Constitution, is always timely and important if it brings to bear some fresh insights concerning the subject matter. And especially if it does so in a way that scholars, policymakers, and the general public alike will find useful and accessible. But, frankly, while the historical period covered by the book only runs through the age of Lincoln, we acknowledge that one real impetus for writing the book arises from the revolutionary influences and impacts of today's digital age.

Without the need for elaboration here, the digital revolution, and the new technologies and business models that it has spawned, undeniably have created new platforms for authors, artists, inventors, and other creators to use to distribute their works and products to the public. In the age of the Internet, these digital platforms allow for such distribution, in most cases, to occur more quickly (virtually instantaneously), more widely (nearly everywhere across the globe), and more economically (often at a near-zero cost) than at any prior time. Overall, the benefits to individuals and society, both social and economic, resulting from the digital revolution and the rise of the Internet are incontrovertibly enormous.

But there are also dark sides to the rise of the Internet and other digital technologies as distribution platforms—and one of them is the ongoing problem of the piracy of a substantial amount of intellectual property. By most accounts, the economic losses from the theft of intellectual property, mostly property subject to copyright, run into billions of dollars per year. It is outside the purpose of this book to address the size and scope of the well-documented piracy problem. But it most assuredly is within the book's purpose—indeed, it is a central aim—to provide a counter to the contemporary "downgrading" or denigration of IP rights in some quarters simply because, it seems, so much information is now readily available on the Internet and can be so easily copied and distributed and recopied and redistributed, *ad infinitum*. This diminishment of IP rights is made easier, if not generated, at least in some minds, perhaps even in the subconscious of some minds, by sloganeering of the oft-repeated "information wants to be free" variety. For digital age dilettantes who find the "information wants to be free" mantra appealing, it is but a short step to convince themselves that theft of intellectual property online is no big deal. Or, worse still, that it is not really theft at all.

But this "IP theft is no big deal" way of thinking represents a very troubling development because it facilitates an unmooring of the protection of intellectual property from its constitutional foundations. The mode of thinking that somehow views IP rights as less deserving of protection than other rights the Constitution authorizes to be secured denigrates not only IP rights but the larger constitutional order. We would be remiss if we did not observe, with some dismay, that many who otherwise proclaim their devotion to constitutionalism and protection of individual rights somehow blithely put IP rights in a different category, less deserving of protection.

So, at bottom, we hope this volume will prove useful to those who want to understand the constitutional foundations of intellectual property and to those who wish to educate others. It should prove especially informative to those who wish to understand the natural rights perspective that, in our view, is integral to a proper appreciation of the foundational principles that are pertinent to IP rights protection. We believe that readers, whether academics, students, policymakers, or just ordinary citizens, will find the book not only useful and informative, but interesting as well, with its blend of history, biography, philosophy, and jurisprudence.

We wish to acknowledge the efforts of the Free State Foundation's Kathee Baker for her excellent assistance throughout the preparation of this manuscript. Kathee's labors range from the more mundane typing and formatting to proofreading and editorial assistance, all tasks crucial to making this a book of which we are proud. As always, Kathee's assistance has been rendered not only without complaint, but with good cheer, and for that we are grateful. We also thank Free State Foundation staff member Michael Horney for his editorial assistance.

Finally, we are grateful for the expert assistance of all those at Carolina Academic Press, without whom this book could not have been completed in such a professional manner. Bringing a book from the idea stage to publication date is always an arduous process, even if a labor of love. Having Carolina Academic Press as a publisher lessens the ardor, leaving more time for the love.

Randolph J. May
Seth L. Cooper

Rockville, Maryland
June 2015

The Constitutional
Foundations of
Intellectual Property

Introduction

An Account of Copyright and Patent Rights Rooted in Natural Rights Principles

This book presents an account of copyright and patent rights as unique types of property rights in American constitutionalism that are ultimately rooted in principles of natural rights. At the outset, it is useful to set forth our understanding of certain key concepts and terminology that are central to the presentation of our ideas.

We use the term "natural right" to mean an inherent right of human nature—a right that belongs to all individuals simply because they are human beings. We conceive of natural rights as derived from and consistent with abstract principles of truth and justice—or what the Declaration of Independence calls "the laws of nature or Nature's God." That is, natural rights are discoverable by reasoning from what the Declaration calls truths that are "self-evident."

By "copyright" we mean the exclusive right of an author in his or her own original writings. It includes the exclusive right to publish copies of original written works, license their commercial use, and to reap any resulting financial returns. Copyright may be obtained in creative works such as books, charts, dramatic plays, engravings, motion pictures, and musical compositions. And by "patent right" we mean the exclusive right of an inventor in his or her original invention, including the exclusive right to manufacture replicas, license their commercial use, and to reap any rewards.

We use the term "property right" to refer to the exclusive ownership of anything to which a person attaches value, including the right of possessing, using, and disposing of it. We use the term "intellectual property" to refer to the ownership of intangible and non-physical goods that are derived from a person's creative activity. For purposes of this book, "intellectual property rights" collectively describe both copyright and patent rights. Other types of intellectual property are not addressed.

The account of copyright and patent rights presented in this book rests upon an argument that reasons from first principles. This account also relies upon the intellectual background, authorities, and history of intellectual property rights in the United States. The initial premise of that argument is that every person has a natural right to the fruits of his or her own labors. The product or expression of a person's creative activity—or resulting mixture of a person's labor with his or her resources to which he or she attaches value— is that person's own by right of original acquisition and first possession. We consider it a self-evident proposition, rooted in the unique rights-bearing nature of human beings, that one person cannot rightfully be deprived of what he or she has earned by force or fraud committed by another person. This natural right necessarily includes the fruits of a person's intellectual labors, such as their writings or inventions.

An accompanying foundational premise is that it is a primary purpose of government to protect every person's right to the fruits of his or her own labors through laws protecting private property. That is, government is obligated to secure the basic rights that all people possess by nature through the enforcement of general, equally applied rules regarding the acquisition and enjoyment of private property. Property laws extend and modify the scope of rights protections in order to facilitate the enjoyment of such rights consistent with the equal rights of all people. By necessity, property laws necessarily depend upon prudential calculations tied to social circumstances. But the core of every person's right to the fruits of that person's labors is unalienable and not surrendered to government.

Our conclusion that government should provide copyright and patent rights protection to authors and inventors, including exclusive rights—for a certain period of time—follows from these premises. Property laws should protect indefinitely the rights that authors hold in their original manuscripts and that inventors hold in their prototypes. By the same token, authors and inventors should enjoy perpetual property rights in any copies or reproductions of their creations that they keep within their respective possession. Importantly, authors and inventors should also be entitled to exclusive rights in all proceeds resulting from public sale and use of reproductions of authored works and inventions.

The just claim of authors and inventors to such proceeds is grounded in the basic premise that one should be able to reap what one has sown. But the claim to proceeds also reflects the social context of property rights and the reciprocal premise that one should not be able to reap what another has sown.

By virtue of the labors and expenses incurred by authors and inventors in bringing their works and discoveries to commercial markets for public consumption, authors and inventors are deserving of reaping the financial returns that might result. At the very least, authors and inventors are more deserving of such proceeds than free riders who have contributed no original creation or useful discovery to society. Indeed, potential rewards resulting from exclusive rights in proceeds provide a critical incentive for would-be authors and inventors to expend intellectual, material, and financial resources in the pursuit of works of art and discoveries intended for public enjoyment. Creativity and discovery may fairly be considered goods in and of themselves, and in many instances human beings may have ample incentive to create and discover for their own sake. However, protections for exclusive rights in proceeds expand the opportunity for authors and inventors to pursue their chosen callings and make more attractive the often laborious pursuit of creativity and discovery.

Copyrights and patent rights are concepts that presuppose a civil society existing under a government of laws. Although property is necessarily rooted in the natural right that all people possess to the fruits of their labors, and intellectual property rooted in the rights of authors and inventors to the fruits of their mental labors, we understand that property law systems must be considered in the contexts of social institutions adjusted to various circumstances, including historical precedents, technological developments, plausibility of enforceability, and costs relative to benefits. In this regard, we do not contend that the justness, incentives, or efficacy of protections for exclusive rights in proceeds to copyrighted works or patented inventions holds indefinitely. This owes largely to the unique features of intellectual property rights as the particular expressions of ideas, to free speech and free enterprise commitments, and to the shortness of lifespans enjoyed by authors, inventors, and their respective children relative to eternity. Therefore, the social context of intellectual property is also reflected in the limited terms of the rights that authors and inventors should enjoy to the exclusive proceeds of their works and inventions.

For that matter, we believe no definitive principle can be ascertained to fix, once and for all, the time period in which authors and inventors should enjoy exclusive rights to the proceeds of their creations and inventions. But this is not to say there is nothing to guide decision-making concerning terms for copyright and patent protections. Here again, the link to every person's natural right to the fruit of their labors provides the necessary grounds to justify copyright and patent rights in proceeds. From that starting point, prudential calculations tied to circumstances should be consulted and periodically reviewed in establishing terms for protections.

Copyright and Patent Rights in the Framework of American Constitutionalism

The general considerations contained in the argument summarized above find more particularized expression in the principles and history of American constitutionalism. Indeed, the central aim of this book is to defend the legitimacy and logic of copyright and patent rights within the framework of the American constitutional order.

It is our contention that the natural rights perspective on intellectual property offered above is consistent with classical liberal concepts concerning the rights of man and responsibilities of government as expounded by thinkers such as John Locke and James Madison. And this perspective is consistent with the ideals expressed in the Declaration of Independence, reflected in common law precedents at the time of American Independence, and embodied in pre-constitutional legislative precedents in the newly-independent United States. In short, the intellectual and historical backdrop in which the Constitution of 1787 was adopted and ratified regarded copyrights and patent rights as forms of private property that are rooted in the natural rights of authors and inventors to secure the fruits of their labors.

In examining the ideological fabric of the American constitutionalism at the nation's founding, historians have variously traced the intellectual lineage through four respective thought systems, namely: (1) natural law or natural rights theories; (2) British common law jurisprudence; (3) civil republicanism or the Commonwealth Men's tradition; (4) and dissenting Protestant theology. This book focuses on natural rights thinking, but it also draws upon insights from British common law. This is not to deny the influence of other thought systems in early America. But we believe that natural rights thinking and insights drawn from British common law are the most relevant to understanding the meaning and place of copyrights and patents in American constitutionalism.

More to the point, this understanding of copyrights and patent rights as property rights rooted in natural rights was embodied in America's written Constitution. As our nation's authoritative charter, the Constitution allocates the powers of the federal government, establishes federal and state relationships, and supplies the basic requirements for the protection of life, liberty, and property under the rule of law. Article I, Section 8, Clause 8 of the Constitution—the Intellectual Property or IP Clause—grants Congress the power "To promote the Progress of Science and useful Arts, by securing for limited Times to Authors and Inventors the exclusive Right to their respective Writings and Discoveries." The IP Clause makes copyrights and patent rights a unique area in which the federal government—rather than the states—is expressly charged with protecting private property rights. Our examination thus excludes other forms of intellectual property, such as trademarks and trade secrets, which the Constitution does not expressly address. As will be seen, forms of intellectual property are readily conformable to the key components of the Constitution's rule of law.

The timeframe that is the focus of this book extends through the first century of our nation's existence, dating from the Declaration of Independence through the Civil War era. During that span, regard for copyrights and patent rights as constitutionally recognized property rights grounded in natural rights was widely reiterated in public discussions, legal advocacy, judicial interpretations, legislative pronouncements, and executive actions. American constitutionalism's embodiment of a natural rights perspective toward intellectual property shaped the development and expansion of copyright and patent right protections up through the time of the Declaration's Centennial Celebration.

Drawing upon Key Historical Figures, Authorities, and Events

As readers will surmise, a basic presupposition of this book is that the Constitution provides the legitimate and authoritative framework for our federal government's powers, for its relationship to the states, and for protection of fundamental individual rights, including life, liberty, and property. Another presupposition of this book is that the Constitution properly should be interpreted and considered in light of its original understanding—that is, the Constitution should be viewed according to the meaning of the written text as understood by those who adopted, ratified, and debated its provisions in the public square. The Constitution's written text should control the exercise of government power. Moreover, the fundamental principles and ideals of American constitutionalism—including those stated in the Declaration of Independence—offer important guidance when applying constitutional provisions to contemporary factual circumstances. Therefore, our exploration of the constitutional foundations of copyrights and patent rights is undertaken in light of the written text and the broader principles and ideals that stand behind the text.

At its core, our case for the constitutional legitimacy and importance of copyrights and patents from a natural rights perspective is an appeal to first principles, not an appeal to history. This book does not attempt a comprehensive historical survey of intellectual property rights in America. But we undoubtedly draw upon key historical figures, authorities, and events that illuminate the constitutional foundations of intellectual property.

History also offers a compelling and accessible introduction to the meaning and place of intellectual property rights in American constitutionalism. The contributions of figures such as John Locke, James Madison, Noah Webster, Daniel Webster, Abraham Lincoln, and more are unquestionably crucial to the establishment and development of copyrights and patent rights in American constitutionalism. Those figures likewise remain a point of reference for many Americans. By connecting constitutional concepts of copyrights and patents to the likes of Locke, Madison, the Websters, and Lincoln, we offer readers a familiar starting place from which to approach these concepts and to grasp their pedigree.

In presenting a case for copyright and patent rights from first principles, this book therefore aims to move the basics of intellectual property rights from the area of technical or policy expertise to the realm of common-sense constitutionalism—to "We the People." Skilled technical knowledge may be necessary to grasp adequately some of the intricate facets of copyright and patent administration or complex licensing arrangements. But the basic meaning and place of copyrights and patents rights in the American constitutional order may be comprehended by any elected official, public policy analyst, or citizen who is so interested.

Our aim is not to meticulously rebut or critique any specific criticisms by intellectual property experts offered over the last several years. The primary aim of this book is to offer our own affirmative case. But we make this case with the basic conviction that the constitutional legitimacy and importance of copyrights and patent rights are widely unappreciated, or at least underappreciated. It is our sense that the foundations of intellectual property rights have been subject to increasing attacks, including attacks premised upon the idea that such rights are mere legal conventions that may be readily curtailed or even rescinded. As will be seen, we maintain that such attacks on copyrights and patent rights are unfounded and ought to be rejected.

We hope that this book contributes to public understanding of intellectual property and ultimately deepens respect for the constitutional legitimacy and importance of copyrights and patents. In presenting a natural rights perspective, we offer a viewpoint that is often overlooked in 21st century considerations of intellectual property. A natural rights grounding for copyrights and patent rights undoubtedly diverges from more utilitarian or pragmatic defenses of intellectual property that have been ably advanced in recent years by such eminent scholars as Richard Epstein, Ronald Cass, and Keith Hylton. While our respective accounts may differ, we nonetheless commend their scholarship for the many helpful insights they offer regarding intellectual property issues. We similarly commend the scholarship of Adam Mossoff and Mark Schultz to anyone who is interested in better understanding these issues. Particularly to the extent that a natural rights perspective countenances a critical role for prudential judgments based on existing circumstances in shaping the outer contours of protectable intellectual property rights, we believe that the viewpoints of those scholars are in many respects parallel to our own. Rather than dwell on differing conceptual underpinnings, our preferred approach is to offer a natural rights perspective on copyrights and patent rights that can stand alongside more utilitarian or pragmatic perspectives and make common cause in defense of intellectual property rights.

Because the focus of this book is on the constitutional foundations of copyright and patent rights, we do not address contemporary public policy issues or debates about copyright or patent reform. We do not expect the principled considerations explored here to yield a set of specific answers to current legislative, regulatory, or judicial controversies or disputes. Rather, our purpose is to bring to light those foundational principles of copyright and patent rights that should inform future reform efforts and guide the pursuit of solutions to such disputes.

A Sketch of the Book's Chapters

The chapters that follow were originally published as separate essays as part of the Free State Foundation's *Perspectives from FSF Scholars* series. They have been revised, mostly modestly, in preparing for the publication of this book. Each chapter contains an introductory section that summarizes the chapter's contents as well as a brief conclusion. In addition to a list of "Sources" at the end of each chapter, an extensive Bibliographical Essay in narrative form at the back of the book briefly discusses authorities cited in each chapter and offers insightful suggestions for further reading. Together, the "Sources" cited at the end of the chapters and the narrative Bibliographic Essay will provide scholars, students, policymakers, and lay readers with the authorities upon which we principally have relied in researching and writing the material presented in the book.

Although there is some overlap in the content of certain chapters, this is primarily attributable to the fact that the chapters are of two basic types that mutually reinforce one another. Certain chapters are organized primarily around critical conceptual aspects of copyrights and patent rights related to American constitutionalism. Other chapters are organized primarily around significant historical figures, authorities, and events that shed light on the constitutional foundations of copyrights and patent rights. But this dichotomy should not be viewed too strictly. As the reader will discover, several chapters certainly mix elements of the conceptual with discussion of historical figures and events. After all, this is the way history is made and understood, including, of course, the history of ideas.

Chapter 1, which serves as the fountainhead for the rest of the book, introduces both foundational conceptual principles upon which intellectual property rights rest and key historical figures. We consider the classical liberal political philosophy that was a formative influence on the framers and ratifiers of the U.S. Constitution. This philosophy, particularly as espoused by the 17th century philosopher John Locke, defined "property" broadly to include one's person, one's faculties, and the fruits of one's labor. And it regarded protection of property as the central purpose of government. Chapter 1 succinctly describes how Lockean natural rights philosophical premises, as understood and adopted by our nation's Founding Fathers, confirm the status of copyrights and patents as genuine forms of property, on par with real or personal property.

Chapter 2 defends copyrights and patent rights as unique forms of property rights. As we explain, classical liberal philosophy had a two-track understanding of property. In addition to its broad meaning, "property" also had a narrower meaning. This narrower meaning referred to the rights of persons in the actual productions of their labors or their actual possessions. The existence of rights of property in this narrower sense depended upon civil laws. While not synonymous with natural rights, this narrower understanding of property rights nonetheless maintained a link to natural rights. Intellectual property also fits within classical liberal philosophy's narrower definition of property. Thus, we briefly describe how civil laws expand and create new forms of property, including intellectual property, thereby facilitating the enjoyment of natural rights. The dependence of copyright and patent rights upon civil laws in no way diminishes their status as genuine property rights, since other forms of property rights similarly depend upon civil laws for protection. Indeed, the classical liberal understanding of property includes things both tangible and intangible, and no persuasive reason exists for excluding intangibles from the category of property. Moreover, property plays a critical institutional role in defining and limiting the powers of government by securing individual freedom and promoting individual initiative. Both intellectual property and physical property partake of that role. In sum, whether made wittingly or unwittingly, attacks on intellectual property are in large measure attacks on property itself.

Next, Chapter 3 spotlights the alliance between Noah Webster—"The Father of Copyright"—and James Madison—"The Father of the Constitution"— in securing protection for copyright in the newly independent states, and, ultimately, in the U.S. Constitution. Webster and Madison's collaboration advanced a public understanding of copyright as a form of "literary property," grounded in a person's basic right to the fruits of his or her own labor. That understanding and grounding should inform our reading of the IP Clause and should continue to guide copyright policy today.

In Chapter 4, we defend copyrights and patent rights from claims that intellectual property rights are illegitimate government-conferred monopolies or that they are contrary to the anti-monopolistic outlook of America's Founders. Government-conferred monopolies over commerce, trade, and occupations are, in fact, essentially anathema in the American constitutional order. Indeed, the Founding Founders held a generally anti-monopolistic outlook. But, significantly, at the same time they supported limited protections for copyright and patent, placing the power in Congress to establish those protections into the fundamental law of the land. At the time of the nation's founding, critical differences between odious monopolies and individual intellectual property rights were perceived. A property rights approach to copyrights and patent rights ties limited protections to the creation of specific literary works and inventions. By its mode of operation, a property rights approach respects the freedom of all to create and invent without geographical or occupational barriers to entry.

Chapter 5 considers copyrights and patent rights from the constitutional viewpoint expressed in *The Federalist Papers*. The Constitution's IP Clause is briefly addressed in *Federalist No. 43*. An examination of that passage in light of other *Federalist Paper* essays and contemporary writings by James Madison reveals a rich understanding of the nature and place of copyrights and patents in the U.S. constitutional order. In subtle and succinct fashion, *Federalist No. 43* traces copyright and patent back to an individual's natural right to the fruits of his or her own labor. As *Federalist No. 43* points out, securing an individual's IP rights, consistent with the rules of justice, also furthers the public good by incentivizing further investments and discoveries that promote the "progress of science and useful arts." *Federalist No. 43*'s passage regarding the IP Clause also describes the usefulness to the Union of a congressional power for protecting copyrights and patent rights and, by contrast, it points to the relative inability of the states separately to provide the necessary safeguards for those rights.

The Federalist's insight into constitutional meaning extends far beyond a reading of the IP Clause, of course. Some scholars say that *The Federalist Papers* are an even better source for understanding the political science that stands behind the Constitution than they are a source for the meaning of the Constitution's textual provisions. To an important degree, therefore, *Federalist No. 43* informs the entirety of our book's examination of the constitutional foundations of copyrights and patent rights. We cite to it liberally in several chapters.

The focus of Chapter 6 is the significance of the First U.S. Congress to the meaning and place of copyrights and patent rights in American constitutionalism. The so-called "Constitutional Congress" that met between 1789 and 1791 passed a series of momentous measures that still shape the contours of American constitutionalism, including the Bill of Rights. That the most important Congress in American history included the first Copyright and Patent Acts in its legislative agenda suggests its members found intellectual property rights essential to the new nation's economic, artistic, and technological progress. The fact that President George Washington signed them into law is also indicative of a consensus regarding the legitimacy and efficacy of intellectual property rights. Equally critical, the First Congress's securing of copyrights and patent rights amidst its other constitution-implementing business bolsters the conclusion that intellectual property rights fit within the basic logic of American constitutionalism as understood by the Founders.

No book on intellectual property rights in American constitutionalism would be complete without considering Thomas Jefferson. This we do in Chapter 7, supplying something of a backstory to events recounted in the preceding chapters and answering what might be deemed a natural rights counter-perspective on copyrights and patent rights. Jefferson's primary contribution to American constitutionalism was in shaping the American philosophical understanding of the nature and purpose of government in the Revolutionary Era. But a "Jeffersonian mythology" has overstated his role in shaping the constitutional contours of patent and copyright protection. To the extent Jefferson expressed anti-IP views in private letters during America's founding period, we deem them ultimately unpersuasive and hardly influential with respect to the Constitution that was drafted and ratified while he was away in France. Nearer to the end of his time abroad, Jefferson appeared somewhat reconciled to the Constitution's IP Clause and its purpose. And as both Washington's Secretary of State and as President, Jefferson oversaw the implementation and even the expansion of copyright and patent protections. Just as significantly, we reiterate in Chapter 7 that copyright and patent rights fit within the conceptual framework for limited government and protection of individual rights eloquently espoused by Jefferson.

Chapter 8 addresses rule of law implications of the Constitution's recognition of copyrights and patent rights as private property rights. The rule of law is an essential attribute of a free and just society. In theory and in practice, intellectual property rights are readily conformable to the key components of the rule of law as well as to the unique institutional context for their application within American constitutionalism. This chapter explains how copyrights and patent rights accord with the structural roles assigned to the branches of government in order to limit and control the exercise of government power. It also addresses some basic rule of law implications for intellectual property rights related to various individual rights provisions of the Constitution, such as due process, equal protection, and vested rights protections.

Conceptually, Chapter 8 is sequel to Chapter 2. But its survey of the rule of law ranges from the contributions of classical liberal philosophers and British common law jurists to American constitutional insights developed in the late 18th and 19th centuries. Accordingly, the chapter finds a fitting place next to our treatment of intellectual property rights in the Antebellum Era.

In Chapter 9 we explore how American constitutional concepts of copyrights and patent rights were reinforced and expanded during the time period between the War of 1812 and the Civil War. Following in the thought paths of Founding era predecessors, prominent Antebellum era thinkers overwhelmingly regarded copyrights and patents in light of natural rights and property rights principles. As a result, the Antebellum era was a period of advancement for the protection of IP rights. Prominent law writers such as Chancellor James Kent and Justice Joseph Story characterized copyrights and patents as private property acquired by an individual's intellectual labors. Antebellum era decisions by the Supreme Court and lower courts developed legal doctrines for protecting and ascertaining the scope of intellectual property rights. Importantly, Daniel Webster—known as the "Defender of the Constitution"—also defended copyrights and patent rights in his capacities as orator, constitutional lawyer, and statesman of the Antebellum era. Indeed, congressional and presidential actions provided parallel reinforcement and expansion of copyrights and patent rights.

Finally, Chapter 10 analyzes copyrights and patents in light of the impact of the sectional conflict, Civil War, and Reconstruction Amendments on American constitutionalism. The significance and permanency of change to the nation's fundamental law formally achieved through Civil War and the Reconstruction Amendments to the Constitution makes it an essential reference point for any analysis of constitutional powers and rights. Antislavery thought concerning "free labor" offers a logical and compelling account for protection of intellectual property rights. Our analysis therefore draws upon free labor ideology, particularly as expressed in the political philosophy, constitutional thought, and actions of Abraham Lincoln. The free labor concept held that a person has a natural right to the fruits of his or her own labor. And, significantly, Lincoln himself linked the concept of free labor to intellectual property rights.

Chapter 10 also considers the sectional crisis and Civil War as a clash over the Constitution's relationship to property rights. Antislavery thinkers such as

Lincoln rejected the concept of "property in men" that rivals contended either was expressly or implicitly affirmed in the Constitution. We observe that the "Freedom National" program—little remembered today—informed Lincoln administration policy, effectively settling that free blacks would be issued copyrights and patents. And by virtue of Congress's adoption of legislation expanding copyrights and patent rights contemporaneously with its passage of the Reconstruction Amendments, we conclude that intellectual property rights were conceptually consistent with the antislavery principles and views of property that were vindicated by the Union victory and that influenced those amendments to the Constitution.

The foregoing description of the book's individual chapters offers a taste of what's to come. Our hope is that, considered as a whole, at the very least the book will serve to stimulate discussion and debate among scholars, students, policymakers, and interested citizens concerning the constitutional legitimacy and importance of copyrights and patents. Beyond that objective, if the book deepens the respect of the reader for the constitutional legitimacy of intellectual property rights, and for American constitutionalism more generally, then we will consider our efforts to have been all that we possibly could have envisioned and hoped for when we began our journey.

Chapter 1

The Constitutional Foundations of Intellectual Property

Introduction

Intellectual property (IP) protection is indispensable to enabling and advancing a healthy and vibrant digital age economy. This reflects the indispensability of property protection in general to enabling and advancing overall economic prosperity. As innovation and value increasingly take intangible form, securing intellectual property rights becomes ever more critical to fostering the creation and marketing of goods and services to consumers. To this end, the need to prevent the improper expropriation of value created by authors and inventors makes enforceable systems of copyright and patent essential.

Long before the digital age began, intellectual property rights were secured in the U.S. Constitution's so-called Intellectual Property (IP) Clause. Article I, Section 8, Clause 8 provides: "The Congress shall have Power ... To promote the Progress of Science and useful Arts, by securing for limited Times to Authors and Inventors the exclusive Right to their respective Writings and Discoveries."

For that matter, the foundations for intellectual property predate the Constitution. Classical liberal political philosophy supplied a logical framework and reference point for the framers and ratifiers of the Constitution. According to this philosophy, especially as exemplified by the works of John Locke, free governments are established by social compact to protect persons' natural rights to life, liberty, and property. Classical liberal philosophy defined "property" broadly to mean all of a person's rights, including everything for which a person labors and to which he or she attaches value. Put differently, according to classical liberal doctrine, property encompassed one's person, one's faculties, and the fruits of one's labor.

Copyright and patent fit within classical liberal philosophy's broad meaning of property. That is, natural rights premises, as understood and adopted by James Madison and other of our Founders, confirm the status of copyrights and patents as genuine forms of property. According to the logic of natural rights, intellectual property is on par with real or personal property.

The Constitution's Intellectual Property Clause is premised on natural rights or Lockean philosophical precepts. By its terms it expressly recognizes the exclusive rights of authors and inventors, for limited times, as part of the fundamental law of the land. Putting copyrights and patents on a constitutional footing secures the legitimacy of intellectual property from spurious attacks. Increasingly in fashion in some circles are dubious claims that intellectual property is not property at all, or that somehow it must be "reconstructed" on different analytical grounds. But such supposed "reconstruction" of intellectual property is inconsistent with fundamental principles concerning our rights that are firmly embodied in the American constitutional order grounded in classical liberal principles.

Government's Purpose:
Protecting Natural Rights to
Life, Liberty, and Property

The U.S. Constitution is the defining document of the American constitutional order. After all, American constitutionalism uniquely insists upon the primacy of a written constitution. Yet, for all the Constitution's preamble, grant of limited powers, division of powers between branches, definition of relationships to and between state governments, protections for individual rights, and provisions for formal amendment, the written Constitution contains only a basic framework for a working government. The Constitution's drafting work, ratification, and initial implementation all took place in light of an intellectual backdrop of philosophical ideals, historical understandings, and legal doctrines.

In *Federalist No. 39*, James Madison maintained that the Constitution was premised on "fundamental principles of the revolution." He similarly asserted in *Federalist No. 43* that its authority was derived from "the transcendent law of nature and of nature's God."

The Constitution dates its own completion in Convention at the twelfth year of "the Independence of the United States of America." And, to be sure, the Declaration of Independence contains a brief expression of philosophical ideals that formed a critical part the Constitution's intellectual backdrop:

> We hold these truths to be self-evident, that all men are created equal,
> that they are endowed by their Creator with certain unalienable Rights,

that among these are Life, Liberty and the pursuit of Happiness.—
That to secure these rights, Governments are instituted among Men,
deriving their just powers from the consent of the governed,—That
whenever any Form of Government becomes destructive of these ends,
it is the Right of the People to alter or to abolish it, and to institute new
Government, laying its foundation on such principles and organizing its powers in such form, as to them shall seem most likely to effect their Safety and Happiness.

The document's principal drafter, Thomas Jefferson, wrote in an 1825 letter to
Henry Lee that "the object of the Declaration of Independence" was "[n]ot to
find out new principles, or new arguments, never before thought of ... but to
place before mankind the common sense of the subject." Jefferson added, "all
its authority rests then on the harmonizing sentiments of the day, whether expressed in conversation, in letters, printed essays, or in the elementary books
of public right, as Aristotle, Cicero, Locke, Sidney, etc."

Thus, the Constitution, like the Declaration, was the product of American understanding of philosophical ideals about government powers and individual rights. That inherited understanding was also modified in light of
colonial experience and practical circumstances. But it was more than historical backdrop. The Declaration endures as an expression of defining principles to guide the course of American constitutionalism. Hence, Abraham
Lincoln's 1857 pronouncement of the Declaration as a "standard maxim for
free society" to be "constantly looked to, constantly labored for" still res-
onates today.

Reduced to its most basic components, the political philosophy of natural
rights prevailing at the time of the American Revolution and at the adoption
of the Constitution recognized that free governments are established by a social compact based on the consent of all persons acting through a majority of
the whole for the purpose of securing their equal natural rights to life, liberty,
and property. Stated differently, the central purpose of government is to protect rights of "property"—conceived broadly to mean a person's property in
all of their rights and everything for which they have labored and to which
they attach value.

Thus, a natural rights approach to the origins and purpose of government
as well as its relationship to property rights is ultimately based on abstract
principles rather than on historical authorities or precedents. Even so, the exploration and articulation of those principles by historically significant philosophers and polemicists are important to consider insofar as they reflect the same
basic principles understood and applied by the Founding Fathers.

The Natural Rights Basis
of Locke's Political Philosophy

John Locke, the prominent 17th century English philosopher, articulated the classic liberal theory of natural rights. Locke was a patron of Whig opposition leader Anthony Ashley-Cooper. He apparently began composing his *Two Treatises of Government* (1689) during the so-called "Exclusion Crisis," in which the British House of Commons attempted to pass a bill excluding James II from being eligible to ever ascend the throne then occupied by his older brother, Charles II. Locke and others faced personal danger for their unsuccessful opposition to the Stuart royal dynasty, particularly when Charles II died and James II succeeded him. Cooper and Locke both spent time in exile. The abdication of James II and ascension of William of Orange to the British throne in the Glorious Revolution of 1688 allowed for Locke's safe return. Locke's subsequently edited his *Two Treatises* for anonymous publication, suggesting in a preface that it was written to justify the Glorious Revolution.

Locke's *First Treatise of Government* was a critical response to arguments for the divine right of kings contained in Sir Robert Filmer's posthumously published *Patriarcha* (1680). Locke's *Second Treatise of Government* presented a theory of civil government, the authority of which rests upon principles of natural law. While Locke's major political writings were undoubtedly shaped by existing circumstances in British politics, his ideas cannot be reduced to such circumstances. His ideas drew upon principles of political philosophy that had been the topic of discussion for centuries. As the historian and law professor Edwin S. Corwin wrote in *The Higher Law Background of American Constitutional Law* (1955), "Locke himself would have been the first to own his indebtedness to [Hugo] Grotius and [Samuel von] Puffendorf and ultimately to [Marcus Tullius] Cicero; while his citations of 'the judicious [Joseph] Hooker,' a still earlier apostle of Ciceronian revival, outnumber those of any other writer."

According to Locke, individuals residing in a state of nature — that is, people living outside of any political system — are accountable to certain laws of nature — or to what various political philosophers have also called "higher laws" or "first principles of moral reasoning." Such natural laws stand for both an ontological and ethical truth: all persons are inherently equal and have basic rights. On the basis of that equality, persons cannot be subject to the capricious will of others. As Locke summed up matters in his *Second Treatise*: "The state of nature has a law of nature to govern it, which obliges every one: and reason, which is that law, teaches all mankind, who will but consult it, that being all equal and independent, no one ought to harm another in his life, health, liberty, or possessions."

However, humans are also naturally self-seeking. Indeed, they are prone to outright selfishness and to passions that override their right reasoning, prompting them to deviate from the moral or ethical standards of the laws of nature. Disparate personal interests and passions inevitably lead to interpersonal clashes, endangering enjoyment of natural rights. Thus, a referee is needed to secure persons in their natural rights by impartially adjudicating disputes regarding their lives, liberty, and property, and by defending life, liberty, and property from foreign aggression.

Owing again to the principle of human equality, persons can only bind themselves to a governing political power by consenting to a social compact with others. Wrote Locke:

> Men being, as has been said, by Nature, all free, equal and independent, no one can be put out of this Estate, and subjected to the Political Power of another, without his own *Consent*. The only way whereby any one devests himself of his Natural Liberty, and *puts on the bonds of Civil Society* is by agreeing with other Men to joyn and unite into a Community, for their comfortable, safe, and peaceable living one amongst another, in a secure Enjoyment of their Properties, and a greater Security against any that are not of it.

According to Locke, people form civil societies and establish civil governments in order to preserve their lives, liberty, and property.

Locke maintained that such consent may be offered either expressly or tacitly through acceptance of the benefits of safety and order provided by political society. Locke's *Second Treatise* also offered rudiments of rule of law and separation of powers principles as necessary for keeping political authority limited to its central purpose: protecting the "lives, liberties, and estates of the people":

> Whoever has the legislature or supreme power of any commonwealth, is bound to govern by established standing laws, promulgated and known to the people, and not by extemporary decrees, by ... upright judges, who are too decide controversies by those laws; and to employ the force of the community at home only in the execution of such laws; or abroad to prevent or redress foreign injuries and secure the community from inroads and invasion. And all this is to be directed to no other end but the peace, safety, and public good of the people ...
>
> Whensoever, therefore, the legislative shall transgress this fundamental rule of society, and either by ambition, fear, folly, or corruption, en-

deavor to grasp themselves, or put into the hands of any other, an absolute power over the lives, liberties, and estates of the people, by this breach of trust they forfeit the power the people had put into their hands for quite contrary ends, and it devolves to the people; who have a right to resume their original liberty, and by the establishment of a new legislative (such as they shall think fit), provide for their own safety and security ...

Political scientist Steven M. Dworetz conducted a close review of American colonists and revolutionaries' citations of Locke and use of Lockean concepts for his book, *The Unvarnished Doctrine: Locke, Liberalism, and the American Revolution* (1994). According to Professor Dworetz, "[t]hey used Locke's political theory ... to define the inherent moral limits of civil authority with respect to liberty (civil as well as religions) and property and to justify resistance and revolution when government exceeds, or threatens to exceed, those limits." As Dworetz has explained, "[i]n Revolutionary America the colonists embraced the distinctively Lockean conception of property insofar as it essentially contained the notion of consent." In other words, Parliament's attempts to tax colonists without representation denied them the right to consent to the disposal of their property. American colonists and revolutionaries therefore invoked the *Second Treatise's* eleventh chapter in connection with consent to disposal of property as a safeguard against arbitrary power:

> [T]he supreme power cannot take from any man any part of his property without his own consent ... [N]o body hath a right to take their substance or any part of it from them, without their own consent; without this, they have no property at all. For I have truly no property in that which another can by right take from me, when he pleases, against my consent.

Locke on the Origin and Broad Meaning of Property

In Professor Corwin's estimation, "[t]he two features of the *Second Treatise* which have impressed themselves most definitely upon American constitutional law are the limitations which it lays down for legislative power and its emphasis on the property right." The fifth chapter of Locke's *Second Treatise*, titled "Of Property," presents what is commonly known as the "labor theory of value." This theory offers a justification for the acquisition and enjoyment of private property and also provides a defense for the existence of inequalities or disparities in the relative amounts of property possessed by different persons. As Locke explained:

Though the Earth, and all inferior Creatures be common to all Men, yet every Man has a *Property* in his own *Person*. This no Body has any Right to but himself. The *Labour* of his Body, and the *Work* of his Hands, we may say, are properly his. Whatsoever then he removes out of the State that Nature hath provided, and left it in, he hath mixed his *Labour* with, and joyned to it something that is his own, and thereby makes it his *Property*. It being by him removed from the common state Nature placed it in, hath by this *labour* something annexed to it, that excludes the common right of other Men. For this *Labour* being the unquestionable Property of the Labourer, no man but he can have a right to what that is once joyned to, at least where there is enough, and as good left in common for others.

Notably, Locke used the term "property" in a broad sense to refer to the rights a person has in his or her own self, thereby encompassing all of a person's rights. Distilled to its essence, government therefore exists to protect self-ownership. This understanding of property includes protection of the property to which persons claim by original right of acquisition through their labors and which they come to value.

As will be discussed, Locke's grounding of property rights in a person's natural right to the fruits of his or her own labor formed a fundamental part of the Constitution's intellectual backdrop.

Locke in Relation to Other Transmitters of Natural Rights Concepts

Locke was by no means the only political philosopher who transmitted natural rights concepts that would later form—to use Corwin's term—the Constitution's "higher law background." It would be a mistake to ignore the contributions of other political philosophers, polemicists, and statesmen to the formation of the American consciousness during the Colonial and Revolutionary eras.

Algernon Sidney was a contemporary of Locke. Sidney's *Discourses Concerning Government* (1698) was known and cited in early America. Although many modern historians group Sydney within the "classical republican" school of political thinkers that emphasized cultivating public virtue above protecting personal liberty or property rights, other scholars giver greater credence to the principles of natural liberty Sydney espoused. Political scientist Thomas G. West has observed:

Sidney is as much a natural rights and contract man as Locke. Both advocate government by elected representatives. Both maintain that natural liberty is governed by the natural law. Both argue for limited government and the people's right to revolution. Both are spirited proponents of liberty. Sidney and Locke are 'republicans' as well as 'liberals.'

Summarizing Sydney's argument in his *Discourses*, West has written that "the purpose of government, discovered by reason, is to protect the people in their natural liberty as far as that is prudent." Sydney's discussion of property is more muted than Locke's, but his *Discourses* connect property with liberty in a manner that parallels his contemporary:

Property ... is an appendage to liberty; and 'tis impossible for a man to have a right to lands or goods, if he has no liberty, and enjoys his life only at the pleasure of another, as it is to enjoy either when he is deprived of them. He therefore who says kings and tyrants are bound to preserve their subjects' lands, more than the significance of their pleasure, seeks to delude the world with words which signify nothing.

Although Locke should certainly not be considered the sole source of natural rights thinking in early America, his voice nonetheless appears to have carried more weight than others with American colonists and revolutionaries. As historian Forrest McDonald explained in *Novus Ordo Seclorum: The Intellectual Origins of the Constitution* (1985), "[t]he Patriots had turned to Locke rather than to the other natural-law theorists—Hugo Grotius, Samuel von Puffendorf, Thomas Rutherforth, [Jean Jacques] Burlamaqui, [Emmerich de] Vattel—for the reason that none of the others was so well adapted to their purposes," including "a clear-cut rationale for independence."

Professor McDonald observed that Locke's *Two Treatises* "was the subject as well as the source of a large amount of polemical writing during the eighteenth century." It was through subsequent public writings and discussions that Lockean concepts and basic intuitions grew ascendant in early American political thinking. Borrowing and building on basic notions derived from Locke, Lockean thinking thereby expanded beyond the particular works of one late 17th century English Whig.

Certainly, natural rights concepts espoused by Locke were reflected in American Revolution era writings by James Otis, Thomas Paine, and Thomas Jefferson. All of them invoked the logic of natural rights as part of their constitutional arguments. McDonald has suggested that "ordinary people probably got their ideas about a 'Lockean' state of nature not from Locke but from

[Daniel] Defoe's *Robinson Crusoe* (first published in 1719), the underlying political philosophy of which—though Defoe counted himself a Lockean—differs in subtle but important ways from Locke." Not to be overlooked, scholars such as Professor Dworetz have likewise observed the extent to which New England clergy modified and expounded Lockean concepts in sermons delivered up through the time of the American Revolution.

Jeffersonian and Madisonian Adaptations of Lockean Natural Rights Concepts

The political thought of Thomas Jefferson and James Madison offer a window into American adaptation and elaboration of Lockean ideals to suit the practical circumstances of America in the late 18th century. Among the Founding Fathers, Jefferson and Madison are perhaps the most well-known for drawing upon the logic of natural rights in laying out the foundations for American constitutionalism.

In *The Political Philosophy of Thomas Jefferson* (1991), Garrett Ward Sheldon wrote of the Declaration of Independence's principal drafter: "Jefferson's legal studies imbued him with principles generated by the English political turmoil from 1660 to 1688, especially the Ancient Constitution and Locke's natural rights philosophy, which he adapted in his ideological struggles for colonial independence." More particularly, Jefferson fitted Lockean concepts to the situation of the American colonies, then existing as part of a "federated empire under an arbiter-king":

> Jefferson's earliest and most familiar perception of freedom was expressed in the Declaration of Independence, and entails a freedom from arbitrary, tyrannical government defined according to Locke's psychology of free, equal, and independent individuals possessed of natural rights who must legitimately submit only to limited authority to which they consent in order to protect their material self-preservation. However ... this liberal creed, designed by Locke for use by free and independent individuals in a state of nature, was adapted by Jefferson for free and independent states ... against the arbitrary and corrupt rule of distant, commercial regimes.

Principles of the Declaration relating to property—and, by implication, to intellectual property—will be further considered in Chapter 7. Suffice it for now to recognize the Declaration's embodiment of natural rights ideals.

James Madison's contributions to the establishment of the U.S. Constitution and to our understanding of its meaning are likewise rooted in his own grasp of natural rights concepts. Although not a statement of natural rights *per se*, the U.S. Constitution presumed a specifically American application of Lockean concepts. Madison played no small part in supplying those premises. As Gary Rosen has explained:

> [T]he social compact was indeed the fundamental idea of Madison's political thought. Its influence is evident both in his general political goals (popularly established government, fidelity to written constitutions, security and prosperity) and in the philosophical idiom (the statue of nature, natural rights, the original compact and its stages, necessity versus liberty) that he used to discuss them.

Consistent with the political philosophy of Locke—as well as with the practice of early American colonial charters and the first State Constitutions—Madison maintained that the natural rights of individuals are secured by governments established by social compact. As he wrote in his essay "On Sovereignty" (1835): "All power in just & free Govts. is derived from Compact, that where the parties to the Compact are competent to make it, and where the Compact creates a Govt, and arms it not only with a moral power but the physical means of executing it." Madison described the compact as based on "the Theory, which contemplates a certain number of individuals, as meeting & agreeing to form one political Society, in order that the rights the safety & the interest of each may be under the safeguard of the whole." Continued Madison: "[T]he theory further supposes, either that it was a part of the original compact, that the will of the majority was to be deemed the will of the whole; or that this was a law of nature, resulting from the nature of political society, itself the offspring of the natural wants of man." Madison regarded the majority as both empowered and constrained, with a charge to do anything that could otherwise rightfully be done by the unanimous consent of the people, in order to best ensure the security of the people and their happiness.

Madison's understanding of the social compact as a deliberate political agreement of a majority of the people acting on behalf of the whole in establishing new forms of government to protect individual rights was realized in the very process by which the Constitution was established and ratified. That is, the drafting of the Constitution by the Constitutional Convention of 1787 and the process of ratification through state conventions established by popular elections were concrete manifestations of Lockean concepts, suited to the American experience and sensibilities. Madison explained the necessity of this process and defended its legitimacy in *Federalist Papers Nos. 37–40*.

Appropriation of Lockean concepts by Madison is also especially evident with respect to the role of government in securing rights of private property.

In his 1792 *National Gazette* essay "On Property," James Madison offered a broad definition of property that echoes Locke and is worth careful attention: "In its larger and juster meaning, it embraces every thing to which a man may attach a value and have a right; and which leaves to every one else the like advantage." Included in this "larger and juster meaning" of property, Madison explained "a man has property in his opinions and the free communication of them," "a property of peculiar value in his religions opinions, and in the profession and practice dictated by them," "a property very dear to him in the safety and liberty of his person," and "an equal opportunity in the free use of his faculties and free choice of the objects on which to employ them." As Madison summed up: "In a word, as a man is said to have a right to his property, he may be equally said to have a property in his rights." Stated more emphatically: "If the United States mean to obtain or deserve the full praise due to wise and just governments, they will equally respect the rights of property, and the property in rights."

In his essay, Madison also refers in Lockean terms to the natural right to the fruits of one's own labor. He described "that sacred property, which Heaven, in decreeing man to earn his bread by the sweat of his brow, kindly reserved to him, in the small repose that could be spared from the supply of his necessities." Madison listed individuals' "labor that acquires their daily subsistence" among the broad class of property that government is entrusted with safeguarding. As Madison explained:

> Government is instituted to protect property of every sort; as well that which lies in the various rights of individuals as that which the term particularly expresses. This being the end of government, that alone is a just government, which impartially secures to every man, whatever is his own.

This Lockean-Madisonian formulation of government's proper purpose — to protect "the rights of property, and the property in rights" — is crucial to appreciating the original understanding of the American constitutional order. It is also crucial to understanding the place of intellectual property rights within American constitutionalism. A Lockean-Madisonian approach grounds intellectual property in natural right.

Intellectual Property: Safeguarding the Fruits of One's Labor in Civil Society

While Locke's *Second Treatise* did not speak directly to the matter of intellectual property, IP fits within the broad Lockean conception of property. Recall how, by Locke's definition, "every Man has a *Property* in his own *Person*. This no Body has any Right to but himself. The *Labour* of his Body, and the *Work* of his Hands, we may say, are properly his." Similarly, Madison defined property "[i]n its larger and juster meaning," as "embrac[ing] every thing to which a man may attach a value and have a right; and which leaves to every one else the like advantage." Authors and inventors certainly attach value to their writings and inventions, with their creative labors supplying their rightful claims to such value.

Further, although copyrights and patents confer exclusive rights to authors and inventors, all other members of civil society remain free to author and invent their own works, profiting thereby. So long as copyright and patent protections apply to specific creative works or discoveries made by particular authors, such protections are not, to use Madison's terms, "arbitrary restrictions and monopolies [that] deny to part of its citizens the free use of their faculties, and free choice of their occupations."

Nor is it of consequence that creative works or discoveries involve things non-physical or intangible, rather than physical or tangible things such as land, ground minerals, or other natural resources. Madison expressly included intangibles in the "larger and juster meaning" of property that he wrote about. Not only did Madison believe that "a man has property in his opinions and the free communication of them," he also maintained that "[c]onscience is the most sacred of all property ... being a natural and unalienable right." There may be differences between tangibles and intangibles, just as there are differences even between various kinds of tangibles. But nothing in that distinction alone puts copyrights or patents beyond Madison's "larger and juster meaning" of property.

Thus, and this is a key point, a Lockean-Madisonian approach also bolsters the property rights status of copyright and patent protection systems in the face of modern—or perhaps we should say post-modern—criticisms of intellectual property. In recent years, some academics and public policy advocates, even those who at times consider themselves "conservative" or "constitutionalist," have suggested that intellectual property should not be regarded as property at all. It has likewise been suggested that intellectual property should be "rebuilt" or reformulated on different philosophical grounds. This criticism of intellectual property is profoundly wrong. And it misunderstands or ignores important founding principles of our constitutional order.

Intellectual Property as Constitutional Law

That individuals, by nature, possess a property right to the fruits of their own labor does not necessarily mean that individuals, by nature, in all cases and for all times possess enforceable copyrights or patent rights. As will be addressed further in Chapter 2, Locke, Madison, and the framers and ratifiers of the Constitution recognized that life in civil society requires government to establish, adjust, and enforce particular rules that may modify the exercise of those rights individuals possess by nature. This modification ensures that the core of those natural rights may be exercised, consistent with the equal exercise of rights by others in civil society. Importantly, the Constitution applies this recognition to the subject of IP rights.

Article I, Section 8, Clause 8 of the U.S. Constitution grants Congress power "To promote the Progress of Science and useful Arts, by securing for limited Times to Authors and Inventors the exclusive Right to their respective Writings and Discoveries." The Lockean-Madisonian principles addressed above are integral to understanding and informing its purpose. By securing to authors and inventors exclusive but time-limited rights to their work, the Intellectual Property Clause is best understood as safeguarding the natural right to the fruits of one's labor in a civil society. The IP Clause protects the core of that right for authors and inventors, granting Congress authority to establish a uniform system of exclusive rights in intellectual property, while also setting limits on that authority.

Express recognition of the exclusive rights of authors and inventors in the fundamental law of the land establishes the importance and respect with which these rights should be regarded. Even those unfamiliar with Lockean or Madisonian political philosophy should regard the IP Clause's express constitutional recognition of copyrights and patents as authoritative.

Of course, appeals to natural rights premises don't provide answers when it comes to setting specific rules respecting intellectual property. The IP Clause's high-level requirement that the exclusive rights of authors and inventors be secured "To promote the Progress of Science and useful Arts ... for limited Times" says little about the particular contours of intellectual property policy. Fixing terms for copyrights or patents, defining fair use of copyrighted works, and setting appropriate enforcement penalties and the like, necessarily involve policy judgments for Congress. Contextual considerations, including potential trade-offs, incentives, and consequences weigh heavily in setting precise rules for safeguarding intellectual property. However, the complexities and uncertainties involved in defining precise boundaries of copyright and patent protection in no way undermine the core property rights protection rationale recognized by Lockean-Madisonian premises and the IP Clause.

Conclusion

The classical liberal philosophy of John Locke and other writers conceived free governments to be established by social compact to protect persons' natural rights to life, liberty, and property. This included a definition of "property" that extended to all of a person's rights, including everything to which a person labors and attaches value. Natural rights supplied the intellectual backbone of the Declaration of Independence and were presupposed by the framers and ratifiers of the Constitution. The idea of intellectual property rights in writings and inventions fit squarely within this larger meaning of property that encompasses one's person, one's faculties, and the fruits of one's labor.

The IP Clause makes intellectual property a normative feature of the American constitutional order. It substantiates not only the value but also the right that creators have in their own intellectual property—the fruits of their own labor. Any supposed latent questions or ambiguities as to whether copyrights or patents truly constitute forms of property are answered by the Constitution itself.

Sources

Declaration of Independence (1776).
Thomas Jefferson, Letter to Henry Lee (1825).
Abraham Lincoln, *Speech on the Dred Scott Decision* (1857).
John Locke, *Two Treatises of Government* (1689).
James Madison, "On Property," *National Gazette* (1792).
James Madison, "On Sovereignty" (1835).
Publius (James Madison), *Federalist No. 39* (1788).
Publius (James Madison), *Federalist No. 43* (1788).
Algernon Sidney, *Discourses Concerning Government* (1698).

* * *

Edward S. Corwin, *The "Higher Law" Background of American Constitutional Law* (1955).
Steven M. Dworetz, *The Unvarnished Doctrine: Locke, Liberalism, and the American Revolution* (1994).

Forrest McDonald, *Novus Ordo Seclorum: The Intellectual Origins of the Constitution* (1985).

Garrett Ward Sheldon, *The Political Philosophy of Thomas Jefferson* (1991).

Thomas G. West, "Foreword," in Algernon Sydney, *Discourses Concerning Government* (1698) (Revised ed., Liberty Fund 1996).

Chapter 2

Reasserting the
Property Rights Source
of Intellectual Property

Introduction

"The entire U.S. economy relies on some form of IP, because virtually every industry either produces or uses it." This remarkable conclusion was contained in a March 2012 report released by the U.S. Commerce Department. According to the report, "IP-intensive industries directly accounted for 27.1 million American jobs, or 18.8 percent of all employment in the economy, in 2010." And "IP-intensive industries accounted for about $5.06 trillion in value added, or 34.8 percent of U.S. gross domestic product (GDP), in 2010."

Despite the dramatic rise in intellectual property as a source of value and a key driver of economic progress, intellectual property rights have come under fire. Wrongly in our view, some academics and public policy analysts have called into question the institutional legitimacy of intellectual property. Economic prosperity generated by and through intellectual property is dependent upon the existence of the same conceptual and legal framework applicable to property rights more generally. Of course, such framework may be adapted in certain appropriate ways to take into account the advances of the Information Age. But there is no justification for excluding intellectual property from fundamental principles of property law that government is charged with enforcing.

Intellectual property and physical property share the same conceptual foundations. Thus, attacks on intellectual property are in large measure attacks on property itself, even though they may not be characterized as such or even recognized as such by those attacking IP. The foundational source of property rights and the status of intellectual property therefore need to be reasserted and defended.

A comprehensive understanding of property prevailed among the Founding Fathers at the time of the U.S. Constitution's framing and ratification.

James Madison, often described as "the Father of the Constitution," exemplified this understanding. He defined property "[i]n its larger and juster meaning," as "embrac[ing] every thing to which a man may attach a value and have a right" and which "leaves to every one else the like advantage." This broad definition of property included the rights individuals by nature possess to "their persons," "their faculties," "their actual possessions," and "the labor that acquires their daily subsistence." Intellectual property and physical property share this common grounding in natural right. Certainly, the concept of rights in an author's writings and an inventor's discoveries are encompassed within this broad understanding of property.

But Madison and the Founding Fathers held a two-track understanding of property. They also understood property "in its particular application." This narrower definition separated "personal" rights—including public communication of opinions, liberty of conscience, and free use of one's faculties—from "property" rights in actual possessions, such as "a man's land, or merchandize, or money."

This "particular application" or narrower understanding of property was likewise rooted in natural right. But it also depended upon civil society. That is, laws established by governments expanded the scope of protected property and reflected social and technological progress. Intellectual property and physical property both share this necessary connection to the laws of society. And both copyrights and patents fit within the meaning of property in this narrower sense of the term.

Stated somewhat differently, in the broad understanding of property held by Madison and the Founding Fathers, a person has a natural right to the fruits of their labors. The right to make use of one's faculties as a means to acquiring property is a personal right, and the right to the actual productions of one's labors is a property right, in the narrow understanding of the term.

That individuals, by nature, possess a property right to the fruits of their own labor, does not necessarily mean that individuals, by nature, in all cases possess enforceable copyrights or patent rights. Certainly, coherent and functional copyright and patent systems seem to presuppose a vibrant civil society under a duly constituted governing authority that must establish and enforce intellectual property systems. But civil law does not sever the connection between property rights and natural rights. Rather, as Sir William Blackstone observed in his *Commentaries on the Laws of England* (1765), the purpose of civil law is to fulfill natural rights of property by expanding property, creating new forms of property as society progresses, and ensuring mutual enjoyment of property rights by all persons.

Civil laws apply in unique ways to different types of property. The need for different rules regarding different kinds of intangible property is akin to the need for different rules for different kinds of tangible property, whether in real property, minerals, water, or personal property. But this in no way suggests that, in a foundational sense, intangible property rights are any less grounded in natural right, or in our constitutional order, than tangible property rights.

Article I, Section 8, Clause 8 of the U.S. Constitution delegates to the federal government a responsibility for securing the exclusive rights of authors and inventors for limited times. Fixing terms for copyrights or patents, defining fair use of copyrighted works, and setting appropriate enforcement penalties necessarily involve policy judgments for Congress. The IP Clause's recognition of the exclusive rights of authors and inventors in the fundamental law of the land conveys the importance and respect with which these rights should be regarded.

Even those unfamiliar with the two-track definition of property held by the Founding Fathers should regard the IP Clause's express constitutional recognition of copyrights and patents as authoritative. This should foreclose any notion that government can denigrate the idea of property in intangibles or reduce intellectual property to second-class status.

Intellectual and Physical Property Are Both Encompassed Within Classical Liberalism's Broader Understanding of Property

As recounted in Chapter 1, the classic liberalism of the 17th and 18th Centuries fostered a comprehensive understanding of property that included the full sweep of all of a person's rights. Such an understanding was advanced by John Locke, who wrote in his *Second Treatise of Government* (1689) that "every Man has a *Property* in his own *Person*. This no Body has any Right to but himself. The *Labour* of his Body, and the *Work* of his Hands, we may say, are properly his." Property, so broadly defined, was invoked by those who declared America's Independence. And it was presupposed by those who drafted and ratified the U.S. Constitution. In the words of the man regarded as "the Father of the Constitution"—James Madison: "In its larger and juster meaning, it embraces every thing to which a man may attach a value and have a right; and which leaves to every one else the like advantage." Stated somewhat differently: "In a word, as a man is said to have a right to his property, he may be equally said to have a property in his rights." For Madison, this also included persons' "free use of their faculties, and free choice of their occupations." Chapter 1 explained that this broad, classical liberal understanding of property includes both things tangible and intangible.

Classical Liberalism's Narrower Understanding of Property

But Madison and the Founding Fathers held to a two-track definition of property. The broad understanding encompassed one track. And a narrower understanding constituted the second track.

In this, the Founders followed John Locke. The *Second Treatise* sets out Locke's labor-mixing theory of property ownership, whereby "[w]hatsoever then he removes out of the State that Nature hath provided, and left it in, he hath mixed his *Labour* with, and joyned to it something that is his own, and thereby makes it his *Property*." But in this respect, Locke was referring to the "original Law of Nature for the *beginning of Property*." Locke recognized that property, although grounded in natural right, was secured by "the Civiliz'd part of Mankind, who have made and multiplied positive Laws to determine Property." Much of what American colonists found especially attractive about Locke's *Second Treatise* were the principles for limited constitutional government that it set out to guide the operation of all laws related to property.

So, too, the Founders' two-track understanding of property reflected concepts espoused by Sir William Blackstone. His *Commentaries on the Laws of England* (1765) was widely printed in early America and read by students in the law, including Madison. In his *Commentaries*, Blackstone defined property as "that dominion which one man claims and exercises over the external things of the world, in exclusion of every other individual." Madison quoted this definition in his *National Gazette* essay, "On Property" (1792), and referred to it as property "in its particular application."

Madison's narrower definition of "property" separated "personal" rights— including public communication of opinions, liberty of conscience, and free use of one's faculties—from "property" rights in actual possessions, such as "a man's land, or merchandize, or money." This distinction between personal and property rights would become familiar in American constitutionalism. As Madison declared in his speech before the 1829 Virginia Constitutional Convention: "It is sufficiently obvious, that persons and property are the two great subjects on which Governments are to act; and that the rights of persons, and the rights of property, are the objects, for the protection of which Government was instituted. These rights cannot well be separated."

Thirty years later, Abraham Lincoln would touch upon the relationship between personal rights and property rights. In his April 6, 1859, letter to Henry L. Pierce, Lincoln recalled how "the Jefferson party were formed upon its supposed superior devotion to the *personal* rights of men, holding the rights of *property* to be secondary only, and greatly inferior." Proceeding to his own time,

Lincoln reflected: "The democracy of to-day hold the *liberty* of one man to be absolutely nothing, when in conflict with another man's right of *property*. Republicans, on the contrary, are for both the *man* and the *dollar*; but in cases of conflict, the man *before* the dollar." Aspects of property's relationship to the "pursuit of happiness" and to the idea of "property in men"—slavery—are discussed in Chapters 7 and 10, respectively. Suffice it here to observe that personal and property rights both find their origin in natural right. Both are entrusted to the government for protection. Lincoln's conferral of priority on personal rights over property rights was rooted in principles of self-ownership and human equality. Those principles Lincoln identified with Jefferson, his 1859 letter deeming them "the definitions and axioms of free society."

The connection between natural rights, personal rights, and property rights—narrowly defined—is further touched on by Madison in his essay "On Property." Wrote Madison, persons' "free use of their faculties, and free choice of their occupations ... not only constitute their property in the general sense of the word; but are the means of acquiring property strictly so called." To state the matter somewhat differently, the broad understanding of property held by Madison and the Founders recognized a person has a natural right to the fruits of his or her labors. The right to make use of their faculties as a means to acquiring property is a personal right, and the right to the actual productions of their labors is a property right, in the narrow understanding of the term.

In grasping the two-track definition of property, the critical takeaway is that both copyrights and patents fit within the meaning of property in this narrower sense of the term.

Blackstone on Property's Origins in the Laws of Nature and Laws of Society

That individuals, by nature, possess a property right to the fruits of their own labor, does not necessarily mean that individuals, by nature, in all cases possess enforceable copyrights or patent rights. Coherent and functional copyright and patent systems seem to presuppose a vibrant civil society under a duly constituted governing authority that must establish and enforce intellectual property systems. After all, the state of nature, in its Lockean sense, referred to the situation of persons living outside of political systems of government with enforceable civil laws. But this in no way undermines the case for copyright or patent. Civil law builds upon the natural rights basis for intellectual property in the labors of authors and inventors.

Locke made this very point in the *Second Treatise*, where he wrote that "the obligations of the Law of Nature cease not in society but only in many cases are drawn closer, and have by human laws known penalties annexed to them to enforce their observation." Following in Locke's footsteps, Blackstone offers illumination. For Blackstone, the laws of England did not abridge natural rights in property but instead gave them fuller expression. According to historian Daniel Boorstin in *The Mysterious Science of Law: An Essay on Blackstone's Commentaries* (1941):

> The English constitution, according to Blackstone, had fulfilled and enlarged the right of property in many ways. English law had, for example, found an owner for everything that was by its nature capable of ownership, even where nature had neglected to make an assignment. Forests, waste grounds, wrecks, estrays, game, and all the things that had not been 'appropriated in the general distribution' had been distributed by the laws of England according to the natural cannons.

In the Blackstonian view, wrote Boorstin, "the law had enlarged the right of property even beyond the form which it had in nature" and "the state was continually creating new forms of property, to meet the needs of men." For Blackstone, law was necessary to ensure all persons could exercise dominion over their property consistent with the like right of others—for example, by preventing the taking of property by force or fraud. Whereas Blackstone regarded occupancy as the original and exclusive means of securing property by natural right, positive law restrained and abridged the exercise of occupancy to prevent violent conflicts thereby realizing natural rights in modern society. The law also provided mechanisms for transferring title to property through enforceable contracts or wills, further facilitating harmonious possession and use of rights originating in nature.

Unhelpfully, Blackstone sometimes appeared to describe property as originating solely in nature, and at other times property was described as originating solely through society. But as Boorstin explained, Blackstone ultimately held nature and society together in rooting rights of property:

> Thus, whatever confusion there may at first seem to have been in saying that property had been commanded by Nature and had been created by the state, Blackstone actually made the two ideas complementary. The law of nature had made property possible and necessary but the laws of England had fulfilled the possibility, and had shown new aspects of ownership which Nature herself had not dreamed of. By attributing property to this double source, the *Commentaries* had strengthened its sanctions. Every right of property which was protected by the law of England in Blackstone's day thus had ultimately the protection of Nature and of Nature's God.

Both intellectual property and physical property depend upon the laws of society for their existence and enforcement. Particular provisions of the law regarding title, use, or transfer of copyrights or patents should not be simply equated with natural rights. But neither should the need for such laws be read as somehow eviscerating the basis for copyrights and patents in the intellectual labors of authors and inventors. Instead, civil laws of property—in the narrow sense—exist to ensure enjoyment of natural rights of property—in the broad sense.

Intellectual and Physical Property Share the Same Institutional Role in Defining and Limiting Governmental Power

Tasking government to protect intellectual property rights and administer intellectual property systems implicates the same basic set of government responsibilities and public benefits associated with physical property. Property is protected through government-adopted rules to clarify boundaries of ownership and usage rights. This ensures individuals have the ability to enjoy their rights, free from interference but consistent with the rights of others. It also facilitates individuals' ability to make intelligent choices about what to do with their resources and enables planning for the future.

In addition, government has an important role in establishing and administering a records system to clarify and document property ownership and to streamline title transfers. Such systems help ensure that rightful owners maintain title. They also help reduce transaction costs when property is sold, thereby facilitating transfer of property to individuals who value it the most.

A critical byproduct of the protection of property rights by government is the safeguarding of individualized decision-making in economic and personal matters. Individuals are at liberty to pursue their own ends, rather than be made subservient to government interests. Individuals remain free to utilize their first-person knowledge and skills in pursuing opportunities and adjusting to market changes. Most obviously, property ownership provides the best economic incentives for investment and innovation, since individuals are then free to reap financial rewards for their efforts. This property-centric approach to governance is opposed to command-and-control economies where governments coordinate activities through top-down rules or arbitrary action.

Protection of property rights also implies government conformity to the rule of law. As Madison wrote, "[t]hat is not a just government, nor is property secure under it, where the property which a man has in his personal safety and personal liberty, is violated by arbitrary seizures of one class of citizens for the service of the rest." Property's function in confining government actions to the rule of law is further addressed in Chapter 8.

Importantly, these institutional functions of property rights in defining the duties and limits of government power do not trade upon whether any particular species of property resides in intangible or tangible form. When it comes to the purpose and scope of government power, the case for intellectual property rights and the case for physical property rights are one in the same.

Protection of property extends to the fruits of one's labors. This is the grounding of intellectual property rights, not the good graces of government. It is immaterial whether the fruits of one's labors result from cultivating one's land, manufacturing physical goods, authoring literary works, or inventing innovative products. There is no principled reason for excluding any of these forms of property, whether tangible or intangible, from protection under law.

Intellectual property and physical property operate as part and parcel of this conceptual and legal framework for decentralized decision-making. Both forms of property check the tendency toward government centralization of decision-making.

Despite Differences, Intellectual and Physical Property Share the Same Source

Intellectual property and physical property are different in certain respects. But such differences in no way undermine the common source of both types of property rights. Oft-cited differences between intellectual and physical property are important insofar as they inform judgments about the particular rules best suited to clarify ownership and use limits. One commonly observed difference between intellectual and physical property is the non-rivalrous nature of the former and the rivalrous nature of latter. Intellectual property can be possessed and used by many individuals at the same time without causing interference with such possession or use. Physical property, however, cannot be successfully possessed and used by many individuals simultaneously.

Another commonly observed difference between intellectual and physical property is the non-exhaustible nature of the former and the exhaustible nature of the latter. Intellectual property is not depleted with usage or repeated usage, although increased or universal access to intangible property by numerous users can deplete its market value. But physical property typically is depleted with usage.

Additional differences between intellectual and physical property include the ease with which the former generally can be used and transferred compared to the latter. Modern industrial production techniques and digital technologies have made replication and simultaneous access and use of inventions and created works increasingly easy and less costly in many instances. And policing efforts to prevent or prosecute such unauthorized reproductions and their usage is increasingly difficult.

But none of those asserted differences in the attributes of intangibles and tangibles should cause one to overlook that rights in both types of property are grounded in natural right. Both intellectual property and physical property fall within the broad understanding of "property." And there is nothing about those differences that would put copyrights or patents beyond the narrower understanding or "particular application" of the term "property."

Properly understood, non-rivalry and non-exhaustibility are characteristics of various kinds of property. But those characteristics do not define property as such. The presence or absence of non-rivalry and non-exhaustibility are factors that bear on the realistic expectations of ascertainable property ownership and beneficial usage. The extent to which certain types of property exemplify non-exclusivity and non-rivalry are circumstances that should inform the administration of property rights systems. Ease of use and transfer are also contextual factors that should influence the contours of property rules regarding ownership and use. Calibrating the rules of property according to those dynamics may be necessary to ensure and facilitate the use and transfer of property by its respective owners.

Aspects unique to various types of physical property require particular adjustments and periodic readjustments to the rules of property. But the fundamental property rights status remains whether those rights are in minerals, water, real property, or personal possessions. So it is with different types of intellectual property, whether in copyrights or patents. That the rules of property must be tailored to the unique features of different types of intellectual property is typical of property systems.

A Property Rights Approach to Intellectual Property Reform

Appeals to natural rights do not provide specific answers when it comes to setting specific rules respecting copyrights or patents. The IP Clause's high-level requirement that the exclusive rights of authors and inventors be secured "To promote the Progress of Science and useful Arts ... for limited Times" says little about the particular contours of intellectual property policy. Fixing terms for copyrights or patents, defining fair use of copyrighted works, and setting appropriate enforcement penalties and the like, necessarily involve policy judgments for Congress. Contextual considerations, including potential trade-offs, incentives, and consequences weigh heavily in setting precise rules for safe-guarding intellectual property. However, the complexities and uncertainties involved in defining precise boundaries of copyright and patent protection in no way undermine the core property rights protection rationale for intellectual property. The placement of copyright and patent protection in the Constitution bespeaks the critical importance of intellectual property to the nation's commercial marketplace.

Recent data reinforces the increasingly essential role of copyrights and patents to our nation's economy. According to a U.S. Commerce Department's report published in 2012, "IP-intensive industries directly accounted for 27.1 million American jobs, or 18.8 percent of all employment in the economy, in 2010." That same year, "IP-intensive industries accounted for about $5.06 trillion in value added, or 34.8 percent of U.S. gross domestic product (GDP)."

In his book *The Noblest Triumph: Property and Prosperity Throughout the Ages* (1998), Tom Bethell wrote that "the sudden rise of intellectual property is the legal expression of this transition" from the Industrial Age into the Information Age. However, Bethell also directed attention to a conundrum created by new technological capabilities: "An information economy is one in which the value added by intellectual goods, such as songs and films and software, is higher at the margin than that added by steel and oil. But thanks to the possibility of almost costless replication, that 'value added' is threatened with collapse."

Economists Carl Shapiro and Hal R. Varian identified these same considerations in *Information Rules: A Strategic Guide to the Networked Economy* (1998). Shapiro and Varian recognized the "danger" that "if copies crowd out legitimate sales, the producers of information may not be able to recover their production costs." Nonetheless they pointed out that "[t]he very technology that makes rights management more difficult—the dramatic reduction in costs of copying and distribution—also offer a fantastic opportunity for owners of intellectual content."

Protecting the intellectual property rights of creators and inventors is a mission-critical public policy challenge in the Information Age. This includes preserving intellectual property owners' opportunity to recover production costs and obtain profits. Preventing improper expropriation of the fruits of their labors and preserving incentives to further innovation are therefore essential.

Meeting this challenge may likely require periodic adjustments to the rules of intellectual property to reflect the changing landscape of digital technologies and Internet communications. But reforms made in this regard should reflect, and be consistent with, government's primary purpose: protecting property rights.

Conclusion

A comprehensive understanding of property prevailed among the Founding Fathers. James Madison defined property "[i]n its larger and juster meaning," as "embrac[ing] every thing to which a man may attach a value and have a right" and which "leaves to every one else the like advantage." This broad definition of property included the rights individuals by nature possess to "their persons," "their faculties," "their actual possessions," and "the labor that acquires their daily subsistence." Intellectual property and physical property share this common grounding in natural right. Certainly, the idea of rights in writings and inventions are encompassed within this broad understanding of property.

But Madison and the Founders also understood property "in its particular application." This narrower definition separated "personal" rights from "property" rights in actual possessions. This "particular application" or narrower understanding of property was likewise rooted in natural right. But it also depended upon civil society. That is, laws established by governments expanded the scope of protected property and reflected social and technological progress. Intellectual property and physical property both share this necessary connection to the laws of society. And, importantly, both copyrights and patents fit within the meaning of property in this narrower sense of the term.

Any adjustments to intellectual property rules must ultimately respect the right of individuals to the fruits of their own labors. Property rights of authors and inventors, both in the broader and narrower meaning, must be respected. This means rejecting any notion that government can jettison the idea of property in intangibles or reduce intellectual property to second-class status in property's realm. Attacks on intellectual property are attacks on property itself. And attacks on intellectual property should be resisted by recourse to the principles upon which all property rights depend.

Sources

William Blackstone, *Commentaries on the Laws of England* (1765).
Abraham Lincoln, Letter to Henry L. Pierce, & Others (1859).
John Locke, *Second Treatise of Government* (1689).
James Madison, "On Property," *National Gazette* (1792).
James Madison, *Speech at the Virginia Convention* (December 2, 1829).

* * *

Tom Bethell, *The Noblest Triumph: Property and Prosperity Throughout the Ages* (1998).

Daniel Boorstin, *The Mysterious Science of Law: An Essay on Blackstone's Commentaries* (1941).

The Commission on the Theft of American Intellectual Property, The IP Commission Report (2013).

Carl Shapiro and Hal R. Varian, *Information Rules: Information Rules: A Strategic Guide to the Networked Economy* (1998).

Chapter 3

Literary Property: Copyright's Constitutional History and Its Meaning for Today

Introduction

The efforts of Noah Webster—"The Father of Copyright"—and James Madison—"The Father of the Constitution"—are important to understanding the constitutional foundation of copyright, even though these efforts are little known by some. Separately and jointly, these two prominent figures in early American history called attention to the need for copyright protection in our newly independent nation. They played leading roles in successfully obtaining protection for copyright in several states, and, ultimately, in the U.S. Constitution.

Recalling this oft-overlooked historical alliance between the Father of Copyright and the Father of the Constitution sheds light on the nature and meaning of copyright in our nation's fundamental law. Significantly, Webster and Madison both advanced a public understanding of copyright as a form of "literary property," grounded in a person's basic right to the fruits of his or her own labor. This understanding and grounding should inform our reading of the U.S. Constitution's copyright provision and should continue to guide copyright policy today.

Unlike James Madison, Noah Webster—a lawyer, statesman, author, and lexicographer—is an oft-forgotten figure today. But he played a pivotal role in fixing copyright into American constitutionalism. During the time of the Articles of Confederation, Webster personally lobbied the Confederation Congress as well as several state legislatures for adoption of laws securing authors' exclusive rights to the proceeds attributable to their labors. Webster's efforts were largely successful in the states. In large part, this success owed to Webster's close connections with prominent statesmen of the day, including George Washington and James Madison.

43

James Madison's contributions to American constitutionalism are so significant and wide-ranging that it is easy to overlook the key role he played respecting copyright's place in our constitutional order. Madison pushed through the Confederation Congress a resolution urging all states to adopt uniform laws securing rights in literary property. For his part, Madison also helped pass Virginia's copyright law in 1785. Madison regarded the lack of uniform protection of literary property in the states to be a vice in the regime that prevailed under the Articles of Confederation. He did not want to see this same vice carried forward into the new constitutional order.

With Webster's backing, Madison would eventually propose to the 1787 Constitutional Convention a provision for protecting copyright and patent. That provision is contained in the Article I, Section 8, Clause 8 of the U.S. Constitution—the Intellectual Property (IP) Clause. Both Madison and Webster believed that a uniform copyright system was a necessary component of a more perfect Union, to promote progress in science and the arts, as well as commerce.

Copyright's constitutional history—and the contributions of Webster and Madison, in particular—should serve as an important backdrop to today's public deliberations about copyright policy. In particular, Webster's and Madison's view of copyright as literary property arising out of the fruits of one's labor and deserving uniform protection should redirect policymaking to government's primary purpose under the Constitution—protecting rights of property in all its facets. Recognizing copyright in the fundamental law of the land conveys its importance as a means of promoting progress in science and useful arts, as well as in commerce. And by recognizing an individual's rights to the fruits of his or her labor, copyright not only promotes progress and commerce, but also secures a space for individual entrepreneurship free from government control or taking.

For policymakers and analysts today, the IP Clause makes copyright a normative feature of the American constitutional order, deserving of respect. Of course, we do not maintain that the terms of Article I, Section 8, Clause 8 definitively settle all boundaries regarding scope of ownership and terms of protection. But we do maintain that copyright's status as a constitutionally protected property right does require that all policy touching on such rights comport with the rule of law.

Webster's State Copyright Quest

Noah Webster's late 1782 petition to the Connecticut General Assembly seeking copyright protection for authors was the first effort in the United States to obtain passage of a copyright law, earning Webster the title "Father of Copyright." Early in 1783, a Connecticut Assemblyman presenting Webster's petition convinced that state's legislature to adopt a copyright law granting authors exclusive rights to earnings from their publications for a term of fourteen years.

Connecticut's 1783 "Act for the encouragement of literature and genius" included a preamble that expressly rooted copyright in the natural rights of authors:

> Whereas it is perfectly agreeable to the principles of natural equity and justice, that every author should be secured in receiving the profits that may arise from the sale of his works, and such security may encourage men of learning and genius to publish their writings; which may do honor to their country, and service to mankind.

Webster's lobbying coincided with promoting his *American Spelling Book*—or "blue back speller," as it was popularly known. Webster sought to protect his spelling instruction book from unauthorized copying. In the words of Webster biographer Joshua Kendall, "Webster invented the modern book tour and drafted America's first copyright laws."

Webster's efforts in lobbying state legislatures—whether through petitions and personal visits or through correspondence and acquaintances—helped secure copyright laws in the newly independent states. New York, Massachusetts, New Jersey, South Carolina, Virginia, and Maryland were among the states passing copyright laws at Webster's urgings.

Along with Connecticut, most of the states passing copyright legislation included preambles that linked copyrights to natural rights. For instance, on March 17, 1783, Massachusetts passed "An Act for the purpose of securing to authors the exclusive right and benefit of publishing their literary productions, for twenty-one years." The Massachusetts copyright act included a whereas clause that declared:

> [T]he Improvement of knowledge, the progress of civilization, the public weal of the community, and the advancement of human happiness, greatly depend on the efforts of learned and ingenious persons in the various arts and sciences: As the principal encouragement such persons can have to make great and beneficial exertions of this nature, must exist in the legal security of the fruits of their study and industry to themselves; and as such security is one of the natural rights of all men, there being no property more peculiarly a man's own than that which is produced by the labour of his mind.

That same year, New Jersey, New Hampshire, and Rhode Island passed copyright laws prefaced by a whereas clause nearly identical to the one in the Massachusetts act. A supplemental whereas clause in New Jersey's "Act for the promotion and encouragement of literature" further declared:

> [L]earning tends to the embellishment of human nature, the honour of the nation, and the general good of mankind; and as it is perfectly agreeable to the principles of equity, that men of learning who devote their time and talents to the preparing treatises for publication, should have the profits that may arise from the sale of their works secured to them.

In addition, North Carolina's 1785 "Act for securing literary property" began with a whereas clause declaring:

> [N]othing is more strictly a man's own than the fruit of his study, and it is proper that men should be encouraged to pursue useful knowledge by the hope of reward; and as the security of literary property must greatly tend to encourage genius, to promote useful discoveries, and to the general extension of arts and commerce.

Noah Webster's persistence in advocating copyright laws was bolstered by a principled set of arguments he advanced on their behalf. Specifically, he contended for copyright legislation as a measure to promote and protect the rights of authors to the fruits of their labor. Webster regarded publication proceeds as the exclusive property right of authors. For example, in his plea to the New York State Legislature, Webster sought "to secure to your petitioner the benefit of his own labors to which he conceives himself solely entitled but which are not protected by the laws that protect every other species of property."

Reflecting the views espoused by Webster, New York's 1786 "Act to promote literature" declared:

> [I]t is agreeable to the principles of natural equity and justice that every author should be secured in receiving the profits that may arise from the sale of his or her works; and such security may encourage persons of learning and genius to publish their writings, which may do honour to their country and service to mankind.

The whereas clause contained in Georgia's 1876 "Act for the encouragement of literature and genius" closely mirrored New York's act.

According to Webster, works of the mind constitute a species of property on par with physical types of property. As he declared in his petition to the state legislature in Delaware:

> Among all modes of acquiring property, or exclusive ownership, the act or operation of *creating* or *making* seems to have the first claim. If

anything can justly give a man an exclusive right to the occupancy and enjoyment of a thing it must be that he *made* it. The right of a farmer and mechanic to the exclusive enjoyment and right of disposal of what they *make* or *produce* is never questioned. What, then, can make a difference between the produce of *muscular strength* and the produce of the *intellect*?

Although Delaware apparently passed no copyright act, the legislatures of all of the other original thirteen American states saw fit to pass legislation securing the exclusive rights of authors to the proceeds of their creative labors.

Virginia's Copyright Law: Webster and Madison Joined in Alliance

Of special interest, from a constitutional history standpoint, is Noah Webster's connection to copyright legislation in Virginia. In the early 1780s, Webster had become an acquaintance and correspondent with George Washington and James Madison. Both Virginians were familiar with Webster's fifty-page pamphlet calling for constitutional reform and national unity, *Sketches of American Policy* (1785). *Sketches* would advance a "Plan of policy for improving the advantages and perpetuating the union of the American states." The pamphlet would also anticipate aspects of the future U.S. Constitution, such as the separation of powers and the presidency.

To ensure legislative action to secure copyright protection in Virginia, Webster obtained letters of introduction from George Washington to the state's governor and legislative leaders. Armed with Washington's letters, Webster travelled to Richmond in late 1785. According to Webster biographer Harlow Giles Unger:

> Webster met with James Madison, who greeted the New Englander warmly and recalled their previous meeting and subsequent correspondence with enthusiasm. He "spoke with praise of [the] contents" of the *Sketches*, which Washington had shown him and which he had studied carefully. Madison's newfound enthusiasm combined with Washington's letter to win passage of copyright legislation.

The next month, Webster would write to Washington: "For this success I acknowledge myself indebted, in some measure, to your politeness." In his memoirs, Webster would later recall that in the very same session, the Virginia legislature would invite other states to meet in Annapolis, Maryland, in order to "form some plan for investing Congress with the regulation and taxation of commerce." The Annapolis Convention, which Madison attended, would become a precursor to the 1787 Constitutional Convention in Philadelphia.

Protecting Literary Property: Copyright During the Articles of Confederation

Noah Webster's previous interaction with James Madison likewise involved the subject of copyright. In fact, Webster's effort to obtain state copyright legislation was preceded by his lobbying of the Confederation Congress at the end of 1782. Madison was a member of the Congress and took active interest in the matter.

The *Journal of the Continental Congress* records a March 1783 motion: "That a committee be appointed to consider the most proper means of cherishing genius and useful arts through the United States by securing to the authors or publishers of new books their property in such works."

Madison was named to that committee. In May of that same year:

> The committee, consisting of Mr. [Hugh] Williamson, Mr. [Ralph] Izard and Mr. [James] Madison, to whom were referred sundry papers and memorials from different persons on the subject of literary property, being persuaded that nothing is more properly a man's own than the fruit of his study, and that the protection and security of literary property would greatly tend to encourage genius, to promote useful discoveries and to the general extension of arts and commerce, beg leave to submit the following report:
>
> Resolved, That it be recommended to the several states, to secure to the authors or publishers of any new books not hitherto printed, being citizens of the United States, and to their heir or assigns executors, administrators and assigns, the copyright of such books for a certain time, not less than fourteen years from the first publication; and to secure to the said authors, if they shall survive the term first mentioned, and to their heirs or assigns executors, administrators and assigns, the copyright of such books for another term of time not less than fourteen years, such copy or exclusive right of printing, publishing and vending the same, to be secured to the original authors, or publishers, or their assigns their executors, administrators and assigns, by such laws and under restrictions as to the several states may seem proper.

Along with Webster's lobbying efforts, the Confederation Congress's resolution helped to prompt passage of copyright legislation by twelve of the thirteen states. For instance, the Congress's resolution was expressly recognized in Pennsylvania's 1784 "Act for the encouragement and promotion of learning by vesting a right to the copies of printed books in the authors or purchasers of such copies, during the time therein mentioned."

More than that, the Confederation Congress's resolution urging the states to secure copyright protection to authors offers insights into the nature and purpose of copyright in the mind of Madison and in other American statesmen leading up to the Constitution's drafting and ratification. Madison and his colleagues regarded copyright as a type of property—"literary property" they sometimes called it—grounded in the rightful ownership of the fruits of one's labor. And they believed that the promotion of arts, discoveries, and commerce depended upon the securing the rights to such property.

Operating under the Articles of Confederation, however, the Confederation Congress lacked any power to adopt or enforce copyright laws. This prompted Webster to pursue his state-by-state strategy. But it also factored into Madison's deeper and broader thinking about the structural defects and other deficiencies of government under the Articles as well as the problems arising in the states.

According to Madison constitutional biographer William Lee Miller, in the 1780s Madison would undertake a vigorous personal study of systems of government, including the fall of ancient republics and confederations. That study, as well as his reflections on the situation in America, would be reflected in some key memoranda written by Madison. *Vices of the Political System of the United States* (1787) is one such memorandum. Therein Madison listed a dozen deficiencies of government among the several states and under the Articles of Confederation. Under the memo's heading for vice number 5, "want of concert in matters where common interest requires it," Madison wrote:

> This defect is strongly illustrated in the state of our commercial affairs. How much has the national dignity, interest, and revenue suffered from this cause? Instances of inferior moment are *the want of uniformity in the laws concerning* naturalization & *literary property* ...

As Miller observed, "Madison certainly would get a lot of mileage out of his memos. He drew heavily upon them in his speeches in the Federal Convention in Philadelphia."

Copyright at the 1787 Constitutional Convention

It is well known that Madison's speeches, committee work, and lobbying of fellow delegates played a pivotal part in shaping the proposed Constitution.

But it is much less well known that Noah Webster was likewise in Philadelphia during the Convention's meeting during the summer of 1787. "Throughout that summer, Webster was spending a lot of time with 'Convention Men,'" wrote Joshua Kendall. And Webster also socialized with the Virginia delegates, including James Madison and Convention President George Washington. Webster was only too eager to take advantage of opportunities to promote his ideas for a strengthened union and for copyright protection in his visits with Convention delegates.

Thus, in Philadelphia in 1787, the efforts of both the Father of Copyright and the Father of the Constitution came to ultimate fruition. Madison's *Notes of Debates in the Federal Convention of 1787* (1840) for Saturday, August 18 reads: "In Convention Mr. Madison submitted ... the following powers as proper to be added to those of the General Legislature ... To secure to literary authors their copy rights for a limited time." There is no indication of any contentious debate on this point. And so the Convention's proposal would come to include the "IP Clause" in Article I, Section 8, which provides that "Congress Shall have Power ... To promote the Progress of Science and useful Arts, by securing for limited Times to Authors and Inventors the exclusive Right to their respective Writings and Discoveries."

Copyright and Constitutional Ratification

"Even after the convention Madison continued to make use of his memorandums," Miller recounted. In particular, Madison "borrowed from them when he composed his entries in the *Federalist* papers." Reflecting an apparent consensus and lack of debate over the matter of copyright protection, Madison's defense of the IP Clause took only one brisk paragraph of *Federalist No. 43*. Writing under the pen name of "Publius," Madison explained that "[t]he utility of this power will scarcely be questioned" and that "[t]he public good fully coincides [in both the case of copyright of authors and of the right to useful inventions by inventors] with the claims of individuals." Echoing his earlier memorandum, Madison also pointed out that "[t]he States cannot separately make effectual provisions for either of the cases, and most of them have anticipated the decision of this point, by laws passed at the instance of Congress."

In short, Madison in *The Federalist Papers* regarded the IP Clause as a measure to ensure the rights of authors (and inventors) and to further the public good through a national policy of protection and enforcement. For his part, Noah Webster offered high praise of *The Federalist* upon its publication. In his estimation, "It would be difficult to find a treatise ... in which the true principles of republican government are unfolded with such precision." Writing under the pen name "A Citizen of America," Webster offered his own, albeit less sophisticated, defense of the proposed constitution in a pamphlet titled *An Examination into the Leading Principles of the New Federal Constitution Proposed by the Late Convention Held at Philadelphia* (1787). According to Joshua Kendall, "[t]hough the *Federalist Papers* are much better known to history, at the time Webster's pamphlet may well have exerted even more influence, particularly outside New York State."

Conclusion

Knowledge of the efforts of Noah Webster—"The Father of Copyright"—and James Madison—"The Father of the Constitution"—are important to understanding the constitutional history of copyright and its foundational principles. This history reinforces a basic understanding of copyright as a form of "literary property," grounded in a person's fundamental right to the fruits of his or her own labor. Such an understanding and grounding should inform our reading of the IP Clause and continue to guide copyright policy today.

Indeed, Webster's and Madison's view of copyright as literary property arising out of the fruits of one's labor and deserving uniform protection at the national level should focus and redirect policymaking to government's primary purpose under the Constitution—protecting rights of property in all its facets, whether tangible or intangible. Recognizing copyright in the Constitution, the fundamental law of the land, conveys its importance in promoting progress in science and useful arts, as well as commerce.

For lawmakers, policymakers and analysts today, the IP Clause makes copyright a normative feature of the American constitutional order, one deserving of understanding and respect. Copyright's status as a constitutionally protected property right requires that all policy touching on such rights comport with the rule of law.

Sources

A Citizen of America (Noah Webster), *An Examination into the Leading Principles of the New Federal Constitution Proposed by the Late Convention Held at Philadelphia* (1787).

Journals of the Continental Congress (1783).

James Madison, *Vices of the Political System of the United States* (1787).

James Madison, *Notes of Debates in the Federal Convention of 1787* (1840).

Publius (James Madison), *The Federalist*, No. 43 (1788).

Noah Webster, Letter to George Washington (December 16, 1785).
Noah Webster, *Sketches of American Policy* (1787).
Noah Webster, "Origin of the Copy-Right Laws in the United States" (1843).

* * *

Joshua Kendall, *The Forgotten Founding Father: Noah Webster's Obsession and the Creation of an American Culture* (2011).
William Lee Miller, *The Business of May Next: James Madison and the Founding* (1993).
Harlow Giles Unger, *Noah Webster: The Life and Times of an American Patriot* (1998).
U.S. Copyright Office, "Copyright Enactments: Laws Passed in the United States Since 1783 Relating to Copyright," *Bulletin No. 3* (Revised) (1973).

Chapter 4

The Constitution's Approach to Copyright and Patent: Anti-Monopoly, Pro-Intellectual Property Rights

Copyright and patent are rooted in an individual's basic right to the fruits of his or her own labor. Intellectual property (IP) protections are extensions of that basic right. Such protections secure to authors and inventors the financial rewards of their creative works and innovations for limited times, thereby promoting the public good.

Despite the property rights grounding of copyright and patent, some academics and policy analysts have sought, in varying degrees, to undermine the legitimacy of IP rights. One line of attack suggests that IP rights are illegitimate government-conferred monopolies. A related claim is that IP rights are essentially contrary to the anti-monopolistic outlook of America's Founders.

These lines of attack on IP rights are wrong. Government-conferred monopolies over commerce, trade, and occupations are, in fact, almost always anathema to the American constitutional order as well as sound public policy. But basic distinctions set individual intellectual property rights apart from illegitimate government-conferred monopolies. Under a property rights approach to copyright and patent, limited protections are tied to the creation of specific literary works and new inventions. This leaves others like freedom to create and invent, with no geographical or occupational barriers to entry.

Above all else, the U.S. Constitution recognizes the uniqueness of copyright and patent. At the time of the nation's founding, basic differences between government-conferred monopolies and individual IP rights were well known. The Founders were familiar with Britain's sorry history of Crown-chartered monopolies. They were likewise familiar with attempts by British common law courts and by Parliament to restrict such monopolies and to protect IP rights for authors and inventors. Colonial experiences with continuing British monopolistic practices were also a factor in spurring the American Revolution.

While the Founders held an anti-monopolistic outlook, at the same time they supported limited protections for copyright and patent, placing the power to establish those protections in the fundamental law of the land. Article I, Section 8, Clause 8 of the U.S. Constitution grants Congress power "To promote the Progress of Science and useful Arts, by securing for limited Times to Authors and Inventors the exclusive Right to their respective Writings and Discoveries." In other words, it is clear that the framers and ratifiers of the Constitution made a conscious choice to protect individual IP rights and, at the same time, to rely on certain constitutional safeguards against monopolies.

In addition to the limits inherent in the IP Clause, the U.S. Constitution's early supporters stressed structural safeguards against monopolies, including the enumerated powers doctrine. Under this doctrine, Congress could only exercise those legislative powers expressly granted to it, and the U.S. Constitution nowhere granted Congress any power to establish monopolies. Another check against monopolistic abuses was supplied by the republican form of self-government which the U.S. Constitution embodied.

Moreover, concerns regarding government-conferred monopolies over literary publications were expressly addressed in the Bill of Rights. The First Amendment's prohibition on laws abridging the freedom of the press banned government licensing of the press. And it also supplied the federal judiciary with a firm basis for vindicating individual rights to write and publish freely.

Thus, the U.S. Constitution rightfully should be considered to be anti-monopoly and pro-intellectual property rights. Both of these conceptions rightfully coexist in our constitutional order, and they should drive public policy to limit government-conferred monopolies and to promote and protect individual IP rights.

Principled Differences Between Government Monopolies and Individual IP Rights

In recent years, intellectual property rights have come under attack. Some academics and policy analysts have alleged that copyrights and patents amount to little more than illegitimate government-conferred monopolies. IP has also been attacked as a once useful but now dispensable set of government-bestowed privileges.

These broadsides against IP's institutional legitimacy miss the mark. To be sure, anti-monopolistic principles—premised on equal protection under the law, individual liberty, and limited government—are staples of American constitutionalism and deserve careful adherence. Government-conferred monopolies are rightly to be opposed in almost all circumstances. Yet there are obvious differences between illegitimate monopolies over particular industries or occupations and individual copyright and patent protections. Those differences should drive public policy to limit monopolies, on the one hand, and to promote and protect IP rights, on the other.

Government-conferred monopolies are characteristic of arbitrary rule and denial of equal protection under the law. Corruption and self-dealing are all but unavoidable—if not institutionalized—when government issues monopolies to chosen individuals or entities. By granting private entities a monopoly over commercial activity in a certain geographical area or for a particular occupation, government imposes barriers to new entrants and undermines marketplace competition. This violates an individual's basic liberty to engage in commerce and to pursue a lawful occupation of his or her own choice.

Such monopolies are also harmful from a consumer welfare standpoint. They constitute restrictions on outputs of goods or services, encouraging price increases and discouraging innovation. In sum, government-granted monopolies are at odds with principles of free market enterprise.

In contrast, as we explained in Chapters 1 and 2, copyrights and patents are grounded in an individual's basic right—indeed, a natural right—to the fruits of his or her own labor. IP rights protections are extensions of that basic property right. In a civil society, and under our Constitution, IP protections secure to authors and inventors exclusive but time-limited rights to the proceeds of their creations and inventions.

The contours of IP rights protections are guided by public purposes, chiefly incentivizing commercial, artistic, and scientific advances for the benefit of the broader public. According to a 2012 report by the Economics and Statistics Administration and the U.S. Patent and Trademark Office, employment in IP-intensive industries totaled more than 27 million in 2010, with nearly 13 million jobs indirectly associated with those industries. This amounted to 27.7% of jobs in the U.S. economy. That same year, according to the report, "IP-intensive industries accounted for about $5.06 trillion in value added," or 34.8% of U.S. gross domestic product.

Importantly, IP rights are tied to the specific literary works or inventions of respective authors and inventors. And those rights are subject to important limitations regarding scope and term. Literary or artistic expressions can be copyrighted, for instance, but abstract ideas or facts cannot. Fair use of copyrighted materials by the general public is also permitted for purposes of criticism, comment, news reporting, teaching, scholarship, or research. And patents are not granted unless they involve novelty and pass a non-obviousness requirement.

Unlike government-conferred trade monopolies, copyrights and patents do not bar entry into an occupation or prohibit competition in any particular trade. Protection extends only to the proceeds of the author's or inventor's particular literary or artistic work or invention. When copyrights and patents are granted, others remain free to create and invent as they so choose. The liberty of prospective authors and inventors to offer their own creations and inventions as competing alternatives is limited only by their own creative and inventive resources and by the limited rights of original authors or inventors.

IP rights exclude others from using copyrighted materials or patented inventions for commercial gain without permission or licenses. But this exclusionary aspect hardly renders copyright or patent illegitimate kinds of government-conferred monopolies. Exclusion is a common characteristic of property rights. In some instances, the ability to exclude may be an inherent feature of the tangible or intangible good or service in question. By technological design, access to copyrighted information in digital format, like movies or songs, may require an encryption code obtainable only by purchase through a secure platform. Or a particular parcel of land may be protected by natural barriers or by high fences. But as a general matter, exclusion as an attribute of property primarily comes in the form of enforcement through an administrative or legal process. A copyright holder may obtain an award of damages from an infringer through a civil action, for example. Or a trespasser on a property owner's land may be prosecuted.

These basic distinctions between illegitimate government monopolies and limited IP rights for authors and inventors should not be difficult to grasp. Just as importantly, these distinctions were understood in America at the time of the nation's founding. American constitutional history offers lessons in this regard, and these lessons reinforce the uniqueness and importance of IP rights.

The British Backdrop to American Anti-Monopolistic Understanding

Early American understanding about illegitimate government-conferred monopolies as well as individual IP rights was informed by the history of monopolistic abuses by the British Crown. Common law court rulings and statutes of Parliament designed to prohibit or restrict those abuses provided a backdrop to the monopolistic outlook of Colonial-turned-Revolutionary-turned-Independent Americans.

The British Crown granted monopolistic charters as a means of securing revenue apart from a resort to Parliament. Sir Edward Coke's *Institutes of the Law of England* (1664), and abridged versions of the same, were studied and known to early American lawyers. In his *Institutes,* Coke defined a monopoly as an:

> Institution or allowance by the King by his grant, commission, or otherwise to any person or persons, bodies politic or corporate, of or for the sole buying, selling, making, working or using of anything whereby any person or persons, bodies politic or corporate, are sought to be restrainted of any freedom or liberty that they had before, or hindered in their lawful trade.

The printing press, in particular, was also subject to a Crown-granted monopoly. Under the Licensing Act of 1662, no book could be printed in England without prior registration with the Stationers' Company, a Crown-chartered guild of printers and booksellers. The copyrights could only be secured by guild members, could not be bought or sold to non-members in the public marketplace, and lasted forever.

Celebrated cases like *Darcy v. Allen* (1603) struck down royal grants of trade privileges as void under the common law. Coke's report on *Darcy's* case stressed the importance to society of allowing individuals to work freely in trades of their own choosing.

Despite such anti-monopolistic rulings, the Crown's persistence in issuing monopolies prompted Parliamentary response. The Statute of Monopolies (1624) significantly curtailed the British Crown's ability to grant special privileges. One of the Statute's limited exceptions applied in the case of patents on inventions. Such patents were generally limited to 14 years and allowed living inventors to renew them for an additional 14 years.

Also, following the expiration of the Licensing Act in 1695, Parliament enacted the Statute of Anne (1710). This effectively ended the Stationers' Company monopoly. The Statute made authors the original copyright holders, thereby eliminating guild membership requirements. It also imposed term limits on copyrights, generally tracking with the Statute of Monopolies by limiting copyrights to 14 years and allowing living authors to renew their copyrights for an additional 14 years.

Many American Colonists came to believe they were entitled to the protections of British common law and Parliamentary statutes that expressed principles of fundamental law. However, uncertainty revolved around the extent to which British common law and statutes prohibiting or restricting the Crown's monopolistic abuses actually applied to the Colonies.

The Anti-Monopolistic Spur
to the American Revolution

The persistence of British monopolistic policies in the Colonies—and resentment toward such policies—played directly into the American Revolution. British Navigation Acts incurred Colonists' resentment, as those Acts restricted the export of American raw materials to England and likewise prohibited foreign goods and vessels from American ports. A group of Virginians at a meeting presided over by Chairman George Washington described such policies in the *Fairfax County Resolves* (1774):

> [T]he British Parliament have claimed and exercised the Power of regulating our Trade and Commerce, so as to restrain our importing from foreign Countrys, such Articles as they cou'd furnish us with, of their own Growth or Manufacture, or exporting to foreign Countrys such Articles and Portions of our Produce, as Great Britain stood in Need of, for her own Consumption or Manufactures.

Most notably, the Boston Tea Party protest against taxation without representation involved British taxing of tea imported by the East India Company's trade monopoly. The *Fairfax County Resolves* declared:

> [A]s we consider the said Company as the Tools and Instrument of Oppression in the Hands of Government and the Cause of our present Distress, it is the Opinion of this Meeting that the People of these Colonies shou'd forbear all further Dealings with them, by refusing to purchase their Merchandize, until that Peace Safety and Goodorder, which they have disturbed, be perfectly restored.

Undoubtedly, the Colonists regard for freedom of the press from prior restraints or from monopolistic licensing practices was evident in practice. The Colonies saw wide circulation of pre-revolutionary pamphlets by English opposition writers, supplemented by tracts addressed to Colonial concerns at the dawn of the Revolution, such as Thomas Jefferson's *A Summary View of the Rights of British America* (1774) or Thomas Paine's *Common Sense* (1776). As the First Continental Congress declared in its *Appeal to the Inhabitants of Quebec* (1774):

> The last right we shall mention regards the freedom of the press. The importance of this consists, besides the advancement of truth, science, morality, and arts in general, in its diffusion of liberal sentiments on the administration of Government, its ready communication of thoughts between subjects, and its consequential promotion of

union among them, whereby oppressive officers are shamed or intimidated into more honorable and just modes of conducting affairs.

By the time of the 1787 Constitutional Convention, aversion to monopolies and government-conferred privileges had become a key theme in American constitutional thought. But another emerging theme in American constitutionalism was the importance of IP rights.

Anti-Monopoly, Pro-IP Rights: The Constitution's Approach to Copyright and Patent

As previously explained in Chapter 3, James Madison and his colleagues in the 1787 Constitutional Convention regarded copyright as "literary property." And, importantly, as we explained in Chapters 1 and 2, they grounded copyright protection in Lockean principles concerning the rightful ownership of the fruits of one's labor. They believed that the promotion of arts, discoveries, and commerce depended upon the securing of IP rights to authors as well as inventors. Their grasp of the significance of IP rights enabled them to distinguish such rights from illegitimate government-conferred monopolies—and to establish constitutional safeguards against such monopolies.

The IP Clause is contained in Article I, Section 8, Clause 8 of the U.S. Constitution. It grants Congress power "[t]o promote the Progress of Science and useful Arts, by securing for limited Times to Authors and Inventors the exclusive Right to their respective Writings and Discoveries." The IP Clause addressed anti-monopolistic concerns by placing limits on the purpose, scope, and terms of IP rights.

While attuned to the dangers of government-conferred monopolies by history and experience, the framers and ratifiers of the U.S. Constitution made a conscious choice to promote copyrights and patents in the fundamental law of the land. Madison elaborated on that choice in a 1788 letter to Thomas Jefferson, writing:

> With regard to Monopolies, they are justly classed among the greatest nuisances in Government. But is it clear that, as encouragements to literary works and ingenious discoveries, they are not too valuable to be wholly renounced? Would it not suffice to reserve in all cases a right to the public to abolish the privilege at a price to be specified in the grant of it?

While Madison acknowledged wrongfulness of monopolies, he nonetheless thought it unnecessary to adopt a constitutional amendment expressly prohibiting them. In retirement, Madison would restate the distinction between abusive monopolies and beneficial IP rights—and the IP Clause's constitutional policy favoring the latter with limitations. According to his so-called *Detached Memoranda* (circa 1820):

> Monoplies tho' in certain cases useful ought to be granted with caution, and guarded with strictness agst abuse. The Constitution of the U.S. has limited them to two cases, the authors of Books, and of useful inventions, in both which they are considered as a compensation for a benefit actually gained to the community as a purchase of property which the owner might otherwise withold from public use. There can be no just objection to a temporary monopoly in these cases: but it ought to be temporary, because under that limitation a sufficient recompence and encouragement may be given. The limitation is particularly proper in the case of inventions, because they grow so much out of preceding ones that there is the less merit in the authors: and because for the same reason, the discovery might be expected in a short time from other hands.

This distinction between abusive monopolies and beneficial IP rights was also articulated by Noah Webster. The pro-ratification lexicographer Webster was a collaborator with Madison in urging copyright protections for American authors. Webster's *American Dictionary of the English Language* (1828) makes that distinction plain in light of American Revolutionary political theory and history. His dictionary defined "monopoly" as:

> The sole power of vending any species of goods, obtained either by engrossing the articles in market by purchase, or by a license from the government confirming this privilege. Thus the East India Company in Great Britain has a monopoly of the trade to the East Indies, granted to them by charter. *Monopolies* by individuals obtained by engrossing, are an offense prohibited by law. But a man has by natural right the exclusive power of vending his own produce or manufactures, and to retain that exclusive right is not a *monopoly* within the meaning of the law.

The Constitution's Structural Safeguards Against Monopolies

In addition to the inherent limits on copyright and patent protections established in the IP Clause, the proposed U.S. Constitution's structural limits on federal power presumably prohibited federal government-conferred monopolies.

According to Madison in *Federalist No. 45*, "[t]he powers delegated by the proposed Constitution to the federal government are few and defined." Article I, Section 8 nowhere provided Congress a general power to grant monopolies.

Madison also emphasized that the republican form of government, embodied in the U.S. Constitution, provided a vital check on potential monopolistic abuses. In *Federalist No. 39*, he defined the republican form as "a government which derives all its powers directly or indirectly from the great body of the people, and is administered by persons holding their offices during pleasure, for a limited period, or during good behavior." Madison explained:

> It is evident that no other form would be reconcilable with the genius of the people of America; with the fundamental principles of the Revolution; or with that honorable determination which animates every votary of freedom, to rest all our political experiments on the capacity of mankind for self-government.

In his 1788 letter to Jefferson, Madison described the check against monopolistic abuses that would be furnished by self-government under the proposed U.S. Constitution:

> Is there not also infinitely less danger in this abuse in our Governments than in most others? Monopolies are sacrifices of the many to the few. Where the power is in the few it is natural for them to sacrifice the many to their own partialities and corruptions. Where the power as with us is in the many not in the few the danger cannot be very great that the few will be thus favored. It is much more to be dreaded that the few will be unnecessarily sacrificed to the many.

Literary Property and Liberty of the Press: Copyright and the Free Press Clause

A subset of anti-monopolistic concerns that emerged during the U.S. Constitution's ratification debates involved liberty of the press and fears of a federal power grab to license the printing press. Those concerns would eventually be accommodated by the First Congress and state legislatures in proposing and ratifying the First Amendment. The Amendment's Free Press Clause expressly prohibited monopolistic press licensing by the federal government while leaving individual copyright protection intact under the Constitution.

During the ratification period, Anti-Federalist George Mason raised fears over the prospect of the federal government asserting control over the press. James Iredell, a pro-ratification floor leader at North Carolina's unsuccessful first

Ratification Convention and a future member of the U.S. Supreme Court, published *Answers to Mr. Mason's Objections to the New Constitution* (1788). In that pamphlet, Iredell contended that the unamended U.S. Constitution secured liberty of the press while protecting copyright:

> The Liberty of the Press is always a grand topic for declamation; but the future Congress will have no authority over this than to secure to authors for a limited time the exclusive privilege of publishing their works. This authority has long been exercised in England, where the press is as free as among ourselves, or in any country in the world, and surely such an encouragement to genius is no restraint on the liberty of the press, since men are allowed to publish what they please of their own; and so far as this may be deemed a restraint upon others it is certainly a reasonable one, and can be attended with no danger of copies not being sufficiently multiplied, because the interest of the proprietor will always induce him to publish a quantity fully equal to the demand—besides, that such encouragement may give birth to many excellent writings which would otherwise have never appeared.

Iredell also specifically responded to the hypothetical that Congress could grant monopolies in trade and commerce pursuant to the IP Clause. He stated: "I am convinced Mr. Mason did not mean to refer to this clause. He is a gentleman of too much taste and knowledge himself to wish to have our government established on such principles of barbarism as to be able to afford no encouragement to genius."

Similar reassurance regarding liberty of the press under the proposed U.S. Constitution came from pro-ratificationists such as Noah Webster and Alexander Hamilton. In *Federalist No. 84*, Hamilton asked: "Why, for instance, should it be said that the liberty of the press shall not be restrained, when no power is given by which restrictions may be imposed?" Hamilton posed the question in the course of his broader argument against the necessity of adopting a Bill of Rights. One aspect of Hamilton's argument—similar to Madison's arguments against a constitutional provision expressly banning monopolies—was rooted in the republican nature of government under the Constitution. Expressly referring to the liberty of the press, Hamilton wrote:

> [I]ts security, whatever fine declarations may be inserted in any constitution respecting it, must altogether depend on public opinion, and on the general spirit of the people and of the government. And here, after all, as is intimated upon another occasion, must we seek for the only solid basis of all our rights.

New York and ten other states proceeded to ratify the proposed U.S. Constitution, putting the new government into effect. Several ratifying states would pass resolutions calling for a constitutional amendment to guarantee liberty of the press. North Carolina's Convention adjourned without voting on ratification, however, prompting Iredell's published responses to Anti-Federalists in hopes of securing that state's ratification in a subsequent convention.

Madison would ultimately change his mind regarding the efficacy of adopting a Bill of Rights. In his speech to the First Congress introducing a Bill of Rights, Madison expressed the need "to satisfy the public mind that their liberties will be perpetual, and this without endangering any part of the constitution, which is considered as essential to the existence of the government by those who promoted its adoption."

Referring to the refusal of North Carolina and Rhode Island to ratify the Constitution, Madison declared, "[I]t is a desirable thing, on our part as well as theirs, that a re-union should take place as soon as possible." Madison believed that by proposing a Bill of Rights, Congress would induce those two states to ratify, restoring their relations with the other states in the Union. Madison also declared that a Bill of Rights would be enforced by the judiciary to vindicate individual rights from governmental overreach.

Consistent with the views he set out in his 1788 letter to Jefferson regarding the benefits and necessity of constitutional protections for IP rights, Madison did not propose any general anti-monopoly amendment to the U.S. Constitution. He did, however, propose a provision that "[t]he powers not delegated by this constitution, nor prohibited by it to the states, are reserved to the States respectively"—later embodied in the Tenth Amendment. Diverging from his Federalist co-author Hamilton, Madison also proposed a provision securing liberty of the press: "The people shall not be deprived or abridged of their right to speak, to write, or to publish their sentiments; and the freedom of the press, as one of the great bulwarks of liberty, shall be inviolable." This provision would eventually become a part of The First Amendment, which provides, in pertinent part, that "Congress shall make no law … abridging the freedom of speech, or of the press."

Under Madison's leadership, the First Congress proposed—and the state legislatures ratified—an amendment to the U.S. Constitution containing an anti-monopoly component regarding literary publications. The First Amendment's Free Press Clause expressly prohibited what the nation's Founders historically regarded as the primary monopolistic concern regarding literary publications—government control and licensure of the press. The Free Press Clause was thus consistent with the anti-monopolistic but pro-IP rights understanding of the Constitution's framers and ratifiers.

Conclusion

Copyright and patent are rooted in an individual's natural right to the fruits of his or her own labor. Intellectual property protections are inextricable, necessary extensions of that basic right. Such laws secure to authors and inventors the financial rewards of their own creative works and innovations for limited times, promoting the public good.

Despite the property rights grounding of copyright and patent derived from Lockean principles adopted by our Founders and incorporated into the Constitution, some academics and policy analysts have sought to undermine the legitimacy of IP rights by comparing them to illegitimate government-conferred monopolies. Such attacks on IP rights are misguided.

Government-conferred monopolies over commerce, trade, and occupations are anathema to the American constitutionalism. But basic distinctions set copyright and patent protections apart from illegitimate government-conferred monopolies. Under a property rights approach to copyrights and patents, limited protections are tied to the specific literary works and inventions of individuals or individual entities. This leaves others like freedom to create and invent, with no geographical or occupational barriers to entry.

The Founding Fathers held an anti-monopolistic outlook and at the same time supported limited protections for copyright and patent. The Constitution's framers and ratifiers made a conscious choice both to protect individual IP rights and to rely on certain constitutional safeguards against monopolies.

In addition to the limits contained in the IP Clause, the U.S. Constitution's early supporters stressed structural safeguards against monopolies. Congress could only exercise those legislative powers expressly granted to it, and the U.S. Constitution nowhere granted the power to establish monopolies. The republican form of self-government embodied in the U.S. Constitution also checked monopolistic abuses. And the First Amendment's Free Press Clause prohibited government licensing of the press. All told, the U.S. Constitution established an anti-monopoly, pro-IP rights outlook.

Sources

Appeal to the Inhabitants of Quebec (1774).

Sir Edward Coke, *Institutes of the Law of England* (1664).

Fairfax County Resolves (1774).

James Iredell, *Answers to Mr. Mason's Objections to the New Constitution* (1788).

James Madison, *Detached Memoranda* (circa 1820).

James Madison, Letter to Thomas Jefferson (Oct. 17, 1788).
James Madison, Speech to the First Congress Proposing a Bill of Rights (1789).
Publius (James Madison), *Federalist No. 39.*
Publius (James Madison), *Federalist No. 45.*
Publius (Alexander Hamilton), *Federalist No. 84.*
Noah Webster, *American Dictionary of the English Language* (1828).

* * *

Steven G. Calabresi & Larissa C. Liebowitz, "Monopolies and the Constitution: A History of Crony Capitalism," 36 *Harvard Journal of Law & Public Policy* 983 (2013).
Economics and Statistics Administration and United States Patent and Trademark Office, *Intellectual Property and the U.S. Economy: Industries in Focus* (2012).

Chapter 5

The "Reason and Nature" of Intellectual Property: Copyright and Patent in *The Federalist Papers*

Congress's power to secure copyright and patent is expressly granted in the U.S. Constitution's Article I, Section 8 Intellectual Property Clause. It confers on Congress a power "To promote the Progress of Science and useful Arts, by securing for limited Times to Authors and Inventors the exclusive Right to their respective Writings and Discoveries." In order to better grasp the meaning of this power and the rights it is designed to secure, attention undoubtedly should be paid to that repository of American constitutionalism widely regarded to be second only to the Constitution itself: namely, *The Federalist Papers*.

Such attention to *The Federalist Papers* is not merely a matter of historical interest, although the history is certainly interesting. Rather, it is a matter of enhancing our present day understanding of why our Founders thought copyrights and patents important and deserving of protection in our Constitution. So, just what does *The Federalist* have to say about copyright and patent?

James Madison, writing in the guise of "Publius," provided that work's lone direct reference to Congress's power to protect intellectual property rights. In the *Federalist No. 43*, Madison wrote:

> The utility of this power will scarcely be questioned. The copyright of authors has been solemnly adjudged, in Great Britain, to be a right of common law. The right to useful inventions seems with equal reason to belong to the inventors. The public good fully coincides in both cases with the claims of individuals. The States cannot separately make effectual provisions for either of the cases, and most of them have anticipated the decision of this point, by laws passed at the instance of Congress.

A proper reading of that brief passage requires examination of its context within *The Federalist* as well as Madison's other writings from that period. Such an examination reveals a rich understanding of the nature of intellectual property and its place in the U.S. Constitutional order. In subtle and succinct fashion, *Federalist No. 43* identifies the ultimate source for copyright and patent in an individual's natural right to the fruits of his or her own labor. Madison regarded copyright and patent as forms of property that government is established to protect. Additionally, as *Federalist No. 43* and other numbers point out, securing an individual's IP rights, consistent with the rules of justice, also furthers the public good by incentivizing further investments and discoveries that promote the "progress of science and useful arts."

In reading *Federalist No. 43*'s intellectual property passage, one can see it is bookended by considerations about the locus of power for protecting copyright and patent under the proposed Constitution. The opening sentence describes the usefulness to the Union of a congressional power for protecting IP. And the closing sentence recounts both the recognition of IP rights by states as well as the inability of the states separately to provide the necessary safeguards for IP.

Given Madison's use of the terms "utility" and "public good," along with the IP Clause's language about promoting progress, modern minds may be prone to read into *Federalist No. 43* a utilitarian understanding of copyright and patent. In general, however, the utility that *The Federalist* was concerned with is the "Utility to the Union" of lodging certain powers in the federal government. And *Federalist No. 43*'s concern with conferring on Congress the power of protecting IP rights is no exception.

Furthermore, a constructive definition of the term emerges from *The Federalist Papers*. Particularly insightful are *Federalist* essays, such as 10, 37, and 51, that address the finiteness of human perception and communication, the fallibility of human reason, and the depravity in human character. According to *The Federalist*, those aspects of human nature make civil society especially prone to the vice of self-interested factions. Constitutional structures such as the separation of powers and the extended sphere of representative government are required to act as counterweights and to channel self-interests in the service of the public good.

Throughout these essays, "public good" encompasses the interests of all people in the security and enjoyment of their rights to liberty and property, consistent with impartial rules of justice. Therefore, protecting the respective IP rights of authors and inventors "for limited Times" in order "to promote the Progress of Science and useful Arts" in society, fits firmly within Madison's overall understanding of the purpose of a just government: to protect individual rights of liberty and property, in the furtherance of the common good rather than the self-interests of a faction of the people.

Nestled between *Federalist No. 43*'s bookends addressed to federal and state power is a brief and subtle allusion to the underlying nature of IP rights. Madison's meaning is rather easy to misunderstand because of the reference he makes to British common law copyright. But Madison was not making an appeal to binding historical precedent from the Old World. Rather, Madison invoked a historical point of reference in order to address what his co-author Alexander Hamilton, in *Federalist No. 78*, would call "the reason and nature of the thing." What ultimately concerned Madison was certain British common law jurists' identification of an individual's natural right as the *reason* for protecting an author's copyright. Madison appealed to that same reason and advanced its application, in an American constitutional context, to support the protection of both copyright and patent rights.

Thus, in its essence, *Federalist No. 43* traces the reason and nature of intellectual property to an individual's right to the fruits of his or her labor. Madison's short explanation for the IP Clause in *Federalist No. 43* grounds copyright and patent in natural right, not merely utilitarian calculations about the greatest good for the greatest number.

Of course, a natural rights perspective does not eliminate matters of social utility from consideration in defining the dynamics of copyright and patent. Legal or administrative decisions about how best to secure individual IP rights are often complex and fact-intensive. Sound policy demands that both short-term and long-term costs and benefits to society be considered in making such decisions. In the final analysis, however—and this is the important point—such decisions are about how best to protect the core of pre-existing rights of property that do not ultimately depend for their existence upon empirical or intuitive economic calculations. Thus, utility may be said to supply a boundary principle for IP rights, but natural right supplies IP's foundational grounding principle.

The Federalist and Its Constitutional Legacy

Describing *The Federalist Papers* to his audience during the ratification debates over the proposed 1787 U.S. Constitution, James Madison wrote in *Federalist No. 37* that "the ultimate object of these papers is to determine clearly and fully the merits of this Constitution, and the expediency of adopting it." A collaborative effort of Alexander Hamilton, James Madison, and John Jay, *The Federalist Papers* did much more than explain the form and substance of the proposed Constitution. In addition to defending the proposed Constitution from misleading or exaggerated charges made against it by anti-Federalist critics, the co-authors of *The Federalist* assessed the inadequacies of the Articles of Confederation and described the abuses and conflicts stemming from state legislatures. Moreover, *The Federalists'* co-authors contended for the "*utility of the UNION*" to further America's "*political prosperity.*" Indeed, they maintained that the preservation of that Union depended on the ratification of the proposed Constitution. Adoption of the proposed Constitution, they insisted, would help secure republican government, liberty, and property. As Alexander Hamilton wrote to the American public at the beginning of *Federalist No. 1*, the stakes could not be any higher:

> You are called upon to deliberate on a new Constitution for the United States of America. The subject speaks its own importance; comprehending in its consequences nothing less than the existence of the UNION, the safety and welfare of the parts of which it is composed, the fate of an empire in many respects the most interesting in the world. It has been frequently remarked that it seems to have been reserved to the people of this country, by their conduct and example, to decide the important question, whether societies of men are really capable or not of establishing good government from reflection and choice, or whether they are forever destined to depend for their political constitutions on accident and force. If there be any truth in the remark, the crisis at which we are arrived may with propriety be regarded as the era in which that decision is to be made; and a wrong election of the part we shall act may, in this view, deserve to be considered as the general misfortune of mankind.

Articles written under the pen name of "Publius" first appeared in several newspapers. They were subsequently circulated more widely in book form, totaling 85 entries in all. *The Federalist* was admired by contemporaries for its insights into human nature and the character of republican government. It was likewise praised for its lucid review of the proposed Constitution's provisions and its persuasive arguments for their efficacy.

George Washington, for example, secretly transmitted the first seven Federalist essays for wider publication in Virginia after being sent draft versions by Madison on November 18, 1787. In a letter to Hamilton dated August 28, 1788, Washington wrote:

> As the perusal of the political papers under the signature of Publius has afforded me great satisfaction, I shall certainly consider them as claiming a most distinguished place in my Library. I have read every performance which has been printed on one side and the other of

the great question lately agitated (so far as I have been able to obtain them) and, without an unmeaning compliment, I will say, that I have seen no other so well calculated (in my judgment) to produce conviction on an unbiased Mind, as the *Production* of your *triumvirate*. When the transient circumstances and fugitive performances which attended this Crisis shall have disappeared, That Work will merit the Notice of Posterity; because in it are candidly and ably discussed the principles of freedom and the topics of government, which will be always interesting to mankind so long as they shall be connected in Civil Society.

Washington's prediction regarding *The Federalist*'s legacy has proven correct. Its enduring importance depends in no small part on historian John C. Miller's observation that: "Generations of commentators upon the Constitution—John Marshall, Daniel Webster, Joseph Story among them—ranked *The Federalist* second only to the Constitution itself; and in determining the jurisdiction of the national government and the powers of the various departments of that government, they followed Hamilton, Madison and Jay with implicit confidence." Thus, *The Federalist* would quickly assume authoritative status—and continue to grow in stature over time—for its examination of the basic principles of the American constitutional order and for its interpretive insights into the meaning of the Constitution's provisions and terms. Where it speaks to a matter of American constitutionalism, therefore, *The Federalist* merits careful attention.

Federalist No. 43 on Congressional Power, Copyright, and Patent

The U.S. Constitution's Article I, Section 8 Intellectual Property Clause delegates to Congress a power "To promote the Progress of Science and useful Arts, by securing for limited Times to Authors and Inventors the exclusive Right to their respective Writings and Discoveries." *Federalist No. 43*, written by James Madison, marks *The Federalist*'s only direct reference to the IP Clause and to the underlying nature of IP rights that Congress is charged with securing.

Here is what Madison said regarding the IP clause:

The utility of this power will scarcely be questioned. The copyright of authors has been solemnly adjudged, in Great Britain, to be a right of common law. The right to useful inventions seems with equal reason to belong to the inventors. The public good fully coincides in both cases with the claims of individuals. The States cannot separately make effectual provisions for either of the cases, and most of them have anticipated the decision of this point, by laws passed at the instance of Congress.

The foregoing paragraph consists of few words. But a close reading of the passage and an appreciation of its context, including the whole of *The Federalist Papers*, reveal a rich understanding of the nature of IP and its place in the U.S. constitutional order.

Federalist No. 43: Natural Right as the Reasoned Basis for IP Rights

In subtle and succinct fashion, *Federalist No. 43* identifies the ultimate source for copyright and patent in an individual's natural right to the fruits of his or her own labor. This Madison does in a pair of sentences that are easy to misunderstand or misconstrue because of Madison's reference to British common law. However, a careful reading of both sentences suggests that Madison was ultimately concerned with certain British common law jurists' identification of an individual's natural right as the *reason* for copyright. And in an American constitutional context, Madison applied that reason to both copyright and patent.

Confusion Surrounding British Common Law Copyright

Describing the IP rights that Congress is empowered to secure under the proposed Constitution, Madison referenced copyright in British common law. In a handful of cases, British common law jurists deemed copyright a common law right. For instance, in *Millar v. Taylor* (1769), common law luminary Lord Mansfield ruled that authors enjoyed a perpetual common law copyright in their written publications. Sir William Blackstone similarly contended that authors enjoyed a common law right to their manuscripts and to the proceeds resulting from publications.

Incidentally, the section devoted to the IP Clause in Joseph Story's *Commentaries on the Constitution of the United States* (1833) is in many respects a gloss on *Federalist No. 43*. Story, an eminent legal scholar and a Madison appointee to the U.S. Supreme Court, cites *Federalist No. 43* in summing up the historical antecedents for the IP Clause: "It was doubtless to this knowledge of the common law and statuteable rights of authors and inventors, that we are to attribute this constitutional provision."

Mindful of historical developments, some scholars have fixed on the precise status of copyright under British law and suggest that Madison misstated that law in *Federalist No. 43*. Madison made no reference, it is observed, to the

House of Lords ruling in *Donaldson v. Beckett* (1774) that denied a perpetual copyright under the common law. Rather, *Donaldson* held that copyright existed solely because of Parliament's say-so in the Statute of Anne (1717). The implication arising from such observation seems to be that *Federalist No. 43* offers little useful information about IP and perhaps points to the shaky foundations of copyright and patents.

The Lords' decision in *Donaldson* was not without controversy. The Lords' ruling was split, decided by a one-vote margin on account of Lord Mansfield's abstention. Mansfield issued a ruling in a prior stage of the same case to the effect that there was a perpetual common law copyright. *Donaldson* would remain the subject of continuing confusion and legal debate for decades in America. It was unclear to many, for instance, whether *Donaldson* meant that authors still possessed a common law copyright to unpublished manuscripts or whether the Statute of Anne eliminated all common law copyright claims. The matter becomes a bit more confusing given that neither the Statute of Anne nor the Statute of Monopolies—which recognized limited patent rights for inventors—expressly applied to America; and the basic presumption was that those statutes only applied in Britain prior to the Revolution.

This kind of confusion regarding IP vis-à-vis British common law and American law would come as no surprise to Madison. In his discussion of the limitations on human perception and communication in *Federalist No. 37*, Madison explained:

> The experience of ages, with the continued and combined labors of the most enlightened legislatures and jurists, has been equally unsuccessful in delineating the several objects and limits of different codes of laws and different tribunals of justice. The precise extent of the common law, and the statute law, the maritime law, the ecclesiastical law, the law of corporations, and other local laws and customs, remains still to be clearly and finally established in Great Britain, where accuracy in such subjects has been more industriously pursued than in any other part of the world. The jurisdiction of her several courts, general and local, of law, of equity, of admiralty, etc., is not less a source of frequent and intricate discussions, sufficiently denoting the indeterminate limits by which they are respectively circumscribed. All new laws, though penned with the greatest technical skill, and passed on the fullest and most mature deliberation, are considered as more or less obscure and equivocal, until their meaning be liquidated and ascertained by a series of particular discussions and adjudications. Besides the obscurity arising from the complex-

ity of objects, and the imperfection of the human faculties, the medium through which the conceptions of men are conveyed to each other adds a fresh embarrassment.

Explaining Madison's Reference to Common Law Rights of Authors

Unsurprisingly, therefore, *Federalist No. 43* has led to confusion about what Madison meant by his reference to British common law copyright. Scholars have offered a variety of suggestions as to Madison's meaning. According to one account, Madison relied on the first American edition of Blackstone's *Commentaries*, which reported on *Millar's* ruling that recognized the common law right of copyright but not that decision's subsequent overruling in *Donaldson*. By another account, Madison relied on *Burrow's* 1776 published report of *Donaldson*, which described the Statute of Anne as divesting common law copyright entirely. It has also been suggested Madison referred to *Donaldson's* ruling that no perpetual copyright existed under common law because it would apparently be more consistent with the IP Clause's conferring congressional power to secure copyrights and patents "for limited Times." Or perhaps Madison was entirely unaware of the Lords' ruling or had simply forgotten it when writing his hasty defense of the proposed U.S. Constitution in late 1787 and early 1788.

It is also entirely plausible that Madison simply rejected the ruling in *Donaldson*—or that he would have rejected *Donaldson* had he known of it when writing *Federalist No. 43*. After all, the overarching logic of Madison's views concerning constitutionalism and common law cuts against *Donaldson's* ruling in certain respects. Madison was in many ways a critic of British common law. In his October 18, 1787, letter to George Washington—written just three months before *Federalist No. 43*—Madison explained his basic objections to British common law and described how states had limited and modified British common law to suit American constitutional sensibilities:

> The common law is nothing more than the unwritten law, and is left by all the constitutions equally liable to legislative alterations. I am not sure that any notice is particularly taken of it in the Constitutions of the States. If there is, nothing more is provided than a general declaration that it shall continue along with other branches of law to be in force till legally changed ... Since the Revolution every State has made great inroads & with great propriety in many instances on this *monarchical* code ... The abolition of the *right of primogeniture*, which I am sure Col. Mason does not disapprove, falls under this head.

Madison's letter to Washington was occasioned by anti-Federalist George Mason's criticisms that "the Common law is not secured by the new constitution." Writing to Washington, Madison explained the reasoning behind the 1787 Philadelphia Convention's approach to British common law:

> What could the Convention have done? If they had in general terms declared the Common law to be in force, they would have broken in upon the legal Code of every State in the most material points: they wd. have done more, they would have brought over from G.B. a thousand heterogeneous & antirepublican doctrines, and even the *ecclesiastical Hierarchy itself,* for that is a part of the Common law. If they had undertaken a discrimination, they must have formed a digest of laws, instead of a Constitution. This objection surely was not brought forward in the Convention, or it wd. have been placed in such a light that a repetition of it out of doors would scarcely have been hazarded.

Consistent with Madison's concerns about the monarchical, anti-republican aspects of British common law, a case can be made that a decision by the aristocratic House of Lords dismissing common law rights was illegitimate. Such a view carries added plausibility considering *Donaldson* was handed down in 1774, the same year Britain retaliated for the Boston Tea Party with the "Intolerable Acts" and in which Americans would respond by convening the First Continental Congress.

Thus the logic of Madison and like-minded Americans regarding American constitutionalism and British common law also weighs against any easy acceptance of British parliamentary acts eliminating or limiting common law rights. As contemporary common law scholar James Stoner has explained:

> To assume that the Americans of the Revolutionary era simply accepted the dominant understanding of common law in contemporary Britain would be a serious error. Although Blackstone would, within a generation, replace Coke as the favorite authority on common law among Americans, it was understood that his account of parliamentary sovereignty was inapplicable here—it might even be said that the American Revolution was fought against the assertion of that principle in the colonies.

To the extent, therefore, that *Donaldson* claimed to replace the common law's grounding of copyright in natural right with the whim of parliamentary supremacy, there is ample reason to believe that Madison would not find it applicable on American shores. On the other hand, Madisonian logic could accept constitutional limitations on copyright and patent provided for in the IP Clause. The difference being that the source of the limiting power was part of the Constitution to be ratified by the American people and because those limits would be set by members of Congress who are held accountable by the republican principle of representative elections.

Madison's Appeal to the Reason and Nature of IP Rights

Even assuming Madison may have been mistaken about the status of copyright under British common law, that is beside the primary point that Madison was making about IP rights in *Federalist No. 43*. Madison did not invoke British common law as a matter of binding historical precedent. Rather, he made it a historical point of reference in addressing what his co-author Alexander Hamilton in *Federalist No. 78* would call "the reason and nature of the thing." In *Federalist No. 43*, Madison made an implicit appeal to natural right as the underlying reason behind British common law's recognition of copyright. And he extended that same reasoning to patent.

Despite Madison's misgivings of feudal and monarchical aspects of British common law, he was in accord with classical liberal theory and its emphasis on natural rights. And natural right was infused in the common law. As James Stoner has explained:

> By the eighteenth century ... several great attempts at synthesis [between liberal political theory and the common law] were made, first by John Locke, who aimed to reconcile liberal philosophy and the English Constitution, and then by William Blackstone, whose Commentaries on the Laws of England, appearing in the 1760s, reworked the common law from a liberal perspective and presented its chief rules and maxims in accessible, literary form.

In describing the nature of intellectual property rights, Blackstone wrote in his *Commentaries*:

> There is still another species of property, which (if it subsists by the common law) being grounded on labour and invention is more properly reducible to the head of occupancy than any other; since the right of occupancy itself is supposed by Mr. Locke, and many others, to be founded on the personal labour of the occupant. And this is the right, which an author may be supposed to have in his own original literary compositions; so that no other person without his leave may publish or make profit of the copies. When a man by the exertion of his rational powers has produced an original work, he seems to have clearly a right to dispose of that identical work as he pleases, and any attempt

to vary the disposition he has made of it, appears to be an invasion of that right.

Like Blackstone, Madison also accepted Lockean principles regarding rights of private property. Also, like Blackstone, Madison regarded copyrights and patents as forms of individual private property. Madison accepted the natural rights of authors to the fruits of their labors, which—at least formerly—served as the basis for copyright under British common law. And despite patent's lack of recognition under British common law, Madison concluded in *Federalist No. 43*, "with equal reason," that because an individual is entitled to the fruits of his or her own labor that "[t]he right to useful inventions" is a kind of property that should "belong to the inventors."

"Utility to the Union" in *The Federalist*

Federalist No. 43's IP passage is bookended by considerations about the locus of power for protecting copyright and patent under the proposed Constitution. The opening sentence described the usefulness to the Union of a congressional power for protecting IP. And the closing sentence recounted both the recognition of IP rights by states as well as the inability of the states to separately provide the necessary safeguards for IP.

Contemporary minds may be prone to read a utilitarian understanding of IP rights into *Federalist No. 43* by fastening upon its use of the terms "utility" and "public good." But careful attention to context renders a utilitarian interpretation of *Federalist No. 43* unsustainable. While Madison undoubtedly considered copyright and patent to be socially beneficial, his use of terms properly fits within a natural rights framework.

The Utility to the Union of a Congressional Power to Protect IP Rights

To read from Noah Webster's *American Dictionary of the English Language* (1828), utility may be defined as "usefulness," "production of good," or "profitableness to some valuable end." When *Federalist No. 43* used the term "utility," it was not with reference to the usefulness of IP rights as such, let alone to the idea that beneficial aggregate economic consequences form the grounds for the existence of IP rights. Rather, *Federalist No. 43* referred to the efficacy to the Union of lodging a power in Congress for securing copyrights and patents.

At the outset, it should be observed that *The Federalist* uses the term "utility" with regard to the advantages of conferring certain powers upon the Union under the proposed Constitution. For example, the authors of *The Federalist* employ the term "The Utility of the Union" in the title of several essays; namely, "The Utility of the Union as a Safeguard Against Domestic Faction and Insurrection," "The Utility of the Union in Respect to Commercial Relations and a Navy," and "The Utility of the Union in Respect to Revenue."

Federalist No. 43 was the final installment of a discourse that began in *Federalist No. 40* on the quantity of powers conferred by the proposed Constitution on the federal government. "[C]ool and candid people ... will see," wrote Madison in *Federalist No. 41*, "that in all cases where power is to be conferred, the point first to be decided is, whether such a power be necessary to the public good; as the next will be, in case of an affirmative decision, to guard as effectually as possible against a perversion of the power to the public detriment." Madison continued: "That we may form a correct judgment on this subject, it will be proper to review the several powers conferred on the government of the Union." Accordingly, in *Federalist No. 41*, Madison categorized the powers conferred by the proposed Constitution into six classes: (1) "Security against foreign danger"; (2) "Regulation of the intercourse with foreign nations"; (3) "Maintenance of harmony and proper intercourse among the States"; (4) "Certain miscellaneous objects of general utility"; (5) "Restraint of the States from certain injurious acts"; and (6) "Provisions for giving due efficacy to all these powers." *Federalist No. 43*'s brief discussion of the IP Clause was part of Madison's review of "Certain miscellaneous objects of general utility" to be "conferred on the government of the Union." Reading *Federalist No. 43* absent the flow of thought begun in *Federalist No. 40* renders one more likely to miss the crucial context for Madison's use of the term "utility."

Thus, in *Federalist No. 43* Madison addressed the "utility" of the proposed Constitution's shifting of the primary locus of power for protecting IP rights from the states to the government of the Union. This fits with Madison's conclusion, a few sentences later, that the states could not "make effectual provisions" for copyrights or patents. This understanding of the utility of an IP protection power being lodged with the federal Congress is also consistent with Madison's memorandum, *Vices of the Political System of the United States* (1787). In *Vices*, Madison similarly expressed the view that there existed a "want of concert in matters where common interest requires it," among the states, including "the want of uniformity in the laws concerning ... literary property," or copyright. *Federalist No. 43* was one of several instances in which Madison drew on his *Vices* memorandum in publishing his papers in defense of the proposed Constitution.

Madison's explanation that most states "have anticipated the decision of this point, by laws passed at the instance of Congress," referred to the resolution passed by the Confederation Congress in 1783, urging state legislatures to pass laws protecting copyrights and patents. As described in Chapter 3, Madison served on the Confederation Congress committee that issued a report on IP rights and thereby prompted the resolution. Following the adoption of the Confederation Congress's resolution, copyright and patent laws were subsequently adopted by state legislatures. And Madison helped ensure the passage of Virginia's state copyright law in 1785. In *Federalist No. 43*, Madison thus supported giving the federal government lawmaking power to directly protect IP rights through legislation rather than leaving it with a merely declaratory role in supporting IP rights.

The Public Good: Rights of Liberty and Property in the Interests of All, According to the Rules of Justice

Federalist No. 43's conclusion that "[t]he public good fully coincides in both [copyright and patent] cases with the claims of individuals," likewise cannot finally be understood in utilitarian terms. Although Madison does not offer an explicit definition of "the public good" in *Federalist No. 43*, a constructive definition of the term emerges from other papers in *The Federalist*. The "public good," according to the sense of *The Federalist*, encompasses the interests of all people in the security and enjoyment of their rights to liberty and property, consistent with impartial rules of justice—as opposed to the interests of a sect or faction of the people.

In *Federalist No. 10*, Madison described "[t]he diversity in the faculties of men, from which the rights of property originate." Rights to liberty and property belong to individuals by nature. But while every man and woman may possess equal natural rights, inequality inevitably results in their exercise and enjoyments of those rights: "From the protection of different and unequal faculties of acquiring property, the possession of different degrees and kinds of property immediately results; and from the influence of these on the sentiments and views of the respective proprietors, ensues a division of the society into different interests and parties." For Madison, copyrights and patents are "kinds of property," produced by individual faculties for creativity and discovery, and which rightfully belong to authors and inventors.

In explaining the division of society into different interests and parties, Madison concluded that "the most common and durable source of factions has been the various and unequal distribution of property." "By a faction," continued Madison, "I understand a number of citizens, whether amounting to a majority or a minority of the whole, who are united and actuated by some common impulse of passion, or of interest, adversed to the rights of other citizens, or to the permanent and aggregate interests of the community." Factions are all but inevitable as "[t]he latent causes of faction are thus sown in the nature of man." Because mankind is characterized by finiteness in perception, fallibility in reasoning, and by "a degree of depravity" in moral character, activities and circumstances of society that have led them into factions, "inflamed them with mutual animosity, and rendered them much more disposed to vex and oppress each other than to co-operate for their common good."

Thus, in *Federalist No. 51*, Madison stated, "in a state of nature, where the weaker individual is not secured against the violence of the stronger," societies form governments to protect the life, liberty, and property of the individuals composing it. According to Madison, "the protection of these faculties ["of men, from which the rights of property originate"] is the first object of government." This object in protecting individual rights of property Madison identified with the establishment of justice. "Justice is the end of government," concluded Madison in *Federalist No. 51*: "It is the end of civil society."

An eighteenth century audience generally would have understood the term "justice" in its classical sense. According to Webster, "justice" is "[t]he virtue which consists in giving to everyone what is his due; practical conformity to the laws and to principles of rectitude in the dealings of men with each other; honesty; integrity in commerce or mutual intercourse." The term also encompassed notions of "impartiality," "equity," and "agreeableness to right."

For Madison, when it came to contending factions, "[j]ustice ought to hold the balance between them." But "[e]nlightened statesmen will not always be at the helm" to impartially administer a system of rules to protect individual rights. Rather, "the most powerful faction must be expected to prevail," partial to its own interest rather than with "a sole regard to justice and the public good." Given human nature and its tendency toward factionalism, in "a government which is to be administered by men over men," wrote Madison in *Federalist No. 51*, there is a "necessity of auxiliary precautions" to "control the abuses of government." "In the extent and proper structure of the Union," concluded Madison," we behold a republican remedy for the diseases most incident to republican government." One key remedy was the proposed federal Constitution's separation of power between the executive, legislative, and judicial branches. Another remedy was the proposed Constitution's extension of the sphere of representative government. Explained Madison: "In the extended republic of the United States, and among the great variety of interests, parties, and sects which it embraces, a coalition of a majority of the whole society could seldom take place on any other principles than those of justice and the general good."

As observed above, justice, protection of individual rights, and the public good were interrelated concepts in Madison's thought. He believed the proposed Constitution's extended sphere of representative government would make the government more prone to further the interests of all people in the security and enjoyment of their rights to liberty and property, consistent with impartial rules of justice. Madison's constitutional biographer William Lee Miller sheds further light on the matter in describing Madison's answer to the question of how a republic under majority rule can function justly:

> It included protections against that human inclination to neglect the public good, and to prefer private advantage ... but it also presumed a capacity for human beings, to a degree and under the right restraints, to serve justice and the common good. The point of Madison's form of republican government was to arrange institutions so as to encourage that capacity, in part exactly by restraining that inclination.

As previously indicated, Madison regarded copyright and patent as kinds of property, grounded in an individual's right to the fruits of his or her labor. Protecting the IP rights of individuals "for limited Times" in order "To promote the Progress of Science and useful Arts" in society, fits firmly within Madison's overall understanding of the purpose of government: to protect rights of liberty and property, in the furtherance of the common good rather than in the self-interests of a faction of the people, according to rules of justice.

Social Utility Under *The Federalist*'s Natural Rights Framework

A reading of *The Federalist* as a whole, in addition to other contextual factors related to the political philosophy of Madison, suggests his explanation of the IP Clause in *Federalist No. 43* grounded copyright and patent in natural right, not merely utilitarian considerations. A thoroughly primitive eighteenth century utilitarian understanding of IP rights would regard them as a means to the greatest good for the greatest number according to some sort of calculation about collective human pleasure and pain responses. But a utilitarian understanding of human life, liberty, or property devoid of any inherent sense of what is right, just, or good, would have been foreign to those who framed and ratified the U.S. Constitution.

As Madison biographer Ralph Ketcham wrote:

> A great gulf ... separates the thought of Madison (and other Founding Fathers) from that of believers in such later concepts as Benthamite utilitarianism and simple majoritarian democracy, who denied that principles of justice and virtue can be identified and made the foundation of government, and therefore have a higher sanction than the will of the majority.

This is not to deny that Madison regarded IP rights as socially useful. Undoubtedly, he endorsed the IP Clause's express purpose "To promote the Progress of Science and useful Arts." As pointed out previously, Madison suggested that the rights of authors and inventors could be protected consistent with the good of the whole people. The IP Clause was premised on the idea that a genuine harmony of interests between authors, inventors, and the general public existed in principle—even if the human tendency toward factionalism made realization of that harmony more difficult in practice. To quote *Federalist No. 43* once more: "The public good fully coincides in both cases with the claims of individuals." Moreover, a natural rights perspective does not eliminate social utility from consideration in defining the boundaries of copyright and patent.

Since an individual possesses, by nature, a right of property in the fruits of his or her labor, natural right may be said to supply the grounding principle for IP rights. Madison and the Founding Fathers understood, as Locke and Blackstone did before them, that in a civil society, individuals enter into a compact to form a government that will protect liberty and property under positive law. Living in a civil society necessarily requires government to pass laws ensuring that individuals can enjoy their rights of liberty and property consistent with each other. And that inevitably involves government administering rules by which property is acquired, possessed, and transferred. Considerations of overall social utility, including cost-benefit analyses that take into account short-term and long-term gains and losses likely resulting from IP rights and related questions regarding incentives for investment in IP, have an important role to play in determining the scope and degree of protection that the law can and should provide for various "kinds of property" under particular circumstances. The Intellectual Property Clause recognizes this by conferring on Congress the power to secure copyrights and patents "for limited Times."

Legal or administrative decisions about how best to secure copyright and patent are often complex and fact-intensive. But they are matters of deciding how best to protect the core of pre-existing rights of property that do not ultimately depend for their existence upon empirical or intuitive economic calculations. Utility may be said to supply a boundary principle for IP rights, but natural right supplies IP's grounding principle.

Conclusion

Given the inherent qualities and renown of *The Federalist*, anyone interested in understanding the Constitution's IP Clause should carefully consider Madison's meaning in *Federalist No. 43*. That requires examination of its context within *The Federalist* as well as Madison's other writings from that period.

Ultimately, *Federalist No. 43* reveals a rich understanding of the nature of IP and its place in the U.S. constitutional order. In subtle and succinct fashion, *Federalist No. 43* identifies the ultimate source for copyright and patent in an individual's natural right to the fruits of his or her labor. Madison regarded copyright and patent as forms of property that government is established to protect. Additionally, as *Federalist No. 43* and other numbers point out, securing an individual's IP rights, consistent with the rules of justice, also furthers the public good by incentivizing further investments and discoveries that promote the "Progress of Science and useful Arts." Consistent with *Federalist No. 43*, considerations of public good or social utility may be said to supply a boundary principle for IP rights. But natural right supplies IP's grounding principle in Publius's exploration of the U.S. Constitution.

Sources

William Blackstone, *Commentaries on the Laws of England* (1765).

John Locke, *Second Treatise of Government* (1689).

James Madison, Letter to George Washington (October 18, 1787).

James Madison, *Vices of the Political System of the United States* (1787).

Publius (Alexander Hamilton), *Federalist No. 1* (1787).

Publius (James Madison), *Federalist No. 10* (1787).

Publius (James Madison), *Federalist No. 37* (1788).

Publius (James Madison), *Federalist No. 41* (1788).

Publius (James Madison), *Federalist No. 43* (1788).

Publius (James Madison), *Federalist No. 51* (1788).

Publius (Alexander Hamilton), *Federalist No. 78* (1788).

Joseph Story, *Commentaries on the Constitution of the United States* (1833).

George Washington, Letter to Alexander Hamilton (August 28, 1788).

Noah Webster, *American Dictionary of the English Language* (1828).

* * *

Ralph Ketcham, *James Madison: A Biography* (1990).

John C. Miller, *Alexander Hamilton and the Growth of the New Nation* (2003).

William Lee Miller, *The Business of May Next: James Madison and the Founding* (1993).

Thomas Nachbar, "Patent and Copyright Clause," in Edwin Meese III, *et al.* (eds.), *The Heritage Guide to The Constitution* (2005).

Tyler T. Ochoa and Mark Rose, *The Anti-Monopoly Origins of the Patent and Copyright Clause*, 84 J. Pat. & Trademark Off. Soc'y 909 (2002).

James R. Stoner, Jr., *Common-Law Liberty: Rethinking American Constitutionalism* (2003).

Edward C. Walterscheid, *Understanding the Copyright Act of 1790: The issue of Common Law Copyright in America and the Modern Interpretation of the Copyright Power*, 53 J. Copyright Soc. USA 313 (2006).

Chapter 6

Constitutional Foundations of Copyright and Patent in the First Congress

Introduction

The First U.S. Congress is the most important Congress ever convened. Called the "Constitutional Congress" by some historians, the inaugural legislative body that met between 1789 and 1791 passed a series of momentous measures that still shape the contours of American constitutionalism. The accomplishments of the First Congress in implementing the Constitution's many provisions, establishing a working federal government, and defining the relationships among the three branches were praised in its day. In the time since its adjournment, the distinguished membership and record of the First Congress has been acknowledged by figures such as John Marshall and Abraham Lincoln. And the First Congress's actions remain a potent source for insights into the Constitution's meaning.

Therefore, the proceedings of the First Congress inform our understanding of the underlying logic and significance of intellectual property (IP) rights in the American constitutional order. The First Congress not only passed organic acts that set up the federal judiciary, organized the executive departments, established a revenue system, defined legislative roles in federal affairs, selected the permanent capital of the nation, provided for federal control over territories as well as the admission of new states, and drafted the Bill of Rights; it also passed the first Copyright Act and first Patent Act.

That the First Congress saw fit to include copyright and patent in its ambitious, historic legislative agenda suggests its members found intellectual property especially important to furthering the new nation's economic, artistic, and technological progress. Passage of the Copyright and Patent Acts also indicates a consensus regarding the legitimacy and efficacy of a pro-IP rights policy—a consensus conspicuously absent when it came to congressional deliberation on other matters.

The U.S. Constitution's Article I, Section 8 Intellectual Property Clause expressly and unmistakably conferred on Congress the power to protect IP rights: It grants Congress power "[t]o promote the Progress of Science and useful Arts, by securing for limited Times to Authors and Inventors the exclusive Right to their respective Writings and Discoveries." By promptly enacting legislation to protect copyrights and patents, the First Congress confirmed the constitutional status accorded to intellectual property under the Constitution. The Copyright Act provided authors exclusive rights to copy and receive the proceeds from their works for fourteen years with the right to a fourteen-year renewal, upon registering the works at a federal district court. And the Patent Act offered fourteen-year terms of protection to inventors upon obtaining approval by a three-member Patent Board. Both Acts were the fruition of deliberate effort over the course of the previous decade to put IP rights on a more secure footing. That effort preceding the adoption of the federal Copyright and Patent Acts already had resulted in the adoption of various state laws protecting copyrights and patents following the Confederation Congress's 1783 resolution calling for the security of literary property.

Importantly, the First Congress's securing of copyrights and patents amidst all its other constitution-implementing business is indicative of IP's consistency with the logic of American constitutionalism. In particular, protection of IP rights fits squarely within the classical liberal framework of government securing individual property rights under the rule of law. And promotion of "the Progress of Science and useful Arts" through the securing of IP rights fits with the federal government's constitutionally assigned role in fostering an interstate commercial marketplace.

Like many constitutional provisions, the IP Clause is set out in general terms, assigning to Congress the role of adopting legislation adapted to changing circumstances. So it would miss the point to treat legislation adopted by the First Congress as the end-all-be-all. For instance, while the basic structure of the Judiciary Act of 1789 continues to shape the federal judiciary today, Congress has nonetheless expanded and altered the scope and composition of the federal judiciary to address changing caseload needs. Shrinking the functions of today's federal judiciary to 1789 levels would hardly serve current needs regarding the administration of justice.

Likewise, it would make little sense to seek a return to the shorter copyright terms of the Copyright Act of 1790 or the administratively burdensome patent approval process of the Patent Act of 1790. The precedential value of the First Congress's actions derives not so much in the minute details of its legislation, but from its basic approach to implementing the Constitution. That is, the First Congress's record should be respected for the foundation it sets: as a starting point that subsequent legislation should build upon.

Moreover, the role of the first presidential administration should not to be overlooked in understanding the origins and constitutional pedigree of copyright and patent protection. George Washington called upon the First Congress to pass legislation securing IP rights. And President Washington, whose practice was to consider conscientiously the constitutionality of all legislative measures set before him, signed into law both the Copyright Act of 1790 and the Patent Act of 1790.

Of all the First Congress's contributions to American constitutionalism, its role with respect to the Bill of Rights deserves special attention. Significant insights into the American constitutional order derive from the fact that the same Congress that proposed the Bill of Rights also passed the original Copyright and Patent Acts. That the same indispensable Congress approved both our cherished charter of individual liberty and pro-IP rights legislation creates a strong inference that, at a principled foundational level, all of those important measures were considered consistent with one another and mutually reinforcing.

In particular, the legislative record of the First Congress creates a powerful inference that its distinguished members believed that the First Amendment and IP protections are, in their conceptual foundations, in harmony. Merely invoking the record of the First Congress may not resolve particular law and policy debates regarding the constitutionality and efficacy of aspects of contemporary copyright statutes and judicial rulings. But the historical example and constitutional logic demonstrated by the First Congress regarding the compatibility of free speech and protection of intellectual property rights overcomes the occasional claims of contemporary critics that free speech and IP rights are fundamentally at odds.

The record and underlying logic of the First Congress provides critical insights into the coherence and importance of IP within the American constitutional order. For anyone seeking to understand the constitutional foundations of IP, the First Congress should be one of the first sources consulted.

The First Congress's Constitutional Precedent-Setting Role

Future U.S. Supreme Court Justice James Iredell declared before the North Carolina constitutional ratification convention in July 1788 that "the first session of Congress will probably be the most important of any for many years. A general code of laws will then be established in execution of every power contained in the Constitution." In 1789, the *Gazette of the United States* agreed with Iredell's assessment: "No future session of Congress," it editorialized, "will ever have so arduous and weighty a charge on their hands."

While the Constitution established on paper the framework for a workable government, it nonetheless required the Congress to bring a real working government to life. Meeting between 1789 and 1791, the inaugural body of legislators elected to office under the new Constitution would be tasked with establishing a revenue system, setting up executive departments, fleshing out a federal judiciary, defining the roles and relations among the three branches in both domestic and foreign policy, organizing federal territories and the process for admitting future states, determining the location for a permanent national capital, and legislating on a host of additional areas of concern pursuant to the enumerated powers of Congress set out in Article I, Section 8.

Both the American public and the members of the First Congress were well aware of its pivotal and precedent-setting role in expounding and implementing the U.S. Constitution's powers. As James Madison wrote in 1789: "Among other difficulties, the exposition of the Constitution is frequently a copious source, and must continue so until its meaning on all great points shall have been settled by precedents."

Called the "Constitutional Congress" by some historians, the First Congress further distinguishes itself in the American constitutional order for its drafting and proposing the Bill of Rights for ratification in 1790. Within approximately two years' time, ten of the First Congress's twelve proposed amendments would be ratified by the required number of state legislatures and thereby form the U.S. Constitution's renowned charter expressly protecting individual rights.

Did the First Congress rise to the challenges confronting it? According to both contemporary observers and present-day historians, the answer is overwhelmingly "yes." As John Trumbull put it in a letter to Vice President John Adams, "In no nation, by no Legislature, was ever so much done in so short a period for the establishment of Government, Order, public Credit & general tranquility." Consider also the judgment of historians Charlene Bangs Bickford and Kenneth R. Bowling:

> The First Federal Congress was the most important Congress in American history. Its awesome agenda breathed life into the Constitution, established precedent and constitutional interpretation which still guide us two hundred years later, and held the Union together when sectional interests threatened disunion and even civil war. Most significantly, it concluded the American revolution.

Historian Robert Remini offered a similar assessment:

Without question the 1st Congress, despite growing partisan discord, ended its work with 'unbounded success.' Just think. It had inaugurated a strong central government under the Constitution, administered the election and inauguration of President George Washington, established the first executive departments, created the Supreme Court and a federal judiciary system, passed the Bill of Rights and submitted it to the states for ratification, erected a revenue service, provide for the 'uniform regulation of commerce,' fixed the permanent residence of the capital, guaranteed the payment of the national debt, established a national bank, commissioned a regular census and admitted Kentucky and Vermont to statehood. Quite an achievement in just two short years.

Constitutional Credentials of the First Congress's Membership

Attention is also due to the First Congress because of the composition of its membership. According to historians Bickford and Bowling, twenty members of the First Congress were delegates at the 1787 Philadelphia Convention that drafted the Constitution. An even larger number of its members were delegates at the state conventions that ratified the Constitution.

As contemporaries of the Constitution's drafting and ratification processes as well as the surrounding public debate, members of the First Congress possessed a current and up-close understanding of the meaning of the document's terms as well as the circumstances that prompted its adoption. Distinguished members of the first Senate included Oliver Ellsworth of Connecticut, Robert Morris of Pennsylvania, James Paterson of New Jersey, and Rufus King of New York. And such influential statesmen as Roger Sherman of Connecticut, Fisher Ames of Massachusetts, Elias Boudinot of New Jersey, Hugh Williamson of North Carolina, and James Madison of Virginia were members of the first House of Representatives.

The First Congress as Authority on Constitutional Meaning

Owing to both the distinguished composition of its membership and to its pivotal role in making near-contemporaneous, precedent-setting interpretations of the Constitution, the record of the First Congress has achieved authoritative status in the American constitutional order. Over the years, the First Congress has been invoked as an important source for understanding the meaning of the Constitution.

The significance of the First Congress and the constitutional implications arising from its passage of the Judiciary Act of 1789—proclaimed by Bickford and
Bowling as "one of the most outstanding achievements of the First Congress"—
was recognized by no less a figure than Chief Justice John Marshall. Writing for
the Supreme Court in his classic opinion in *Cohens v. State of Virginia* (1821),
Marshall described the Judiciary Act of 1789 as "[a] contemporaneous exposition of the constitution, certainly of not less authority than ... [t]he opinion
of the *Federalist*." Wrote Marshall: "We know that in the Congress which passed
that act were many eminent members of the Convention which formed the
constitution." Marshall said that the concurrence of members of the First Congress "in the same construction of the constitution, may justly inspire some
confidence in that construction."

In another classic Supreme Court opinion, *Martin v. Hunter's Lessee* (1816),
Justice Joseph Story described the same Judiciary Act as a "contemporaneous
exposition" of the Constitution that helped to form a "foundation of authority which cannot be shaken" regarding constitutional doctrine. As Story explained, the Act "was submitted to the deliberations of the first congress,
composed, as it was, not only of men of great learning and ability, but of men
who acted a principal part in framing, supporting, or opposing that constitution." Over the years, other justices of the Supreme Court would consider the
First Congress's record in seeking to ascertain the meaning and scope of constitutional powers.

Perhaps most famously, future President Abraham Lincoln appealed to the
composition and record of the First Congress in establishing the Founding Fathers' understanding of the constitutional power to restrict slavery in federal
territories. In his *Cooper Union Address* (1860), Lincoln explained that "[i]n 1789,
by the first Congress which sat under the Constitution, an act was passed to enforce the Ordinance of '87, including the prohibition of slavery in the North-
western Territory." Lincoln specifically identified sixteen out of thirty-nine
framers of the Constitution as belonging to the First Congress that essentially
re-adopted the Confederation Congress's Northwest Ordinance of 1787. "It
went through all its stages without a word of opposition," declared Lincoln,
"and finally passed both branches without yeas and neighs, which is equivalent to a unanimous passage," with President George Washington approving
and signing the bill. To his Cooper Union audience, Lincoln concluded: "This
shows that, in their understanding, no line dividing local from federal authority, nor anything in the Constitution, properly forbade Congress to prohibit slavery in the federal territory; else both their fidelity to correct principle,
and their oath to support the Constitution, would have constrained them to
oppose the prohibition."

Insofar as Lincoln's address was directed to understanding the constitutional views of congressional power held by "our fathers who framed the government under which we live," Lincoln offered a standard for how all subsequent generations may act in light of their understanding:

> I do not mean to say we are bound to follow implicitly in whatever our fathers did. To do so, would be to discard all the lights of current experience—to reject all progress—all improvement. What I do say is, that if we would supplant the opinions and policy of our fathers in any case, we should do so upon evidence so conclusive, and argument so clear, that even their great authority, fairly considered and weighed, cannot stand; and most surely not in a case whereof we ourselves declare they understood the question better than we.

Copyright and Patent in the Context of the First Congress's Critical Agenda

In light of its precedent-setting role as well as the distinguished composition and position of its membership, the record of the First Congress should still inform our understanding of the underlying logic and significance of intellectual property in the American constitutional order. Consider the First Congress's pro-IP record in light of its legislative agenda as a whole. The First Congress not only passed organic acts to set up the federal judiciary, organize the executive departments, establish a revenue system, define legislative roles in federal affairs, select the permanent capital of the nation, provide for federal control over territories as well as the admission of new states, and draft the Bill of Rights; it also passed the first Copyright and Patent Acts. That the First Congress saw fit to include pro-IP rights legislation in its ambitious, historic agenda suggests its members found IP especially important to furthering the new nation's economic, artistic, and technological progress.

IP rights immediately came to the attention of the members of the First Congress, as the first petition it received upon convening was submitted by author David Ramsay, seeking copyright protection for his books, including *The History of the American Revolution* (1789). In his petition to Congress, Ramsay said that "in reason and justice he ought to be entitled to any Endowments arising from the sale of the aforementioned works as a compensation for his labour and expense," with "the same principle expressly recognized in the new Constitution." Additional petitions by individual authors and inventors seeking IP protection for their respective works and inventions would follow throughout the First Congress. Those petitions were received by the First Congress, referred to committee, and led to the drafting of legislation. Separate bills providing general copyright and patent protection were eventually introduced and passed by Congress.

Passage of the separate Copyright and Patent Acts—and the lack of any seriously heated debate over the bills—also indicates a consensus regarding the legitimacy of IP and the efficacy of pro-IP rights policy. Such a consensus was conspicuously absent when it came to congressional deliberation on other matters. Consideration of IP began during the First Congress's amicable first session—spanning from March 4, 1789 to September 29, 1789, and was adopted during the increasingly rancorous second session—running between January 4, 1790 and August 12, 1790. As widely recognized by historians, the members of the First Congress would engage in heated debates over matters such as federal assumption of state debts; discrimination between original holders of federal bank notes issued during the war, that is, between soldiers of the American Revolution and financiers or speculators; the establishment of the First Bank of the United States; and Secretary of the Treasury Alexander Hamilton's first *Report on Public Credit* (1790). The location of the permanent federal capital even sparked worries over disunion during the second session, before the First Congress would adopt a settlement known today as the "Compromise of 1790," relocating the interim capital to Philadelphia and placing the permanent seat on the Potomac River. Even its adoption of the Judiciary Act of 1789 and its proposal of the Bill of Rights to the states for ratification were not without significant debate. But also widely recognized by historians, both the Copyright and Patent Acts were passed with little debate or disagreement in the First Congress. Pro-intellectual property rights legislation in the First Congress, like the Northwest Ordinance of 1789, rightfully should be classed among the important legislative measures that were enacted into law through broad-based consensus.

Legislation in the First Congress as the Culmination of Concerted, Long-Term Efforts

There is a remarkable consistency regarding the nature and necessity of IP rights, running from the First Congress's passage of pro-IP legislation back to the Confederation Congress's 1783 resolution calling for the security of copyright. The Copyright and Patent Acts were the fruition of deliberate efforts over the course of the previous decade to put IP rights on a more secure footing in the new nation. The Copyright and Patent Acts built upon the record established by a dozen pre-Constitution states that had passed laws protecting IP rights.

Not to be overlooked, a cast of prominent thinkers and statesmen furthered those efforts on repeated occasions in a host of venues. For example, James Madison, who served on the committee of the Confederation Congress that recommended its resolution supporting copyright laws in the states, is widely recognized for his leadership role in the First Congress. In his history of the U.S. House of Representatives, Robert Remini called Madison the "floor manager" of the House in the First Congress. Similarly, Elias Boudinot, who served as President of the Confederation Congress when its pro-copyright resolution was passed, acted as the legislative sponsor of House Resolution 43—what would ultimately become the Copyright Act of 1790. Although Noah Webster was not a member of the First Congress, some historians maintain that Webster prepared the first draft of H.R. 10, titled "a bill to promote the progress of science and useful arts, by securing to authors and inventors the exclusive right to their respective discoveries." The bill was modeled after the British Statute of Anne and involved both copyrights and patents. H.R. 10 was reported to the House by a three-member subcommittee during the first session. Webster, it was observed in Chapter 3, previously lobbied members of the Confederation Congress, numerous legislators in several states, and delegates to the Philadelphia Convention of 1787—all on behalf of IP rights. The consistent, repeated, and deliberate joint efforts of figures like Madison, Boudinot, and Webster to secure protection for IP rights, is suggestive of the high stock we should place in their understanding of the issue and their ultimate achievement in the First Congress.

First Congress's Record Confirms IP's Fit in the American Constitutional Order

As law professor and legal historian David S. Currie has written, "[the First] Congress interpreted a surprising number of provisions of the Constitution." One such provision is the Article I, Section 8 Intellectual Property Clause. It expressly and unmistakably confers on Congress the power to protect IP rights: It grants Congress power "To promote the Progress of Science and useful Arts, by securing for limited Times to Authors and Inventors the exclusive Right to their respective Writings and Discoveries." Copyright and patent legislation offered the First Congress its first opportunity to interpret and implement the IP Clause. Consensus in the First Congress regarding the constitutionality of its pro-IP legislation appears evident. By promptly enacting legislation to protect copyrights and patents, the First Congress confirmed the constitutional status accorded to IP under the Constitution.

The First Congress's securing of copyrights and patents amidst all its other constitution-implementing business is indicative of IP's consistency with the logic of American constitutionalism. In particular, protection of IP rights fits within the classical liberal framework of government securing individual property rights under the rule of law. And promotion of "the Progress of Science and useful Arts" through securing IP rights fits with the federal government's constitutionally assigned role in fostering an interstate commercial marketplace. The record of the First Congress supplies evidence of intellectual property's fit with the internal logic of the American constitutional order.

Recent Supreme Court jurisprudence does, in fact, take stock of the First Congress's exercise of its authority under the IP Clause. In *Ashcroft v. Eldred* (2003), for instance, the Supreme Court referenced the First Congress in upholding the extension of copyright terms of existing works until 70 years after the author's death by the Copyright Term Extension Act of 1998 (CTEA). Factoring into the Court ruling were the facts that "the First Congress accorded the protections of the Nation's first federal copyright statute to existing and future works alike," "that early Congresses extended the duration of numerous individual patents as well as copyrights," and that "renewed or extended terms were upheld in the early days, for example, by Chief Justice Marshall and Justice Story sitting as circuit justices."

Similarly, the Supreme Court's ruling in *Golan v. Holder* (2012) to uphold CTEA's Section 514 referenced the First Congress. *Golan* concerned CTEA's Section 514's restoration of copyright protection to certain foreign works that had entered the public domain. Playing into its ruling to uphold Section 514 was the Court's observation that, "[n]otably, the Copyright Act of 1790 granted copyrights and patents to works and inventions that had lost protections." And so "[th]e First Congress, it thus appears, did not view the public domain as inviolate." It is also relevant that subsequent Congresses passed legislation granting IP protections to inventions and works that had lost protections.

Some scholars have criticized the results and rationales contained in *Eldred* and *Golan*. But even if one disagrees with how the Supreme Court ruled in a specific case on a particular point of law, as a conceptual matter the Court's consideration of the historical record and logic behind the actions of the First Congress is entirely sound. To wit:

> This Court has repeatedly laid down the principle that a contemporaneous legislative exposition of the Constitution when the founders of our Government and framers of our Constitution were actively participating in public affairs, acquiesced in for a term of long years, fixes the construction to be given [the Constitution's] provisions.

So the Supreme Court reiterated the persuasive authority of the First Congress in *Eldred*. Likewise, *Golan* reinforced a premise that must be taken seriously by anyone seeking to ascertain the basic foundations of the IP Clause:

"[The] construction placed upon the Constitution by [the drafters of] the first [copyright] act of 1790 and the act of 1802 ... men who were contemporary with [the Constitution's] formation, many of whom were members of the convention which framed it, is of itself entitled to very great weight."

Basic Principles Prevail over Particulars in Considering the First Congress's Precedents

As Chief Justice John Marshall wrote in *McCulloch v. Maryland* (1819), the U.S. Constitution does not "partake of the prolixity of a legal code," but is limited to marking its "great outlines" and designating its "important objects." Like so many constitutional provisions, the IP Clause is framed in general terms, assigning to Congress the role of adopting legislation adapted to changing circumstances. In delineating rights and developing IP policy designed to address today's world, policymakers would be wise to consult the record of the First Congress. As previously explained, the First Congress's unique role and the composition of its membership shed important light on the nature and meaning of Congress's powers under the IP Clause.

But at the same time, it would miss the point to treat legislation adopted by the First Congress as the end-all-be-all. While the basic principles of the Constitution endure for the ages, it goes without saying that the early 21st century context is far different from that of the late 18th century. For instance, it should be highly unlikely and unexpected that the fourteen-year terms for copyright protection provided by the Copyright Act of 1790 would make sense for today's digital-era marketplace, where the dynamics of authorship, advertising, investment, and other publishing trade press practices are vastly different. Subsequent Congresses saw fit to extend copyright terms and to expand the scope of protection, based on considered judgments about the rights of authors and expedient promotions of literary and artistic progress. Rather than promote the progress of science and useful arts, reverting to the particular terms and provisions of the original Copyright Act and Patent Acts would further an unfortunate regress.

From an administrative standpoint, removing the U.S. Copyright Office from the registration process and transplanting the Copyright Act of 1790's process for registering copyrights at federal district courts to today's federal court system would be just as unwise. Nor would it make sense to resurrect the Patent Board established by the Patent Act of 1790, whereby the patent applications were subject to the approval of the Secretary of State, the Secretary of War, and the Attorney General. While the Patent Board's composition made up of such high officials is highly suggestive of the importance the First Congress placed on the role of patentable inventions to promote the scientific, commercial, and military interests of the new nation, such a Board proved administratively burdensome and overwhelming. The Second Congress would bring more simplicity to the patent process through the Patent Act of 1793, and Congress would establish the Patent Office in 1836.

In considering proper use of the precedent set by the First Congress, consider again the Judiciary Act of 1789. While the basic structure of the Judiciary Act of 1789 adopted by the First Congress continues to shape the federal judiciary today, over the years Congress has nonetheless expanded and altered the scope and composition of the federal judiciary to address changing caseload needs. Just as it would make little sense to readopt the Judiciary Act's minimum amount-in-controversy of $500 as a jurisdictional threshold in diversity cases or limit the scope of original causes of action in federal courts to the terms of the original Judiciary Act, so it would make little sense to seek a return to the shorter copyright terms of the Copyright Act of 1790 or administratively burdensome patent approval process of the Patent Act of 1790.

The precedential value of the First Congress's actions derives not so much in the minute details of its legislation, but from its basic approach to implementing the Constitution. That is, the First Congress's record should be respected for the foundation it sets as a starting point that subsequent legislation should build upon. The First Congress's adoption of modest, general laws to protect and promote intellectual property on a uniform, nationwide basis, with a means of judicial redress for violations of the exclusive rights of authors and inventors, provides a starting point upon which contemporary and future IP policy should build.

The First Presidential Administration's Impact on IP Policy in the First Congress

Not to be overlooked in understanding the origins and constitutional pedigree of copyright and patent protection is the role of the first presidential administration. In his first *Annual Message to Congress* (1790), delivered just prior the First Congress's second session, President George Washington called for legislation securing intellectual property rights. President Washington declared "I cannot forbear intimating to you the expediency of giving effectual encouragement, as well to the introduction of new and useful inventions from abroad, as to the exertions of skill and genius in producing them at home." And likewise he called for "the promotion of science and literature."

It need hardly be mentioned that the first President of the United States was also selected as President of the Philadelphia Convention of 1787 and served as a voting delegate at the Convention with Virginia's delegation. Washington also closely followed the ratification debates, reading and passing on copies of essays comprising *The Federalist* in hopes of influencing a favorable outcome. And prior to the Philadelphia Convention, Washington was personally lobbied by Noah Webster regarding the passage of a copyright law in the Virginia assembly. Washington is noted to have sought out Webster's counsel while the two were in Philadelphia in 1787. Contemporaneous with his assistance to Webster in securing state copyright protection in Virginia, Washington lent personal support to James Rumsey, a Virginia builder and inventor. Rumsey's model for a mechanical boat with propelling capabilities interested Washington, who provided Rumsey with a certificate attesting to the model's usefulness for navigation. Washington also wrote favorably about the model's potential to Virginia's governor. Rumsey subsequently received a patent for his invention from Virginia and in other states.

Washington anticipated the formative role to be played by the first President and First Congress to serve under the Constitution. As he wrote to James Madison in a letter on May 5, 1789: "As the first of everything, in our situation will serve as a Precedent, it is devoutly wished on my part, that these precedents may be fixed on true principles."

According to historian Forrest McDonald's book analyzing the first President's two terms in office, Washington "took seriously his oath to defend the Constitution"—to the point of being "hyper-sensitive" regarding questions of constitutionality. Similarly, Professor Matthew Spalding has written that: "Washington saw the presidency as an equal branch of government and thus an equal defender of the Constitution. He always acted within the confines of the document, but aggressively defended his prerogatives and position when challenged. He understood the precedents that his actions set for the country and future executive officeholders." On particularly contentious matters, such as the establishment of a national bank, Washington even solicited constitutional opinions from his cabinet members. It was the constitutionally conscientious Washington who signed into law both the Copyright Act of 1790 and the Patent Act of 1790. Washington's signature only adds weight to the constitutional imprimatur set upon the pro-IP legislation passed by the First Congress.

The First Congress's Consistency on Copyright and Free Speech

Of all the First Congress's contributions to American constitutionalism, its role with respect to the Bill of Rights deserves special attention. Significant insights into the American constitutional order derive from the fact that the same Congress that proposed the Bill of Rights also passed the Copyright and Patent

Acts. Periodically, scholarly copyright critics or activists will charge that copyright fundamentally infringes free speech, or even that copyright is largely antithetical to the First Amendment. There is no evidence that the First Congress believed this to be so. The history and logic of the First Congress's actions suggest otherwise.

That the same indispensable Congress approved both our cherished charter of individual liberty and pro-IP legislation creates a strong inference that, at a foundational level, all of those important measures were considered consistent with one another and mutually reinforcing. In particular, the legislative record of the First Congress leads to the inference that First Amendment protections of free speech and copyright protections are, at the conceptual level, in harmony.

It bears special consideration that the driving force behind the Bill of Rights in the First Congress's first session was none other than James Madison. Describing Madison's approach in sponsoring "a list of changes that would appease both the friends and the enemies of the Constitution," Robert Remini explained that Madison "realized that by allowing amendments that protected individual liberties he would safeguard the basic structure of the government from further tampering by its enemies." Kenneth Bowling has similarly described Madison's strategy as "Congress recommend[ing] to the states some amendments relating to personal liberty but not altering the basic nature of the Constitution" thereby "protect[ing] it from fundamental structural change."

In his speech introducing the Bill of Rights to the House on June 8, 1789, Madison declared:

> It appears to me that this house is bound by every motive of prudence, not to let the first session pass over without proposing to the state legislatures some things to be incorporated into the constitution, as will render it as acceptable to the whole people of the United States, as it has been found acceptable to a majority of them.

At the same time, however, Madison explained the scope of his proposed amendments:

> I should be unwilling to see a door opened for a re-consideration of the whole structure of the government, for a re-consideration of the principles and the substance of the powers given; because I doubt, if such a door was opened, if we should be very likely to stop at that point which would be safe to the government itself: But I do wish to see a door opened to consider, so far as to incorporate those provi-

sions for the security of rights, against which I believe no serious objection has been made by any class of our constituents, such as would be likely to meet with the concurrence of two-thirds of both houses, and the approbation of three-fourths of the state legislatures.

Thus, to treat any provision contained in the Bill of Rights as somehow conceptually at odds with the unamended Constitution would be completely contrary to the purposes publicly declared by Madison. More particularly, to construe the First Amendment as a repeal or partial repeal of the IP Clause's provision regarding copyright runs contrary to the understanding of the nature of the Bill of Rights as advanced by Madison.

Consider also Madison's consistent track record in promoting individual rights in copyright—or "literary property," as it was often then called. This record was summarized earlier in this chapter and detailed in prior chapters. It strains credulity to believe that in sponsoring what would become the First Amendment that Madison would work at cross-purposes with his pre-constitutional, conventional, and pre-ratification views as well as his support of the Copyright Act in the second session of the First Congress. So it is unlikely in the extreme that Madison would have somehow contemplated a First Amendment that, at the level of principle, would significantly restrict or destabilize Congress's power to promote copyright. And it's equally implausible that, undetected by Madison, there was any principled reason by which the First Amendment would fundamentally upset Congress's powers to protect the exclusive rights of authors to their "literary property."

Here again, Abraham Lincoln's *Cooper Union Address* offers a sensible way of understanding the record and intent of the First Congress, particularly with regard to the constitutionality of legislation passed in close proximity to the Bill of Rights. After making specific reference to the claims that the Bill of Rights' Fifth and Ninth Amendments were supposedly at odds with the legislation passed by the First Congress, Lincoln observed: "Now, it so happens that these amendments were framed by the First Congress which sat under the Constitution—the identical Congress which passed the act already mentioned, enforcing the prohibition of slavery in the Northwest Territory." Lincoln asked: "Is it not a little presumptuous in any one at this day to affirm that the two things which that Congress deliberately framed, and carried to maturity at the same time, are absolutely inconsistent with each other?" To take Lincoln's basic approach and apply it to the First Congress's passage of the Copyright Act and the First Amendment, it would be highly presumptuous to regard the two measures as inconsistent.

It is conceivable that Congress could exercise its power under the IP Clause in such an expansive, aggressive, and abusive way so as to raise the possibility of free speech violations in specific instances. Recent Supreme Court jurisprudence appears to recognize that possibility—while at the same time noting that the "fair use" doctrine, the idea/expression dichotomy that offers copyright protections only to the latter, and various carve-out provisions for educational and other purposes, furthers free speech interests.

A comprehensive analysis of contemporary copyright laws and related judicial doctrines in light of First Amendment rights is far beyond the scope of this paper. And merely invoking the record of the First Congress may not resolve law and policy debates regarding the constitutionality and efficacy of aspects of contemporary copyright statutes and judicial rulings. But the historical example and constitutional logic offered by the First Congress regarding the compatibility of free speech and intellectual property overcomes the claims of some contemporary critics that free speech and IP are fundamentally at odds.

Conclusion

The proceedings of the First Congress should inform our understanding of the underlying logic and significance of intellectual property in the American constitutional order. That the First Congress saw fit to include copyright and patent in its ambitious, historic legislative agenda suggests its members found intellectual property especially important to furthering the new nation's economic, artistic, and technological progress. Passage of the separate Copyright and Patent Acts also indicates a consensus regarding the legitimacy and efficacy of pro-IP policy—a consensus conspicuously absent when it came to congressional deliberation on other matters. Even more important, the First Congress's securing of copyrights and patents amidst all its other constitution-implementing business is indicative of IP's consistency with the logic of American constitutionalism. In particular, the legislative record of the First Congress creates a powerful inference that its distinguished members believed that the First Amendment and intellectual property rights are, at their conceptual foundations, in harmony.

For anyone seeking to understand the constitutional foundations of intellectual property, the First Congress should be one of the first sources to be consulted.

Sources

Copyright Act of 1790.
Abraham Lincoln, *Cooper Union Address* (1860).
James Madison, Speech Introducing the Bill of Rights (1789).

Patent Act of 1790.

George Washington, Letter to James Madison (May 5, 1789).

George Washington, *First Annual Message to Congress* (1790).

* * *

Ashcroft v. Elred (2003).

Cohens v. State of Virginia (1821).

Golan v. Holder (2012).

Martin v. Hunter's Lessee (1816).

McCulloch v. Maryland (1819).

* * *

Charlene Banks Bickford and Kenneth R. Bowling, *Birth of the Nation: The First Federal Congress, 1789–1791* (1989).

Kenneth R. Bowling, "Overshadowed by States' Rights: Ratification of the Federal Bill of Rights," in *The Bill of Rights: Government Proscribed* (Ronald Hoffman and Peter J. Albert, eds.) (1998).

Oren Bracha, "Commentary on the Copyright Act of 1790," in *Primary Sources on Copyright* (1450–1900) (L. Bently & M. Kretschmer, eds.) (2008).

David P. Currie, *The Constitution in Congress: The Federalist Period, 1789–1801* (1997).

William C. diGiacomantonio, "To Form the Character of the American People: Public Support for the Arts, Sciences, and Morality in the First Congress," in *Inventing Congress: Origins and Establishment of the First Federal Congress* (Kenneth R. Bowling and Donald R. Kennon, eds.) (1999).

Edward J. Larson, *The Return of George Washington: 1783–1789* (2014).

Forrest McDonald, *The Presidency of George Washington* (1974).

Robert V. Remini, *The House: The History of the House of Representatives* (2007).

Matthew Spalding, *A Sacred Union of Citizens: Washington's Farewell Address and the American Character* (1998).

Edward C. Walterscheid, "Understanding the Copyright Act of 1790: The Issue of Common Law Copyright in America and the Modern Interpretation of the Copyright Power," 53 *Journal of the Copyright Society U.S.A.* 313 (2005–200).

Chapter 7

Life, Liberty, and the Protection of Intellectual Property: Understanding IP in Light of Jeffersonian Principles

Each year on July 4th, America celebrates its Independence. In its pronouncement of the causes which impelled the United States of America to separate from Great Britain, the Declaration of Independence set out the basic ends of American government: to secure the peoples' unalienable rights to life, liberty, and the pursuit of happiness. As the principal drafter of the Declaration, Thomas Jefferson was an intellectual force for the American Revolution—if not its intellectual leader. The classical liberal principles that Jefferson advanced and articulated formed a critical part of the intellectual backdrop to the U.S. Constitution and Bill of Rights.

But while Jefferson's primary contribution to American constitutionalism was in shaping American philosophical understanding of the nature and purpose of government, his influence on public understanding of intellectual property (IP) is peripheral at best. And yet a "Jeffersonian mythology" has overstated Jefferson's role in shaping the constitutional contours of patent and copyright protection.

To the extent Jefferson expressed anti-IP views in private letters during America's founding period, there is little to no evidence that his sentiments regarding patents or copyrights had any bearing on the Constitution. Jefferson was in Paris during the 1787 Philadelphia Convention and ratification period. He likewise was absent when the Bill of Rights was drafted. Accordingly, his letters appear to have done little or nothing to shape public understanding of the IP Clause.

The Article I, Section 8 IP Clause expressly grants to Congress power to provide patent and copyright protection to inventors and authors, respectively: "The Congress shall have Power ... To promote the Progress of Science and useful Arts, by securing for limited Times to Authors and Inventors the exclusive Right to their respective Writings and Discoveries." So it is self-evidently the case that the Constitution authorizes IP protection. The fact that the Constitution expressly confers on Congress the power to protect copyrights and patents suggests that the few scattered criticisms of IP were, in principle, rejected in the Constitution's formation.

For that matter, it proves too much to read all of Jefferson's concerns about British Crown grants of commercial trade monopolies into his misgivings about IP rights. The Constitution's framers and ratifiers grasped the crucial distinctions between unlimited trade franchise monopolies bestowed by a monarch regime and limited grants of exclusive property rights to inventors and authors under constitutional republicanism. On the one hand, a trade franchise monopoly deliberately places market power in the franchise holder—much in the sense in which we understand "monopoly" in the modern era. While on the other hand, a so-called, but ill-denominated, "limited monopoly" grants a patent or copyright holder the exclusive use of a specified creative work for a limited period of time. Indeed, the patented or copyrighted work might have many close, attractive substitutes in the marketplace. And no entry barriers prevent inventors or authors from bringing forth such substitutes.

It also deserves consideration that Jefferson's misgivings about monopolies and IP were in some measure owing to his attraction to an Enlightenment-influenced 19-year generational theory about when constitutions and laws should expire. That peculiar theory was never incorporated into the U.S. Constitution or otherwise accepted by the American public. Moreover, the extent of Jefferson's opposition to IP has also been overstated at times. While still in Paris, Jefferson appeared at least partially reconciled to the IP Clause and its property rights protections for patents and copyrights. This coincides with Jefferson's overall reconciliation to the Constitution he had initially opposed.

Importantly, patent and copyright protection fits comfortably within the Constitution's classical liberal framework for limited government and protection of individual rights that Jefferson so eloquently espoused. To the extent inventions or literary works themselves constitute fruits of labor, according to this classical liberal framework, inventors or authors by nature possess unalienable rights to those fruits. Through laws guaranteeing exclusive rights to the proceeds of those inventions or works for limited periods, society has established alienable property rights for the respective inventors and authors. In practice, Jefferson, as a public administrator, oversaw the implementation and even the expansion of these intellectual property protections.

Jefferson's ideals for administering the government were thus one in the same with those espoused in the Declaration. Jefferson's *First Inaugural Address* (1801) is the paradigmatic expression of his philosophy for administering the federal government. At the core of that natural rights understanding was a conviction that "a wise and frugal government … shall not take from the mouth of labor the bread it has earned." Inventions and artistic works are the bread that labor has earned and which government should not take. Conferring exclusive property rights in the proceeds of such labor coincides with the rendering of what Jefferson termed "equal and exact justice to all men," rather than granting monopolistic controls over entire commercial enterprises or prohibiting individual industry.

Indeed, at a practical level, IP rights coincided with Jeffersonian administration of government. As President, Jefferson oversaw the modest expansion of IP rights through the appointment of the first Superintendent for the federal government's patent process and by signing the Copyright Act of 1802, conferring copyright protection on maps, charts, engravings, etchings, and prints.

The contributions of Thomas Jefferson to the public philosophy of the Constitution should not be understated. Americans enjoying their unalienable rights to life, liberty, and pursuit of happiness ought to celebrate Jefferson's role in drafting the Declaration of Independence. But his apparent misgivings about IP shouldn't be overstated. Nor should Jefferson's private letter views about IP be read into the Constitution over and against the Intellectual Property Clause's clear recognition of patents and copyrights.

Jefferson's Private Letters on Intellectual Property

It is not uncommon for critics of intellectual property to cite various private letters by Thomas Jefferson in making claims that Jefferson had a fundamental distaste for IP, or that he at least had serious reservations about it. For instance, in letters sent from Paris to James Madison while the Constitution and Bill of Rights were being considered, Jefferson expressed concerns about perpetual government monopolies and the need to restrict or prohibit them. And in a 1788 letter to Madison shortly after the Constitution's ratification, Jefferson opined: "The saying there shall be no monopolies lessens the incitements to ingenuity, which is spurred on by the hope of a monopoly for a limited time, as of 14. years; but the benefit even of limited monopolies is too doubtful to be opposed to that of their general suppression."

Also, intellectual property critics will sometimes quote from Jefferson's letter to Isaac McPherson (1813):

> If nature has made any one thing less susceptible than all others of exclusive property, it is the action of the thinking power called an idea, which an individual may exclusively possess as long as he keeps it to

himself; but the moment it is divulged, it forces itself into the possession of every one, and the receiver cannot dispossess himself of it. Its peculiar character, too, is that no one possesses the less, because every other possesses the whole of it. He who receives an idea from me, receives instruction himself without lessening mine; as he who lights his taper at mine, receives light without darkening me. That ideas should freely spread from one to another over the globe, for the moral and mutual instruction of man, and improvement of his condition, seems to have been peculiarly and benevolently designed by nature, when she made them, like fire, expansible over all space, without lessening their density in any point, and like the air in which we breathe, move, and have our physical being, incapable of confinement or exclusive appropriation.

While the focus of that letter is on patents, IP critics will often extend Jefferson's points to copyrights. And in so doing the name of Jefferson is invoked as part of a claim that property rights in inventions and literary works are illegitimate or at least a serious danger deserving to be severely curtailed.

Of course, IP law's idea/expression dichotomy prohibits patenting or copyrighting mere ideas—as opposed to particular inventions or specific expressions of ideas. Notwithstanding this, criticisms of IP that claim the authority of Thomas Jefferson are misplaced, or at least exaggerated. Indeed, scholars such as Thomas B. Nachbar and Adam Mossoff have persuasively dismantled the "Jeffersonian mythology" that has unnecessarily elevated Jefferson's historical role regarding IP, particularly with regard to patents. Without seeking to retread all the important work of those scholars, Jefferson's relative lack of influence on the drafting of the Constitution and the public meaning of the IP Clause merit further consideration. Limitations and overstatements of Jefferson's opposition to IP rights also deserve cursory examination.

Jefferson's Exaggerated Opposition to IP and Peripheral Influence on Constitutional IP Policy

The Article I, Section 8 IP Clause expressly grants Congress the power to provide patent and copyright protection to inventors and authors, respectively: "The Congress shall have Power ... To promote the Progress of Science and useful Arts, by securing for limited Times to Authors and Inventors the exclusive Right to their respective Writings and Discoveries." So it is self-evidently the case that the Constitution authorizes protection of intellectual property.

But more than that, common sense observations about the Constitution's historical context should lead one to reject the idea that IP is somehow conceptually inconsistent with the Constitution's basic logic.

The private correspondence of the Founders sometimes provides an important source of insight into constitutional meaning and logic. But that doesn't mean all viewpoints ever expressed by individual Founders should be read into the Constitution. The Constitution was a product of political compromise. The 1787 Philadelphia Convention decided certain disputes one way or the other, decided certain other disputes through middle-ground solutions, and left still other disputes unresolved. Owing to the fact that the Constitution is a public document ratified by the people, non-public or obscure intentions of particular Founders should not override or control what "We the People" would have understood its words to mean in 1787–1788.

The fact that the Constitution expressly confers on Congress the power to protect copyrights and patents suggests that the few, scattered criticisms of IP were, in principle, rejected in the constitutional compromise. Moreover, to the extent Jefferson was an anti-IP voice, there is little to no evidence that his sentiments regarding patents or copyrights had any bearing on the Constitution. Jefferson was in Paris during the 1787 Philadelphia Convention and ratification period that followed. According to biographer Dumas Malone, "[i]nsofar as he exerted any influence on opinion this was probably against the Constitution, since his earliest comments were the least favorable and the fight in America was practically over before anybody there was informed of his final acceptance of the new frame of government."

Jefferson was likewise absent when the First Congress proposed the Bill of Rights to the states for ratification. And he arrived at the nation's capital to assume his duties as Secretary of State only a handful of weeks before the Patent and Copyright Acts of 1790 were signed into law.

Indeed, Madison countered Jefferson with respect to patent and copyright protection, writing to Jefferson in Paris on October 17, 1788:

> With regard to monopolies they are justly classed among the greatest nusances in Government. But is it clear that as encouragements to literary works and ingenious discoveries, they are not too valuable to be wholly renounced? Would it not suffice to reserve in all cases a right to the Public to abolish the privilege at a price to be specified in the grant of it? Is there not also infinitely less danger of this abuse in our Governments, than in most others? Monopolies are sacrifices of the many to the few. Where the power is in the few it is natural for them to sacrifice the many to their own partialities and corruptions. Where

the power, as with us, is in the many not in the few, the danger can not be very great that the few will be thus favored. It is much more to be dreaded that the few will be unnecessarily sacrificed to the many.

For that matter, there is good reason to conclude that Jefferson's opposition to IP was less than persuasive, and that the extent of his opposition has also been overstated. It proves too much to take all of Jefferson's misgivings about monopolies and read them into limited grants of exclusive property rights to inventors. In his Paris letters to Madison, Jefferson took particularly sharp aim at commercial trade monopolies. The Crown-chartered monopolies established in Britain undoubtedly factored into his thinking. Colonists protested against monopolies like the East India Company in the lead-up to the American Revolution. Previously, Jefferson attacked British trade monopolies in his pamphlet *A Summary View of the Rights of British America* (1774). No doubt Jefferson was also familiar with Britain's Licensing Act of 1662, which granted a monopoly charter under which copyrights could only be secured by publishers' guild members or sold to members, and they lasted forever.

Of course, in his letters, even Jefferson recognized that patents and copyrights along the lines of the model adopted in nearly every state prior to the Constitution were only limited forms of "monopolies." In any event, he surely understood that they did not constitute monopolies in the same sense we understand and use the term today to assess market power for antitrust purposes. It is true that patent and copyright confer a right to exclude for a limited period of time. But this is only true with regard to specific identifiable discoveries by inventors or creative works of authors. Many substitutes in the marketplace might already exist for such inventions or works, and no barriers prevent such substitutes from being introduced into the market.

The Constitution followed this approach by giving Congress the power to confer on inventors and authors the exclusive rights to the proceeds of their inventions and artistic works, respectively. As a form of property rights established under the Intellectual Property Clause, patents and copyrights could be alienated, and they were not perpetual. (The basic historical background on commercial trade franchises and how they differ from patents and copyrights in American constitutionalism is the subject of Chapter 4.) Jefferson's misgivings about monopolies should therefore be read in light of the crucial distinctions between unlimited trade franchise monopolies conferred by a King or Queen and limited grants of exclusive property rights to inventors and authors under constitutional republicanism.

That Jefferson's misgivings about monopolies were in some measure owing to an Enlightenment-influenced generational theory that was never incorporated into the U.S. Constitution or otherwise accepted by the American public also warrants consideration. In his September 6, 1789, letter to Madison, Jefferson expressed concerns about monopolies as a case in point for his schema for applying the principle that "the earth belongs in usufruct to the living." Out of that general principle Jefferson contrived a 19-year term for each "generation," and posed 19-year lifetimes for all constitutions, laws, and contracts, effectively throwing mankind back into a state of nature every 19 years to allow a new majority will to reconstitute the fundamental laws of society. Interestingly enough, that led Jefferson to express support for an extension of copyright terms to 19 years rather than 14 years—as was the practice under Britain's Statute of Anne, in several states, and under the Copyright Act of 1790.

Jefferson's friend Madison politely rejected the generational theory as a system for constitutionalism in a responding letter sent in February 4, 1790. Madison suggested that concerns about the intergenerational impact of laws constituted "a salutary restraint on living generations from unjust and unnecessary burdens on their successors." As Dumas Malone put it in *Jefferson and the Rights of Man* (1951), "if Jefferson's mind needed to be recalled to American realities too far away for him to see, Madison was the best of all men to point them out."

Two years earlier, writing in *Federalist No. 49*, Madison had similarly rejected as injurious to stability and veneration of good government the idea of frequent appeals to constitutional conventions for rewriting the established forms of government advanced by Jefferson in his *Notes on the State of Virginia* (1784). Apparently, Jefferson later moderated his own position. As he wrote to Samuel Kercheval in 1813: "I am not an advocate for frequent changes in laws and constitutions, but laws and constitutions must go hand in hand with the progress of the human mind." In the end, Jefferson's generational theory was an outlier in the intellectual climate that surrounded the Constitution at its framing. Accordingly, Jefferson's apparent concerns about "monopolies" should be discounted to the extent that such a speculative theory factored into those same generational concerns.

Finally, it should be recognized that while still in Paris Jefferson appeared to be at least somewhat reconciled to the IP Clause and its property rights protections for patents and copyrights. This coincides with Jefferson's overall reconciliation to the Constitution he had initially opposed. In particular, Jefferson's apparent acceptance of IP rights under the Constitution can be found in his August 28, 1789, letter to Madison. There he stated his wish that the proposed Bill of Rights recently drafted by the First Congress and sent to the states for ratification had provided that "[m]onopolies may be allowed to persons for their own productions in literature and their own inventions in the arts for a term not exceeding ___ years but for no longer term and no other purpose." Here Jefferson appears to accept the important distinction between commercial trade monopolies—that were odious to Americans—and IP rights—which were expressly adopted in the U.S. Constitution.

In light of these conceptual and historical considerations about the Constitution and Jefferson's letters from Paris, the important question is the extent to which Jefferson's private sentiments were a significant influence upon or reflection of a broader public understanding about IP at the time of the Constitution's adoption. The stronger inference to be drawn from evidence is that Jefferson's views were *not* a significant influence or reflection of the public understanding of patents, copyrights, or the IP Clause. Jefferson's broader class of concerns about monopolies was widely held in America. But the IP Clause was premised upon crucial distinctions between commercial trade monopolies and the purpose of securing IP rights. And from Jefferson's subsequent acceptance of the Constitution—including its protection of IP—one can also reasonably infer that Jefferson too recognized that critical distinction.

IP Rights in Light of Jefferson's Philosophy of Constitutional Government

Jefferson was not likely an influential force on the shape of constitutional IP policy. But it is useful to consider IP in light of those areas where Jefferson's influence on American constitutionalism was indispensable—namely, American constitutional philosophy. Importantly, patent and copyright protection fits comfortably within the Constitution's classical liberal framework for limited government and protection of individual rights that Jefferson so eloquently espoused.

In the annals of American revolutionary political philosophy, the name of Jefferson stands alongside the likes of James Otis, John Dickinson, John Adams, and Thomas Paine. Although the subject of scholarly debate, Jefferson has reasonably been regarded as the "intellectual leader of the Revolution" for his articulation of the purpose and principles of constitutional republicanism in the years leading up to American independence. His Revolutionary era writings, such as the *Summary View of the Rights of British America* and the *Declaration of the Causes and Necessity of Taking Up Arms* (1775), built upon classic liberal principles previously set out by Algernon Sidney, John Locke, and John Milton.

The Declaration of Independence, of which Jefferson was principal drafter, ranks foremost among Jefferson's contributions to America's constitutional order. As adopted by the Second Continental Congress on July 4, 1776, the

Declaration sets out the conceptual foundation for the American constitutional order in its memorable preamble:

> We hold these truths to be self-evident, that all men are created equal, that they are endowed by their Creator with certain unalienable Rights, that among these are Life, Liberty and the pursuit of Happiness.— That to secure these rights, Governments are instituted among Men, deriving their just powers from the consent of the governed,—That whenever any Form of Government becomes destructive of these ends, it is the Right of the People to alter or to abolish it, and to institute new Government, laying its foundation on such principles and organizing its powers in such form, as to them shall seem most likely to effect their Safety and Happiness.

The context and purpose of the Declaration was recalled nearly a half-century later by Jefferson. In an 1825 letter to Henry Lee, Jefferson wrote:

> [W]ith respect to our rights, and the acts of the British government contravening those rights, there was but one opinion on this side of the water. All American whigs thought alike on these subjects.
> When forced, therefore, to resort to arms for redress, an appeal to the tribunal of the world was deemed proper for our justification. This was the object of the Declaration of Independence. Not to find out new principles, or new arguments, never before thought of, not merely to say things which had never been said before; but to place before mankind the common sense of the subject, in terms so plain and firm as to command their assent, and to justify ourselves in the independent stand we are compelled to take. Neither aiming at originality of principle or sentiment, nor yet copied from any particular and previous writing, it was intended to be an expression of the American mind, and to give to that expression the proper tone and spirit called for by the occasion.
> All its authority rests then on the harmonizing sentiments of the day, whether expressed in conversation, in letters, printed essays, or in the elementary books of public right, as Aristotle, Cicero, Locke, Sidney, &c....

Jefferson deemed the Declaration an "expression of the American mind" and the "common sense of the subject" of the purposes and ends of government.

Of course, several scholars have made Jefferson's draft of the Declaration a focus of study. But the Declaration was ultimately the collective statement of the Continental Congress, not Jefferson alone. As Jefferson himself pointed out, the Declaration expressed "the American mind," not just his mind. The Declaration, as adopted by the Continental Congress and published to the world has been foundational to American constitutionalism. It articulated the intellectual foundation upon which the U.S. Constitution and Bill of Rights were built.

As explained in Chapter 1, the Declaration drew richly from John Locke's *Second Treatise on Government,* in both the concepts and terminology it employed. For instance, Locke described government's role in protecting "life, liberty, and estates." Locke also maintained that "governments of the world that were begun in peace" were "made by the consent of the people." And Locke insisted that when corrupt legislative power breached its trust "it devolves to the people, who have a right to resume their original liberty and, by the establishment of a new legislative, such as they think fit, provide for their own safety and security, which is the end for which they are in society."

The Declaration described the purpose of government to secure unalienable rights to life, liberty, and the pursuit of happiness. But that phrasing's omission of government's role in protecting estates or property by no means marked any rejection of property rights. Had it done so, the Declaration would have been decidedly contrary to "the elementary books of public rights," and unthinkable to property-conscious Americans.

For that matter, Jefferson defended property, in both its broader and narrower senses, throughout his career. Along with John Dickinson, Jefferson was the principal drafter of the Continental Congress's July 6, 1775, *Declaration of the Causes and Necessity of Taking Up Arms.* It opened with a denunciation of the idea that "a part of the human race" could ever rightfully "hold an absolute property in, and an unbounded power over others ... as the objects of a legal domination never rightfully resistible, however severe and oppressive." In making known the justice of their cause in resisting Great Britain, the Continental Congress rooted the rights of their forbearers in establishing settlements in America "[a]t the expense of their blood, at the hazard of their fortunes ... by unceasing labour, and an unconquerable spirit." The *Declaration of the Causes* protested that the British Parliament had "undertaken to give and grant our money without our consent, though we have ever exercised an exclusive right to dispose of our own property"—that is, Parliament imposed taxation without representation. Its protest also included Parliament's "depriving us of the accustomed and inestimable privilege of trial by jury, in cases affecting both life and property." Drawing to a close, the *Declaration of the Causes* asserted: "In our own native land, in defence of the freedom that is our birthright, and which we ever enjoyed till the late violation of it—for the protection of our property, acquired solely by the honest industry of our fore-fathers and ourselves, against violence actually offered, we have taken up arms."

As Garrett Ward Sheldon observed in *The Political Philosophy of Thomas Jefferson* (1991), "Jefferson was Lockean during the revolutionary period, especially in the Declaration of Independence, albeit a Lockean modified by the contingencies of a revolutionary colonist." Following the American Revolution, Jefferson typically emphasized "a more classical republican vision of economically independent, educated citizens participating directly in the common rule of local ward republics," rather than natural rights. But as Sheldon has explained, for Jefferson civic republican was *not* contrary to natural rights. Rather, Jefferson's emphasis shifted in recognition of the social nature of man. He ultimately regarded cultivation of public virtue as a means to protecting natural rights in the context of civil society. Thus, Jefferson remained dedicated to the protection of natural rights, including rights of property. Jefferson's *Second Inaugural Address* (1805), for instance, included a defense of "that state of property, equal or unequal, which results to every man from his own industry, or that of his fathers."

Ambiguity surrounds the reasoning by which Jefferson linked such concepts as natural rights, "unalienable" rights, the pursuit of happiness, and property rights. Unlocking Jefferson's precise understanding of such concepts is certainly difficult, and perhaps even futile. Nonetheless, a few observations about Jefferson's thinking as well as what "the American mind" perceived in that time puts some perspective on the subject of IP rights.

Historian Leonard W. Levy has concluded that the classical understanding of property employed by Locke in the *Second Treatise* and by Madison in his *National Gazette* essay "On Property" was also familiar to Jefferson and other Revolutionary era contemporaries. By this understanding, property was a necessary prerequisite to a person's enjoyment of life and liberty. Accordingly, the classical definition of property is a functional equivalent to the term "pursuit of happiness." Moreover, Professor Levy has argued that while Jefferson regarded the broad understanding of property—that is, the pursuit of happiness—as unalienable, Jefferson regarded the narrower understanding of property—that is, real property and personal possessions—as alienable. James W. Ely, Jr., Dumas Malone, and other scholars have similarly concluded that Jefferson's use of the term "pursuit of happiness" by no means meant to disparage rights of property. Other scholars have suggested that Jefferson borrowed the term from classic liberal Enlightenment thinkers, such as French philosopher Jean-Jacques Burlamaqui or Swiss jurist Emmerich de Vattel, who held to a natural law framework congenial to protection of property as a means for ensuring human happiness.

Jefferson undoubtedly believed a person has a natural right to the fruits of his or her own labors. But he appears to have regarded property primarily as a social institution fitted for sociable human beings. This aspect of Jefferson's thought appears in his letter to Isaac McPherson (1813). Immediately preceding the lengthy section from that letter quoted earlier, Jefferson verbosely and ponderously wrote:

> It is agreed by those who have seriously considered the subject, that no individual has, of natural right, a separate property in an acre of land, for instance. By an universal law, indeed, whatever, whether fixed or movable, belongs to all men equally and in common, is the property for him the moment of him who occupies it, but when he relinquishes the occupation, the property goes with it. Stable ownership is the gift of social law, and is given late in the progress of society.

Intellectual property critics who might rely on Jefferson's letter to McPherson for support of the idea that natural rights don't exist in patents or copyrights should therefore be mindful that Jefferson apparently rejected the idea of natural rights in real property. By treating Jefferson's nuanced rejection of natural rights in patents as a delegitimization of IP it follows that all property would not be legitimate.

However, Jefferson was a defender of property as a social institution throughout his career. Accordingly, from Jefferson's regard for IP as an institution established by society, the most immediate implication appears to be the necessity that society must make discretionary judgments about the scope and boundaries of such IP rights. Of course, society makes precisely those kinds of judgments when it comes to other forms of property.

Another possible inference to be drawn from the premise that IP is a right established by society is that IP rights are not eternally existent. But any need to definitively solve such puzzling issues through speculation is avoided by the IP Clause's express restrictions of patent and copyright protection to "limited Times." Indeed, much of Jefferson's concerns about over-extended patent terms can be squared with the IP Clause and accepted by pro-IP advocates. For example, the idea/expression dichotomy is a widely recognized principle in IP law. That is, mere ideas cannot be patented or copyrighted, but particular expressions of ideas in particular inventions or artistic works might receive protection. Although the idea/expression dichotomy may call for case-by-case application, the principle nonetheless addresses the core of Jefferson's concerns that "an idea, the fugitive fermentation of an individual brain, could, of natural right, be claimed in excusive and stable property."

Of course, the prevailing view of Founding-era IP supporters, such as Noah Webster and James Madison, was that patents and copyrights were ultimately rooted in rights of nature. To the extent inventions or literary works themselves constitute fruits of labor, the inventors or authors by nature possess unalienable rights to those fruits. The IP Clause grants Congress power to guarantee exclusive rights to the proceeds of those inventions or works for limited periods. In so doing American society has established patent and copyright as alienable property rights. Accepting Jefferson's nuanced position that one may not possess an unalienable natural right for all time in a particular expression of an idea does not necessitate a rejection of a natural rights-basis for IP rights. Rather, accepting Jefferson's nuanced understanding about natural rights and all property simply requires a corresponding nuanced understanding about the connection between natural rights and intellectual property rights. So understood, patent and copyright protection fits comfortably within the classical liberal principles of limited government and protection of individual rights that Jefferson eloquently espoused in the Declaration.

IP in Light of Jefferson's Philosophy of Public Administration

Another significant contribution of Jefferson to American constitutionalism is an applied philosophy for administering the government under the Constitution. As Leonard W. White explained in *The Jeffersonians: A Study in Administrative History* (1951), "Jefferson was not interested … in the normal process of day-to-day administration" and "thought administration was mostly common sense applied to concrete situations." Rather, "on the larger scene where administration, policy, strategy, and constitutional relationships were involved, he made contributions of the first order." Thus, Jefferson's "significance in American history flows much less from his contribution to the art of administration than from his convictions about democracy, liberty, and the capacity of the people for self-government."

A similar verdict regarding Jefferson's significance to the administration of constitutional government was rendered by Lynton K. Caldwell in his examination of Jefferson's administrative theory. According to Caldwell:

> Jefferson's contribution to thought on public administration derives from both [practical and intellectual] aspects of his leadership and from the traditions concerning his leadership, but it is fair to say that Jefferson's greater contribution derives from the ideal. For, although ideal ends are distinguishable from means, it is the ends that ultimately determine the nature and direction of the means, and it is the Jeffersonian ideals which in large measure still persist in American political thought which have had a decisive influence in shaping the administrative theories and practices of American government.

Scholars of Jefferson—including both White and Caldwell—pointed to Jefferson's *First Inaugural Address* (1801) as the paradigmatic expression of his philosophy for administering the federal government. Reviewing the *First Inaugural*, Jefferson biographer Dumas Malone wrote that "its enduring appeal may be attributed to its verbal felicity and to the fact that much of it has been deemed timeless." Jefferson's verbal felicity and timelessness are both encapsulated in his *First Inaugural* pronouncement that:

> A wise and frugal government, which shall restrain men from injuring one another, shall leave them otherwise free to regulate their own pursuits of industry and improvement, and shall not take from the mouth of labor the bread it has earned. This is the sum of good government, and this is necessary to close the circle of our felicities.

Among the "essential principles" of his administration Jefferson described a limited federal government based on popular consent, remaining accountable to the people and respecting their individual rights, including property rights. Jefferson's ideals for administering the government were thus one in the same with those espoused in the Declaration of Independence. Whereas the Declaration set out principles upon which government was established, Jefferson's *First Inaugural* invoked those same principles as guideposts for administering the federal government established by the Constitution. Jefferson would later describe the connection of those principles in a letter to Spencer Roane (1819). In admittedly hyperbolic terms, Jefferson described his election and the commencement of his administration as the "revolution of 1800," deeming it "as real a revolution in the principles of our government as that of 1776 was in form." According to Malone, the word "revolution" had a "predominantly political connotation" to Jefferson, akin to the word "restoration." Thus, "[t]he most accurate statement of the matter, it seems, is that in 1801 he was seeking to return to the principles of the American Revolution."

At a conceptual level, protections of limited rights of property for inventors and authors fully coincide with the "essential principles" of Jefferson's philosophy of public administration. Inventions and artistic works are the bread that labor has earned and which government, therefore, should not take "from the mouth of labor." Conferring exclusive property rights in the proceeds of such labor coincides with the rendering of what Jefferson termed "equal and exact justice to all men," rather than granting monopolistic controls over entire commercial enterprises or prohibiting individual industry.

At a practical level, IP rights coincided with Jeffersonian administration of government. Jefferson did not hesitate to take aim at policies he deemed inconsistent with the essential principles he espoused in his *First Inaugural*. Alien and Sedition Act curtailments of the freedom of the press, for instance, did offend those essential principles. Accordingly, pardons were issued and those laws were permitted to expire. Jefferson also signed legislation repealing the Judiciary Act of 1800, thereby rolling back the appointment of "midnight judges" that he believed were intended to thwart the will of the people to govern themselves. But, significantly, Jefferson never publicly attacked the patent or copyright policies that existed when he assumed the presidency.

In fact, as President, Jefferson oversaw the modest expansion of IP rights. First, his Secretary of State James Madison appointed Dr. William Thornton as the first full-time clerk or Superintendent to oversee patent applications. In light of the Jefferson administration's attentiveness to fiscal frugality, the fact that it devoted additional taxpayer dollars to the patent process is not insignificant. Nor should one overlook President Jefferson's 1807 letter to Oliver Evans, in which he wrote that "[c]ertainly an inventor ought to be allowed a right to the benefit of his invention for a certain time," and that "[n]obody wishes more than I do that ingenuity should receive a liberal encouragement." Moreover, President Jefferson signed the Copyright Act of 1802 into law. The 1802 Act expanded the scope of copyright protection, to include maps, charts, engravings, etchings, and prints. Thus, as a public administrator, Jefferson oversaw the practical implementation and even the expansion of those protections.

All told, patent and copyright protections violated no Jeffersonian principle of administration, but such protections were in keeping with the essential principle that the fruits of one's labors not be taken away. And in practice IP rights were not curtailed under the Jefferson administration, but IP rights were modestly expanded.

Conclusion

The contributions of Thomas Jefferson to the public philosophy of the Constitution should not be understated. Americans enjoying their unalienable rights to life, liberty, and the pursuit of happiness ought to celebrate Jefferson's role in drafting the Declaration of Independence. But his perceived misgivings about intellectual property shouldn't be overstated. Nor should Jefferson's private letter views about intellectual property be read into the Constitution over and against the IP Clause's clear recognition of patents and copyrights.

Sources

Declaration of the Causes and Necessity of Taking Up Arms (1775).
Declaration of Independence (1776).
Thomas Jefferson, *A Summary View of the Rights of British America* (1774).
Thomas Jefferson, *First Inaugural Address* (1801).
Thomas Jefferson, Letter to Oliver Evans (1807).
Thomas Jefferson, Letter to Samuel Kercheval (1813).
Thomas Jefferson, Letter to Henry Lee (1825).
Thomas Jefferson, Letter to Isaac McPherson (1813).
Thomas Jefferson, Letter to James Madison (1788).
Thomas Jefferson, Letter to James Madison (1789).
Thomas Jefferson, Letter to Spencer Roane (1819).
Thomas Jefferson, *Notes on the State of Virginia* (1784).
Thomas Jefferson, *Second Inaugural Address* (1805).
John Locke's *Second Treatise of Government* (1689).
James Madison, Letter to Thomas Jefferson (1788).
James Madison, Letter to Thomas Jefferson (1790).
Publius (James Madison), *Federalist No. 49* (1788).

* * *

Lynton K. Caldwell, *The Administrative Theories of Jefferson and Hamilton* (1964).
Justin Hughes, "Copyright and Incomplete Historiographies: Of Piracy, Propertization, and Thomas Jefferson," 79 *Southern California Law Review* (2006).
Leonard W. Levy, "Property as a Human Right," 5 *Constitutional Commentary* 169 (1988).
Dumas Malone, *Jefferson and the Rights of Man* (1951).
Dumas Malone, *Jefferson the President: First Term, 1801–1805* (1970).
Adam Mossoff, "Who Cares What Thomas Jefferson Thought About Patents? Reevaluating the Patent 'Privilege' in Historical Context," 92 *Cornell Law Review* 953 (2007).
Thomas B. Nachbar, "Constructing Copyright's Mythology," 6 *The Green Bag* 37 (2002).
Garrett Ward Sheldon, *The Political Philosophy of Thomas Jefferson* (1991).
Edward C. Walterscheid, "Thomas Jefferson and the Patent Act of 1793," *Essays in History* 40 (1998).
Leonard D. White, *The Jeffersonians: A Study in Administrative History* (1951).

Chapter 8

Intellectual Property Rights Under the Constitution's Rule of Law

Today, the rule of law is all but universally recognized as a fundamental attribute of a free and just society. A "government of laws, not of men" places important limits on government power in order to ensure the protection of individual rights. And a proper understanding of fundamental rule of law precepts plays an important role in securing Intellectual Property (IP) rights.

American constitutionalism supplies the basic conditions for America's unique conception of the rule of law designed to ensure the protection of life, liberty, and property. Intellectual property is a form of property expressly provided for under the Constitution. In theory and in practice, intellectual property is readily conformable to the key components of the rule of law and American constitutionalism, such as according due process and equal protection and protecting vested rights. When IP's critics argue otherwise, including some who otherwise consider themselves respectful of private property rights, they disregard or misunderstand fundamental elements of American constitutionalism and the rule of law.

Typically, the rule of law is characterized in terms of its basic precepts: (1) a system of binding rules; (2) of sufficient clarity, predictability, and equal applicability; (3) adopted by a valid governing authority; and (4) applied by an independent authority.

The building blocks to the rule of law in the American constitutional order were in significant part provided by political philosophers of classical liberalism such as John Locke and Baron de Montesquieu. Prominent jurists of the British common law tradition, including Lord Coke and William Blackstone, similarly informed early American thinking.

America's distinctive contributions to the concept of the rule of law emerged amidst the American Revolution. These contributions found practical application in early state constitutions, such as the Massachusetts Constitution of 1780. Late 18th century American political writers, including the authors of *The Federalist Papers*, also explored rule of law implications flowing from a constitutional republican form of government. And many of those early American insights supplied a critical part of the U.S. Constitution's political backdrop.

American constitutionalism thereby supplies the basic conditions for America's unique conception of the rule of law. Stated succinctly, key components of American constitutionalism include: (1) a written constitution that constitutes the fundamental law of the land; (2) representative government established by democratic elections; (3) division of government authority through the separation of powers and federalism; (4) an enumeration of protected individual rights; and (5) judicial review by an independent judiciary. These key components provide the institutional context for the application of the rule of law within the context of American constitutionalism. They also conform to the classical liberal conception of the basic purpose of government: protecting individual rights of person and property according to equal justice under law.

Copyrights and patents are expressly included in the U.S. Constitution, the supreme law of the land. As the Article I, Section 8 IP Clause states, Congress has the power "To promote the Progress of Science and useful Arts, by securing for limited Times to Authors and Inventors the exclusive Right to their respective Writings and Discoveries." Copyrights and patents are therefore unique types of property that the Constitution designates for protection.

Under the Constitution, IP rights are secured and subject to revision by democratically elected representatives. The Constitution designates Congress as the valid authority for adopting legislation to secure IP rights to authors and inventors. Therefore, it is the constitutional duty of Congress to define the scope of protected IP rights according to generally applicable laws. Whether laws passed by Congress adhere to the rule of law depend on the particular details of such legislation. But at a general level, the IP Clause embodies at least two important limiting principles. First, the IP Clause secures rights to particular writings or discoveries of individual authors and inventors, respectively. It confers no general trade franchise monopolies to entire sectors or segments of trade or commerce. Rather, other authors or inventors are at liberty to employ their own efforts to create and secure IP rights in their own respective writings or inventions. Second, the IP Clause secures rights to particular writings or discoveries only "for limited Times." Setting copyright and patent protection terms of years provides important certainty and predictability to IP rights holders, IP licensees, and others.

American constitutionalism's framework for enforcement of IP rights against infringement before an impartial court of law is also structurally consonant with rule of law precepts. Aggrieved IP rights holders or executive branch law enforcement authorized to enforce IP rights against infringements are required to prove their cases with evidence before impartial tribunals applying statutes, judicial precedents, or terms of enforceable contracts. And congressional statutes and trial court decisions regarding IP rights are subject to review by independent federal circuit courts of appeal and the U.S. Supreme Court.

Especially important rule of law implications follow from IP's status as a constitutionally protected property right. For instance, "due process of law" requirements attach to IP rights. These requirements include protections from legislative deprivations of property interests in copyrights and patents and the guarantee of regular procedures governing individualized proceedings before independent tribunals.

The "equal protection of the law" is a rule of law precept that also has important implications for securing IP rights. Equal protections include the requirement that all property interests in copyright and patents should be treated alike except for those IP rights holders who are differently situated according to a valid public purpose. A related implication is that IP rights should not be subject to discriminatory treatment compared to tangible forms of property rights. Arbitrary classifications are prohibited and reasoned explanations are required to justify differential treatment.

The most basic rule of law implication of the Constitution's Takings Clause's limits regarding IP rights includes a substantive guarantee that IP rights holders be justly compensated for lost profits resulting from government takings of copyrights or patents. An additional implication of the Takings Clause for IP protection is the right to challenge the genuineness of any claimed "public use" before an independent court of law. And finally, vested rights protections recognized for all other property rights should apply where courts of law render judgments regarding those IP rights. For most purposes, IP rights vest through operation of copyright and patent statutes.

Whether or the extent to which contemporary legal doctrines or procedures meet the rigors of the rule of law depends on particularized analysis. What is important is that American constitutionalism supplies a basis for critiquing IP law and policy and for keeping them in conformance with the rule of law.

Therefore, many of today's IP critics are mistaken in regarding IP rights as somehow an aberration from the basic principles of American constitutionalism. At their core, IP rights readily fit within American constitutionalism's framework for the rule of law. Copyrights and patents are specific types of property that the U.S. Constitution was established to protect under law. A disregard for IP rights constitutes an indifference—whether unwitting or not—to principles of American constitutionalism and the rule of law. And such indifference inevitably erodes respect not only for IP rights, but for all property rights.

The Rule of Law in the American Constitutional Order

In *The Rule of Law in America*, Professor Ronald Cass characterized the "core conception of the rule of law" as "government of laws, not of men." Cass and other scholars typically define rule of law in terms of some basic precepts. That is, the rule of law is: (1) a system of binding rules; (2) of sufficient clarity, predictability, and equal applicability; (3) adopted by a valid governing authority; and (4) applied by an independent authority. In a 2011 *National Affairs* article, Professor Richard A. Epstein has similarly described the rule of law as:

> [T]he basic principles of fairness and due process that govern the application of power in both the public and the private spheres. The rule of law requires that all dispute—whether among private parties or among the state and private parties—be tried before neutral judges, under rules that are known and articulated in advance. Every party must have notice of the charge against him and an opportunity to be heard in response; each governing rule must be consistent with all the others, so that no person is forced to violate one legal requirement in order to satisfy a second. In the United States, our respect for such principles has made our economy the world's strongest, and our citizens the world's freest.

Taken together, these basic precepts comprise a formalistic definition of the rule of law. By this understanding, the rule of law is a system of procedures to coordinate and limit government action—but not a system designed to protect any substantive rights as such. However, American constitutionalism contains a core set of individual rights that a government under laws is designed to protect. Protection of individual rights of life, liberty, and property is the central end of American constitutionalism. Intellectual property is a form of constitutionally protected property. IP therefore fits within the central aim of government under the Constitution.

American constitutionalism supplies the basic conditions for a unique conception of rule of law. As constitutional historian Herman Belz has explained, "American constitutionalism insists on fidelity to the text of the written fundamental law." That is, "[w]hen we refer to the United States Constitution, as fundamental law, we mean that it sets the standards by which political and governmental legitimacy are evaluated and determined." The Constitution "expresses the deliberate will of the people under the rule of law, and it is required for the preservation of individual liberty and social freedom in self-governing political communities."

America's constitutional conception of the rule of law was supplied in no small part by classical liberal political theorists. In his *Second Treatise of Government* (1689), John Locke deemed the establishment of government by consent necessary to supply a neutral umpire and enforcer to resolve disputes that inevitably arise when people in society come into conflict over their rights of life, liberty, and property:

> And thus all private judgment of every particular member being excluded, the community comes to be umpire, by settled standing rules, indifferent, and the same to all parties; and by men having authority from the community, for the execution of those rules, decides all the differences that may happen between any members of that society concerning any matter of right; and punishes those offences which any member hath committed against the society, with such penalties as the law has established.

For Locke, only a government acting according to law could act with the impartiality required to protect the individual rights of the governed. "Absolute arbitrary power, or governing without settled standing laws," according to Locke, is contrary to the ends of society and government "to preserve their lives, liberties and fortunes, and by stated rules of right and property to secure their peace and quiet." Exercise of government power by established laws ensures "that both the people may know their duty, and be safe and secure within the limits of the law; and the rulers too kept within their bounds."

Montesquieu added to early American understandings of the rule of law through his emphasis on the separation of powers and the unique role of an independent judiciary. In Book IX of his *Spirit of the Laws* (1748), Montesquieu described the separation of legislative, executive, and judicial powers as a means for holding government accountable to laws and safeguarding against arbitrary exercises of power: "There would be an end of everything, were the same man or the same body, whether of the nobles or of the people to exercise those three powers, that of enacting laws, that of executing the public resolutions, and of trying the causes of individuals."

With an eye toward the British common law, Montesquieu also emphasized an independent judiciary's role in protecting individual rights according to law:

[T]here is no liberty, if the judiciary power be not separated from the legislative and executive. Were it joined with the legislative, the life and liberty of the subject would be subject to arbitrary control; for the judge would then be legislator. Were it joined to the executive power, the judge might behave with violence and oppression.

For that matter, the British common law—a body of judicial precedents applying constitutional and rule of law principles—also influenced Americans in the late 18th century. Adjudication of disputes over rights of private property in courts of law figured central in that tradition. The administration of justice, in turn, depended upon judicial independence. The independence of the judiciary was therefore another critical facet of constitutionalism that Americans received through the British common law tradition.

America's distinctive contributions to the concept of the rule of law came to the fore amidst the American Revolution. Constitutional conditions for applying the rule of law were interwoven into the Declaration of Independence. They figure prominently among the "history of repeated injuries and usurpations" by the King of Britain that impelled the Colonies' separation. Among the Declaration's charges "submitted to a candid world":

He has refused his Assent to Laws, the most wholesome and necessary for the public good;

He has obstructed the Administration of Justice, by refusing his Assent to Laws for establishing Judiciary powers;

He has made Judges dependent on his Will alone, for the tenure of their offices, and the amount and payment of their salaries;

He has combined with others to subject us to a jurisdiction foreign to our constitution, and unacknowledged by our laws; giving his Assent to their Acts of pretended Legislation;

For imposing Taxes on us without our Consent;

For depriving us in many cases, of the benefits of Trial by Jury;

For taking away our Charters, abolishing our most valuable Laws, and altering fundamentally the Forms of our Governments; [and]

For suspending our own Legislatures, and declaring themselves invested with power to legislate for us in all cases whatsoever.

The rule of law found practical application in early state constitutions. Perhaps the paradigmatic example of early state constitutionalism supplying the groundwork for a uniquely American application of rule of law principles is the Massachusetts Constitution of 1780. Principally drafted by John Adams, the Massachusetts Constitution of 1780 set out the basic purpose of government in protecting rights, including property rights. It provides a basic constitutional framework for protecting rights "to the end it may be a government of laws and not of men." Among its provisions:

> [Article I] All men are born free and equal, and have certain natural, essential, and unalienable rights; among which may be reckoned the right of enjoying and defending their lives and liberties; that of acquiring, possessing, and protecting property; in fine, that of seeking and obtaining their safety and happiness;

> [Article IX] All elections ought to be free; and all the inhabitants of this Commonwealth, having such qualifications as they shall establish by their frame of government, have an equal right to elect officers, and to be elected, for public employments;

> [Article X] Each individual of the society has a right to be protected by it in the enjoyment of his life, liberty and property, according to standing laws;

> [Article XI] Every subject of the Commonwealth ought to find a certain remedy, by having recourse to the laws, for all injuries or wrongs which he may receive in his person, property, or character. He ought to obtain right and justice freely, and without being obliged to purchase it; completely, and without any denial; promptly, and without delay; conformably to the laws;

> [Article XII] [N]o subject shall be arrested, imprisoned, despoiled, or deprived of his property, immunities, or privileges, put out of the protection of the law, exiled, or deprived of his life, liberty, or estate; but by the judgment of his peers, or the law of the land; [and]

> [Article XXX] In the government of this Commonwealth, the legislative department shall never exercise the executive and judicial powers, or either of them: The executive shall never exercise the legislative and judicial powers, or either of them: The judicial shall never exercise the legislative and executive powers, or either of them: to the end it may be a government of laws and not of men.

Along with early American state papers such as the Declaration and state constitutions, late 18th century American political writers also explored rule of law implications flowing from constitutional republican form of government. These early American insights into constitutionalism and the rule of law were core components of the intellectual backdrop of the U.S. Constitution.

For their part, the authors of *The Federalist Papers* described the extent to which the U.S. Constitution embodied these rule of law implications and constitutional principles, namely, necessity of a written constitution, separation of powers, federalism, representative elections, and an independent judiciary. Perhaps the best summation of these principles appears in a passage from *Federalist No. 12*:

> The science of politics, ... like most other sciences, has received great improvement. The efficacy of various principles is now well understood, which were either not known at all or imperfectly known to the ancients. The regular distribution of power into distinct departments; the introduction of legislative balances and checks; the institution of courts composed of judges holding their offices during good behavior; the representation of the people in the legislature by deputies of their own election: these are wholly new discoveries or have made their principal progress toward perfection in modern times. They are means, and powerful means, by which the excellences of republican government may be retained and its imperfections lessened or avoided.

In expounding those same principles, *The Federalist Papers* also addressed the necessity that laws be of general application, reasonably clear, and knowable in advance. As James Madison, writing as Publius, explained in *Federalist No. 62*:

> It will be of little avail to the people, that the laws are made by men of their own choice, if the laws be so voluminous that they cannot be read, or so incoherent that they cannot be understood; if they be repealed or revised before they are promulgated, or undergo such incessant changes that no man, who knows what the law is to-day, can guess what it will be to-morrow. Law is defined to be a rule of action; but how can that be a rule, which is little known, and less fixed?

While *Federalist No. 84* advocated against the enumeration of specific individual rights, it did so based on a nuanced argument about the limited scope of federal power and the dangers to the broad scope of individual rights that could result from an attempt to catalog them all. For that matter, essays such as *Federalist No. 78* expounded on the theme of a written constitution as fundamental law, including the idea of judicial review as a necessary component of written constitutionalism. In any event, in the first session of the First Congress, James Madison introduced—and the Congress proposed to the states— what became the Bill of Rights. And as will be discussed in Chapter 10, protections for individual rights under the rule of law, including rights of private property, received their strongest subsequent enhancement through the ratification of the Fourteenth Amendment.

In sum, the key components of American constitutionalism include: (1) a written constitution that constitutes the fundamental law of the land; (2) representative government by democratic elections; (3) division of government authority through the separation of powers and federalism; (4) an enumeration of protected individual rights; and (5) judicial review by an independent judiciary. These key components of constitutionalism are designed to fulfill the basic end of government: protecting individual rights of person and property.

IP's Consonance with American Constitutionalism and the Rule of Law

Since copyright and patent are expressly included in the Constitution, the contours of IP rights are subject to the rule of law. Indeed, in both theory and practice, IP is readily conformable to rule of law norms in the American constitutional order. The U.S. Constitution designates Congress as the valid authority for adopting legislation to secure IP rights to authors and inventors. It is therefore the constitutional duty of Congress to define the scope of protected IP rights according to generally applicable laws.

Whether laws passed by Congress adhere to the rule of law depend on the particular details of such legislation. But at a general level, the IP Clause embodies at least two important limiting principles. First, the IP Clause secures rights to particular writings or discoveries of individual authors and inventors, respectively. It confers no general trade franchise monopolies to entire sectors or segments of trade or commerce. Rather, other authors or inventors are at liberty to employ their own efforts to create and secure IP rights in their own respective writings or inventions. Second, the IP Clause secures rights to particular writings or discoveries only "for limited Times." Setting copyright and patent protection terms of years provides important certainty and predictability to IP rights-holders, IP licensees, and others.

American constitutionalism's framework for enforcement of IP rights against infringement before an impartial court of law is also structurally consonant with rule of law precepts. Aggrieved IP rights holders or executive branch law enforcement authorized to enforce IP rights against infringements are required to prove their cases with evidence before impartial tribunals applying statutes, judicial precedents, or terms of enforceable contracts. And congressional statutes and trial court decisions regarding IP rights are subject to review by independent federal circuit courts of appeal and the U.S. Supreme Court.

Rule of Law Implications of IP as a Constitutionally Protected Property Right

Previous sections primarily explored how intellectual property rights fit within broader political-philosophical themes regarding the rule of law in American constitutionalism. However, rule of law precepts embodied in the Constitution have important implications regarding legal protections for IP rights. While not providing a comprehensive exploration of the subject, this section offers a few basic implications for the protection of IP rights under the rule of law in America's constitutional order.

Certain generalized rule of law implications stemming from IP's status as constitutionally protected property rights can be ascertained from a handful of especially relevant constitutional clauses. The following basic rule of law implications regarding IP should bind or otherwise guide all branches of government policymaking and implementation.

Due Process of Law

Like other property rights, those rightfully possessing IP rights should not be deprived of those rights without "due process of law," as guaranteed by the Fifth and Fourteenth Amendments to the U.S. Constitution. As Professors Nathan Chapman and Michael McConnell have observed, "'[d]ue process of law' is the oldest phrase and the oldest idea in our Constitution." "Fundamentally, it was about securing the rule of law," they explain, "only secondarily about notice and the opportunity to be heard." Professors Chapman and McConnell's scholarship reiterates the original understanding of due process as the conceptual embodiment of the separation of powers. This "due process as separation of powers" logic is evident, for example, in Justice Benjamin Curtis's analysis of the Fifth Amendment Due Process Clause's meaning in *Murray's Lessee v. Hoboken Land & Improvement Co.* (1856):

> The Constitution contains no description of those processes which it was intended to allow or forbid. It does not even declare what principles are to be applied to ascertain whether it be due process. It is manifest that it was not left to the legislative power to enact any process which might be devised. The article is a restraint on the legislative, as well as on the executive and judicial, powers of the government, and cannot be so construed as to leave Congress free to make any process "due process of law," by its mere will. To what principles, then, are we to resort to ascertain whether this process, enacted by Congress, is

due process? To this the answer must be twofold. We must examine the Constitution itself to see whether this process be in conflict with any of its provisions. If not found to be so, we must look to those settled usages and modes of proceeding existing in the common and statute law of England, before the emigration of our ancestors, and which are shown not to have been unsuited to their civil and political condition by having been acted on by them after the settlement of this country.

That is, while due process doesn't impose any particular requirements on the legislative process, it does restrict the contents of legislation that affects rights of property, including intellectual property. Further, the particular procedural requirements due to property rights holders should, at minimum, include those ascertained when "tested by the common and statute law of England prior to the emigration of our ancestors, and by the laws of many of the States at the time of the adoption of this amendment," as well as by "legislative construction of the Constitution, commencing so early in the government ... continued throughout its existence, and repeatedly acted on by the judiciary and the executive." Justice Curtis cited Sir Edward Coke's *Institutes* in observing that "'due process of law' generally implies and includes *actor [plaintiff]*, *reus [defendant]*, *judex [judge]*, regular allegations, opportunity to answer, and a trial according to some settled course of judicial proceedings."

Thus, the rule of law implications of "due process of law" for IP rights include protections from legislative deprivations of property interests in copyrights and patents embodied in regular procedures that must be adhered to as part of individualized proceedings before independent courts of law.

Equal Protection of the Laws

Holders of IP rights are constitutionally guaranteed "the equal protection of the laws" through the Fourteenth Amendment, and, according to Supreme Court precedent, by implication through the Fifth Amendment. While the scope of equal protection is debated, it is widely held that, at minimum, all persons should enjoy equal protection of the same rights protected by the Civil Rights Act of 1866, to wit:

To make and enforce contracts, to sue, be parties, and give evidence, to inherit, purchase, lease, sell, hold, and convey real and personal property, and to full and equal benefit of all laws and proceedings for the security of persons and property ... and shall be subject to like punishment, pains and penalties, and to none other ...

Justice Stephen Field similarly expressed the implications of the Equal Protection Clause in *Barbier v. Connolly* (1885):

> [E]qual protection and security should be given to all under like circumstances in the enjoyment of their personal and civil rights; that all persons should be equally entitled to pursue their happiness, and acquire and enjoy property; that they should have like access to the courts of the country for the protection of their persons and property, the prevention and redress of wrongs, and the enforcement of contracts; that no impediment should be interposed to the pursuits of anyone, except as applied to the same pursuits by others under like circumstances; that no greater burdens should be laid upon one than are laid upon others in the same calling and condition, and that in the administration of criminal justice no different or higher punishment should be imposed upon one than such as is prescribed to all for like offenses ... Class legislation, discriminating against some and favoring others, is prohibited; but legislation which, in carrying out a public purpose, is limited in its application, if within the sphere of its operation it affects alike all persons similarly situated, is not within the amendment.

The rule of law implications of "equal protection of the laws" for IP rights include the requirement that all property interests in copyright and patents should be treated alike—except for IP rights holders who are differently situated according to a valid public purpose. A related implication is that IP rights should not be subject to discriminatory treatment compared to tangible forms of property rights; arbitrary classifications are prohibited and reasoned explanations are required to justify differential treatment.

No Takings for Public Use Without Just Compensation

Describing the Fifth Amendment Takings Clause's requirement that "private property shall not be taken for public use without just compensation," Justice Joseph Story declared in his *Commentaries on the Constitution of the United States* (1833) that:

> This is an affirmance of a great doctrine established by the common law for the protection of private property. It is founded in natural equity, and is laid down by jurists as a principle of universal law. Indeed, in a free government, almost all other rights would become utterly worthless, if the government possessed an uncontrollable power over the private fortune of every citizen. One of the fundamental ob-

jects of every good government must be the due administration of justice; and how vain it would be to speak of such an administration, when all property is subject to the will or caprice of the legislature, and the rulers.

In modern times, the Supreme Court has not definitively opined on the application of the Takings Clause to IP. However, there is nothing in the text, structure, or logic of the Constitution to suggest the Clause's non-applicability to IP. Rather, IP's consonance with American constitutionalism and the express inclusion in the IP Clause in the Constitution makes the Takings Clause's application to IP rights a straightforward matter.

Professor Adam Mossoff's scholarship has shed important light on "The Historical Protection of Patents Under the Takings Clause." That history includes *McKeever v. U.S.* (1878), wherein the Supreme Court concluded that the Takings Clause secured patents as constitutionally protected private property. Accordingly, the most basic rule of law implications of the Takings Clause's limits regarding IP rights include a guarantee that IP rights holders be justly compensated for lost profits resulting from government takings of copyrights or patents.

Moreover, it seems difficult to conceive of legitimate "public uses" of individual IP rights resulting from government taking. For instance, laws seeking to turn protected copyrights and patents over to the public domain appear contrary to any straightforward understanding of public use. Thus, another obvious implication of the Takings Clause for IP protection is the right to challenge the genuineness of any alleged "public use" before an independent court of law.

Vested Rights

The Constitution also implies protection of vested rights in property—including IP—from infringement by arbitrary retroactive laws. Vested property rights arise from constitutional requirements of due process, limits on takings, prohibitions on laws impairing obligations of contracts, and prohibitions on *ex post facto* laws. The vesting of rights is also rooted in the logic of private property and basic rule of law precepts.

Where rights secured under the laws vest, they are protected from subsequent attempts by government to retroactively undo the law and legal expectations that secured those rights. Although the vested rights doctrine does not enjoy the robust application it received in earlier times at the hands of jurists such as Chief Justice John Marshall, vested rights principles remain a fixed part of modern jurisprudential understanding. A summation of vested rights principles was given by the Supreme Court in *McCullough v. Virginia* (1898). In that case the Court observed: "It is not within the power of a legislature to take away rights which have been once vested by a judgment. Legislation may act on subsequent proceedings, may abate actions pending, but when those actions have passed into judgment the power of the legislature to disturb the rights created thereby ceases."

To be sure, where IP rights are in dispute in particular instances, those same vested rights protections recognized for all property rights should apply where courts of law render judgments regarding those IP rights. As Professor Mossoff's scholarship in constitutional history reminds us, in *McClurg v. Kingsland* (1843) the Supreme Court concluded that "Congress could not *retroactively* limit property rights that had been secured in now-repealed patent statutes." With equal reason, those same vested rights protections should protect copyrights from congressional repeals of earlier copyright statutes.

But as a general matter, court judgments should be unnecessary to secure vested IP rights. Rather, for most purposes, IP rights should vest through operation of copyright and patent statutes. Those laws specify the terms by which authors or inventors secure rights to the proceeds of their respective writings or inventions. As Chief Justice John Marshall observed in his opinion for the Circuit Court in *Evans v. Jordan* (1813), an inventor possesses an "inchoate property which [is] vested by the discovery" and "perfected by the patent." The Supreme Court made a similar observation about the vesting of patents by law in *Gayler v. Wilder* (1850). Even at common law, authors had a recognized property right in their unpublished manuscripts, giving authors the basis for copyright protection even prior to publication. And the same logic regarding vested property rights as applied to inventions also applies to copyright post-publication.

* * *

The extent to which modern congressional legislation or judicial precedents meet the rigors of the rule of law depends on particularized analysis. But one need not delve far into the intricacies of the Constitution's specific clauses and modern jurisprudence in order to grasp the basic rule of law implications of recognizing copyright and patents as private property.

Conclusion

American constitutionalism supplies the basic conditions for America's unique conception of rule of law—designed to ensure the protection of life, liberty, and property. Copyrights and patents are special types of property that the U.S. Constitution was established to protect under law. In theory and in practice, IP is readily conformable to the key components of American constitutionalism and to the rule of law. And American constitutionalism supplies a basis for critiquing IP law and policy and for keeping them in conformance with the rule of law.

IP critics are therefore mistaken in regarding IP rights as an aberration from the basic principles of American constitutionalism. A disregard for IP rights constitutes an indifference—whether unwitting or not—for principles of American constitutionalism and the rule of law. Such indifference inevitably tends to erode respect not only for intellectual property rights, but for all property rights.

Sources

Declaration of Independence (1776).
John Locke, *Second Treatise of Government* (1689).
Massachusetts Constitution of 1780.
Baron de Montesquieu, *The Spirit of the Laws* (1748).
Publius (Alexander Hamilton), *Federalist No. 12* (1788).
Publius (James Madison), *Federalist No. 62* (1788).
Publius (Alexander Hamilton), *Federalist No. 78* (1788).
Publius (Alexander Hamilton), *Federalist No. 84* (1788).
Joseph Story, *Commentaries on the Constitution of the United States* (1833).

* * *

Barbier v. Connolly (1885).
Evans v. Jordan (1813).
Gayler v. Wilder (1850).
McClurg v. Kingsland (1843).
McCullough v. Virginia (1898).
Murray's Lessee v. Hoboken Land & Improvement Co. (1856).

* * *

Herman Belz, *Constitutionalism and the Rule of Law in America* (2009).
Ronald A. Cass, *The Rule of Law in America* (2001).
Ronald A. Cass, "Property Rights Systems and the Rule of Law," *The Elgar Companion to Property Right Economics* (Enrico Colombatto, ed., 2003).
Nathan S. Chapman and Michael W. McConnell, "Due Process As Separation of Powers," 121 *Yale Law Journal* 1672 (2012).
Richard A. Epstein, *Design for Liberty: Private Property, Public Administration, and the Rule of Law* (2011).
Richard A. Epstein, "Government by Waiver," *National Affairs*, Issue Number 7 (Spring 2011).

Richard A. Epstein, "The Perilous Position of the Rule of Law and the Administrative State," *Perspectives from FSF Scholars*, Vol. 8, No. 6 (February 28, 2013).

Adam Mossoff, "Patents as Constitutional Private Property: The Historical Protection of Patents Under the Takings Clause," 87 *Boston University Law Review* 689 (2007).

Brian Z. Tamanaha, *On the Rule of Law: History, Politics, Theory* (2004).

Chapter 9

Reaffirming the Foundations of Intellectual Property Rights: Copyright and Patent in the Antebellum Era

The principles established in the U.S. Constitution underwent significant development during the Antebellum era. Generally considered the time book-ended by the conclusion of the War of 1812 and the beginning of the Civil War, the Antebellum era was a period in which the Founding era's solicitude for protection of individual private property rights was solidified and received extended application. In the time between the War of 1812 and the Civil War, the justice and economic imperative of protecting intellectual property (IP) rights was widely perceived and appreciated. As a result, the Antebellum era was a period of advancement for the protection of copyright and patent rights.

By the early 1800s, protection of copyright and patent rights had become established concepts within the American constitutional order. Article I, Section 8 of the U.S. Constitution included the IP Clause, empowering Congress to guarantee to authors and inventors the exclusive rights to the proceeds of their writings and inventions for limited periods. The First Congress enacted the Copyright and Patent Acts of 1790. Subsequent Congresses made minor amendments to the federal patent registration process and expanded copyright protection to historical prints, etchings, and engravings in 1793 and 1802, respectively. Authors and inventors began registering their writings and inventions under the new laws. And courts of law opened their doors to the first copyright and patent infringement lawsuits.

Over the next half-century, American constitutional concepts of copyright and patent protection were reinforced and expanded. Following in the thought paths of Founding era predecessors, prominent Antebellum era thinkers overwhelmingly regarded copyrights and patents in light of natural rights and property rights principles. According to this view, persons are by nature entitled to the fruits of their labor—that is, to their property. Government exists to safeguard individual rights to acquire, use, and transfer property according to just and equal laws.

This natural rights basis for copyright and patent is evidenced in the works of prominent law writers of the Antebellum era. In their highly influential legal treatises on American law and constitutionalism, Chancellor James Kent and Justice Joseph Story emphasized the protection of property rights as a core function of government. Both Kent and Story characterized copyrights and patents as private property acquired by an individual's intellectual labors. Story considered it "a poor reward, to secure to authors and inventors, for a limited period, only, an exclusive title to that, which is, in the noblest sense, their own property." Regarding the Intellectual Property Clause's provision for securing copyrights and patent rights, Story contended "it is impossible to doubt its justice, or its policy, so far as it aims at their protection and encouragement." Kent similarly wrote in favor of the "justice and the policy of securing to ingenious and learned men the profit of their discoveries and intellectual labor."

A natural rights understanding of copyright and patent also figured prominently in U.S. Supreme Court and federal circuit court jurisprudence. Antebellum era decisions by the Supreme Court and lower courts developed legal doctrines for protecting IP rights and for ascertaining the limits of those rights. Court decisions by Chief Justice John Marshall and others applied to patents the vested rights doctrine—also rooted in natural rights principles. And the courts would apply legal doctrines related to real property to IP claims. Justice Story advocated a liberalized understanding of patent law that promoted IP protections for inventors. In this, Story was urged on by Chancellor Kent and by Daniel Webster. As a statesman and as the most influential constitutional lawyer of the Antebellum era, Webster—often called the "defender of the Constitution"—was a defender of patents and copyrights.

While the most notable Supreme Court decision of the era, *Wheaton v. Peters* (1834), rejected the idea of a perpetual common law copyright, it did so based principally on federalism considerations. Despite their differences, the justices of the Supreme Court in *Wheaton v. Peters* agreed on the conceptual premise that an individual's rights to the fruit of his or her intellectual labors was the subject entrusted to Congress under the Constitution's Article I, Section 8 Intellectual Property Clause. Rather than rely on a substantive body of federal common law of copyright inherited from Britain, *Wheaton v. Peters* offered a more plausible and straightforward application of the IP Clause's provision that "The Congress shall have Power ... To promote the Progress of

Science and useful Arts, by securing for limited Times to Authors and Inventors the exclusive Right to their respective Writings and Discoveries."

Legal doctrinal developments related to IP rights were paralleled by congressional and presidential actions reinforcing and expanding copyright and patent protections. The first major revisions to federal copyright and patent laws since the 1790s took place during the Antebellum era, enhancing IP rights in copyrights and patents. Legislative reforms expanded protection terms for both authors and inventors. And legislation improved administrative processes for copyright registrations and patent applications.

In 1831, Congress passed its first major revision to U.S. copyright laws since the First Congress. In conjunction with adoption of the Copyright Act of 1831, author and lexicographer Noah Webster vigorously urged a natural rights understanding of literary property. The 1831 Act expanded copyright terms, and permitted the heirs of authors to claim a right in the renewal of those terms. Additional legislation amending copyright laws passed in 1819, 1834, 1846, 1855, 1856, 1859, and 1861, supported by the likes of statesmen such as Henry Clay and Daniel Webster.

Likewise, in 1836, Congress passed its first major revision to U.S. patent laws since 1793, again at the urging of Clay and others. The Patent Act of 1836 officially established the United States Patent Office and provided for additional personnel to process patent applications. The 1836 Act also included expanded protection terms to inventors. Congress passed other patent law amendments in 1832, 1837, 1839, 1842, 1848, 1849, 1851, and 1861. That Congress, in an era of property rights consciousness, would so frequently pass legislation congenial to copyright and patent protection, indicates the solicitude of lawmakers toward the IP rights of authors and inventors.

The fact that Jacksonian hostility to monopolies and perceived monopolies held currency at least among certain segments of the population in the decades leading up to the Civil War should not be overlooked. Yet, significantly, politicians who railed against monopolies endorsed IP rights at the same time. Avowed anti-monopolists such as Andrew Jackson, Martin Van Buren, and James K. Polk signed legislation expanding copyright as well as patent protections. They also signed individual patent approvals as part of their presidential duties. That indicates recognition of principled differences, rooted in the Constitution, between mere government favoritism in the form of business or industry charters on the one hand and baseline protection of an individual's rights to the proceeds from his or her writings or inventions on the other.

All told, Antebellum era legal treatises, Supreme Court and federal circuit court jurisprudence, as well as adoption and implementation of congressional legislation evidence a common conceptual understanding about copyright and patent protection rooted in natural rights principles. In this respect, Antebellum era thinking marked the continuation of a consistent line of thought about the basic nature of intellectual property rights in the American constitutional order. Recognizing the principled commitment to copyright and patent protection that permeated this important period of history should lead to a renewed understanding and appreciation that those enduring intellectual property rights principles remain true today.

The Natural Rights Basis for Private Property in the Antebellum Era

In the early years of the 19th century, the U.S. Constitution's provisions on the whole had received only modest interpretations and applications by the executive, legislative, and judicial branches of government. During the half-century to follow, many of the Constitution's structural principles and terms found occasion for interpretation and application by the three branches. State government institutions as well as constitutional and legal thinkers in the public square also examined and debated constitutional meaning during the decades that bridged the War of 1812 and the Civil War.

In fleshing out the basic meaning of the Constitution's many clauses, Antebellum-era thinking built upon Founding-era understanding that it is a fundamental purpose of government in a free society to protect an individual's rights to private property. As described throughout previous chapters, it is a principle of the Declaration of Independence, enshrined in the Constitution, that all persons possess a right to the fruits of their own labor. In turn, as Chapter 8 explained, that right is safeguarded from unjust deprivation by rule of law principles embodied in the Constitution, including the Fifth Amendment's provisions regarding due process of law and just compensation. Antebellum thinking reaffirmed this natural rights basis for the institution of private property and its protection under law.

Professor James W. Ely, Jr., provided an overview of the development of property rights in the Antebellum era in his book *The Guardian of Every Other Right: A Constitutional History of Property Rights*. According to Ely, "[l]egal scholarship reinforced the importance of property rights in antebellum jurisprudence." Ely specifically identified the legal scholarship of New York Chancellor James Kent. Often known as "the American Blackstone" or the "father of American jurisprudence," Kent wrote "the popular and influential *Commentaries on American Law* (1826–1830), providing a definitive interpretation of American law" and resulting in "an enormous impact on subsequent legal developments." Kent's work was strongly supportive of the view that the acquisition and enjoyment of private property ranked among the "absolute rights of individuals" that government was obligated to protect. As Professor Ely summed up, "Kent believed that the security of property ownership and corporate enterprise encouraged economic growth, and consequently he emphasized the constitutional restrictions on governmental authority over property."

A paradigmatic Antebellum era restatement of the natural rights basis for property is provided in Kent's *Commentaries*:

> The sense of property is inherent in the human breast, and the gradual enlargement and cultivation of that sense, from its feeble force in the savage state, to its full vigor and maturity among polished nations, forms a very instructive portion of the history of civil society. Man was fitted and intended by the Author of his being for society and government, and for the acquisition and enjoyment of property. It is, to speak correctly, the law of his nature; and by obedience to this law, he brings all his faculties into exercise, and is enabled to display the various and exalted powers of the human mind.

The role of government in securing rights of property that individuals possess by nature is amplified by the equally esteemed Antebellum era academic and jurist, Justice Joseph Story. Writing for a unanimous Supreme Court in *Terrett v. Taylor* (1815), Justice Story described "a great and fundamental principle of republican government, the right of the citizens to the free enjoyment of their property legally acquired." Similarly, Story wrote in *Wilkinson v. Leland* (1829) that "[t]he fundamental maxims of a free government seem to require that the rights of personal liberty and private property should be held sacred." Judicial biographer Kent Newmyer described Story's outlook regarding the governmental role in protecting property in no uncertain terms: "Security of property rights, including the right to deploy property freely and enjoy fully the fruits of one's deployment, was the foundation of the whole dynamic moral structure of free enterprise and of free government itself."

Supreme Court and federal circuit court jurisprudence solidified and extended those property rights principles in cases involving the Constitution and federal laws. The primacy of property rights in America's constitutional order was an indispensable feature of the judicial opinions of Story's senior colleague, Chief Justice John Marshall. Marshall's tenure as Chief Justice lasted from 1801 to 1835. During most of that span, Marshall possessed an uncanny ability to obtain a consensus among his judicial colleagues. The length of his tenure as well as his congeniality heightened the prestige of the Supreme Court as a co-equal branch and similarly increased popular respect for the federal judiciary's judgments—even when subject to public criticism. As a result, the emphasis on property rights in Marshall's countless opinions for the High Court and as a federal circuit judge bolstered the institution of private property and indelibly shaped constitutional law for decades to come.

As Ely has explained, "To Marshall, property ownership both preserved individual liberty and encouraged the productive use of resources. Security of private property promoted the public interest by quickening commercial activity and thereby increasing national wealth." But Marshall's most basic assumptions about the primacy of property rights in American constitutionalism were widely shared by other jurists. In Ely's words, "Antebellum legal culture placed a high value on the security of property. Despite their differences, the leading jurists of this period, Marshall, [Chief Justice Roger] Taney, Story, and Kent, envisioned respect for property rights as the basis for both ordered liberty and economic development."

Indeed, respect for property rights was vigorously pressed at the bar of the Supreme Court. Perhaps no constitutional lawyer of the Antebellum era put greater stress upon the primacy of property rights than Daniel Webster—the "Defender of the Constitution." According to Webster biographer Maurice Baxter: "Like most of his contemporaries, he believed there were universal laws of natural justice anterior to positive, man-made laws ... Foremost among these first principles, he thought, was the right to hold property." Webster fervently contended that the Constitution confirmed fundamental principles such as the right to own and use property. He urged constitutional protections for property in numerous appearances before the Supreme Court. As Baxter explained: "In the formative years from the end of the War of 1812 through the famous Compromise of 1850, no lawyer had more effect upon the United States Supreme Court ... than Daniel Webster."

Webster's profound impact on Antebellum constitutional jurisprudence regarding property rights protections is aptly summed up by Professor Baxter:

> By mid century Webster could feel assured by the steadily expanding body of precedents available for the protection of property. In the cases he and his colleagues had argued they had asked the Court to go very far in that end. Often it had consented. Not only did the contract clause of the Constitution become a trustworthy shield for private rights of many kinds against state power, but the common law and principles of natural justice were valuable supplements. Inherent judicial power, exclusive of constitutional and statutory authority, was also a possible instrument for the purpose. But usually there were laws and public policy, state or national, upon which to rely.

During the Antebellum era, development of constitutional protections for private property rights was particularly evident in the Supreme Court's decisions interpreting the Constitution's Contracts Clause contained in Article I, Section 10. In leading decisions such as *Fletcher v. Peck* (1810) and *Dartmouth College v. Woodward* (1819)—the latter argued by Daniel Webster—Chief Justice Marshall's opinions for the Supreme Court offered a broad construction of the Contracts Clause. Those decisions extended strong constitutional protections to contractual obligations—and the property transfers and interests comprising those obligations—from infringement by state legislation. Supreme Court and circuit court opinions by Justice Story and other justices also emphasized a broad construction of the Contracts Clause to protect property interests.

It was primarily—but by no means exclusively—in the context of contracts that the Court under Marshall developed the vested rights doctrine in American constitutional law. According to Professor Ely, the vested rights doctrine is rooted in "the precepts of natural law." As he has explained, the Supreme Court:

> [A]dopted the doctrine of vested rights to protect established property rights from legislative interference. According to the doctrine of vested rights, property ownership was a fundamental right. Laws that disturbed such rights were void because they violated the general principles limiting all constitutional governments.

Regarding the Fifth Amendment's property protections, Ely has observed that, "like the takings clause, the due process clause of the Fifth Amendment did not play a large role in the constitutional safeguarding of economic interests before the Civil War." During this era, however, both constitutional clauses received interpretations friendly to property rights that laid the groundwork for future development of property protections in constitutional law.

The federal government seldom exercised eminent domain during this period, so there was little occasion for considering the Takings Clause. And in *Barron v. Baltimore* (1833), Chief Justice Marshal's opinion for the Supreme Court expressly concluded that the Fifth Amendment restricted only the federal government, not the states. The implication of Marshall's opinion was that the entire Bill of Rights limited only federal power. Thus, federalism considerations also played into the modest role of the Takings Clause during this era. Nonetheless, Professor Ely has pointed out that Webster "attacked legislative discretion over eminent domain and urged judicial supervision by the federal courts" in *West River Bridge Company v. Dix* (1848). "Webster's plea was unheeded before the Civil War, but later in the nineteenth century the Supreme Court began to fashion the takings clause of the Fifth Amendment into a more powerful shield for property owners."

While the Fifth Amendment's Due Process Clause was only modestly interpreted and applied during this time, Ely has observed that by the end of that era, "Federal courts also adopted the view that due process limited legislative discretion." This is perhaps best reflected in *Murray's Lessee v. Hoboken Land and Improvement Co.* (1856), wherein it was recognized that the Due Process Clause is "a restraint on the legislative as well as the executive and judicial powers of government, and cannot be so construed as to leave Congress free to make any process 'due process of law,' by its mere will."

Not to be overlooked, Baxter has pointed out that "the rationale of vested rights became closely associated with separation of powers between legislative and judicial departments," and therefore associated with due process of law. Particularly for Webster, in cases involving private rights of property, "'due process of law' demanded that the property holder have a fair trial in the circumstances and with legal protection that a politically minded legislature could never afford."

Of course, basic considerations of the nature of property rights and the importance of safeguarding those rights under law were by no means confined to the Supreme Court. During this period, state courts also demonstrated a commitment to natural rights and property rights principles. That commitment was embodied in the development of state court jurisprudence protective of property rights.

On this score, Professor Ely has recounted:

> Following *Barron*, the states took the lead in fashioning the contours of eminent domain ... Reflecting the influence of the Fifth Amendment, the constitutions of the newer states, such as Ohio and Tennessee, usually included a just compensation provision. Moreover, even when the state constitution did not expressly provide for payment, state courts reasoned that just compensation must be made under the principles of common law or natural justice. Thus, the prominent New York jurist James Kent, in *Gardner v. Village of Newburgh* (1816) equated due process with natural equity and barred an uncompensated taking of property.

And further to the point:

> Because property ownership had long been closely associated with individual liberty, by mid-nineteenth century judges increasingly invoked substantive due process to defend property rights against economic regulations. Courts broadly reviewed and struck down laws deemed unreasonable as deprivations of property without due process of law.

Importantly, regard for property rights rooted in natural rights provided the crucial context in which Antebellum legal jurists developed constitutional legal doctrines for the protection of copyright and patent.

Antebellum Legal Treatises Reflect Property Rights Understanding of IP

The natural rights understanding of the basis for copyright and patent is evidenced in the works of highly influential legal treatises of the Antebellum era. One of the most enduring of such treatises is Justice Joseph Story's *Commentaries on the Constitution* (1830). Story's *Commentaries* has been described by judicial biographer Kent Newmyer as "the logical successor to the *Federalist Papers*." According to Newmyer, the response to Story's *Commentaries*— even from critics—"marked them at once as the leading nationalist work on the Constitution, a position of authority that remained unchallenged throughout the nineteenth century." In 1840, Story published an abridgement of his *Commentaries* for popular consumption for non-lawyers and for use in schools, titled *A Familiar Exposition of the Constitution of the United States*.

In the *Exposition*'s section on copyrights and patents, Story quotes the Intellectual Property Clause and paraphrases *Federalist No. 43* regarding the utility of granting Congress the power to secure IP rights and the ineffectualness of leaving that power to the states. What then follows is one of Story's most succinct statements about justification for recognizing and protecting copyrights and patents:

> No class of men are more meritorious, or are better entitled to public patronage, than authors and inventors. They have rarely obtained, as the histories of their lives sufficiently establish, any due encouragement and reward for their ingenuity and public spirit. They have often languished in poverty, and died in neglect, while the world has derived immense wealth from their labors, and science and the arts have reaped unbounded advantages from their discoveries. They have but too often possessed a barren fame, and seen the fruits of their genre gathered by those, who have not blushed to purloin, what they have been unable to create. It is, indeed, but a poor reward, to secure to authors and inventors, for a limited period, only, an exclusive title to that, which is, in the noblest sense, their own property; and to require it ever afterwards to be dedicated to the public. But, such as the provision is, it is impossible to doubt its justice, or its policy, so far as it aims at their protection and encouragement.

As indicated earlier, Chancellor James Kent authored his own multi-volume treatise that was widely read and held sway for decades to follow. Historian Daniel Walker Howe has written that Kent "spread the influence of Story's judgments through his famous *Commentaries on American Law*." Lecture 36 of Kent's *Commentaries* is devoted to the subject of title to personal property by original acquisition. In Kent's words, "[t]he right of original acquisition, may be comprehended under the heads of occupancy, accession, and intellectual labor." Kent characterized the right of acquisition of property by intellectual labor as follows:

> Another instance of property acquired by one's own act and power, is that of literary property, consisting of maps, charts, writings, and books; and of mechanical inventions, consisting of useful machines or discoveries, produced by the joint result of intellectual and manual labor. As long as these are kept within the possession of the author, he has the same right to the exclusive enjoyment of them, as of any other species of personal property; for they have proprietary marks, and are a distinguishable subject of property. But when they are circulated abroad, and published with the author's consent, they become common property, and subject to the free use of the community. It has been found necessary, however, for the promotion of the useful arts, and the encouragement of learning, that ingenious men should be stimulated to the most active exertion of the power of genius, in the promotion of works useful to the country, and instructive to mankind, by the hope of profit, as well as by the love of fame, or a sense of duty. It is just that they should enjoy the pecuniary profits resulting from mental as well as bodily labor. We have, accordingly, in imitation of the English jurisprudence, secured by law to the authors and inventors, for a limited time, the right to the exclusive use and profit of their productions and discoveries. The jurisdiction of this subject is vested in the government of the United States, by that part of the constitution, which declares, that Congress shall have the power 'to promote the progress of science and useful arts, by securing, for limited times, to authors and inventors, the exclusive right to their respective writings and discoveries.' This power was very properly confided to Congress, for the states could not separately make effectual provision for the case.

The above-quoted passages served as introductions to the particulars of copyright or patent rights, primarily under British common law or under congressional statutes. During the Antebellum era, the Supreme Court and federal circuit courts would address constitutional issues related to the scope of copyright and patent protection pursuant to the IP Clause. At its early stages of development, American constitutional jurisprudence regarded both copyright and patent as property rights protected by law.

Antebellum Copyright Jurisprudence Reinforces a Property Rights Understanding of IP

The Supreme Court addressed the nature and scope of copyright protection accorded to authors under the IP Clause in *Wheaton v. Peters* (1834). Oddly enough, the case involved a dispute between two different Supreme Court reporters regarding copyrights in published Supreme Court opinions and accompanying publisher notes. Then-Supreme Court reporter Richard Peters published a multi-volume edition report of Supreme Court cases that included cases reported by its former reporter, Henry Wheaton. A lawsuit was filed by Wheaton, who sought a permanent injunction against publication of the previously published materials. Co-Counsel Daniel Webster and Elijah Paine, Jr., a future New York judge, represented Wheaton before the Supreme Court.

Paine's argument in the case traced the natural rights' logic for literary property:

It would seem needless to discuss those general principles on which an author's property is based. They are the same as give man a title to any species of property. An author acquires a property in his works, because they are the product of his own labour, bestowed with the declared and known intention of appropriating such product exclusively to himself. They are his, because the natural law makes it necessary for man to labor for his subsistence, and therefore secures to him what he thus acquires in obedience to its commands. They are his, because the law forbids a dependance upon casual acquisitions, but enjoins the duty of providence, and of course protects those stores which by labour he seeks to lay by for the future. They are his, because the object of all labor is acquisition; because man must depend upon his labor alone for subsistence, and the products of his labour, are therefore, absolutely necessary to his being. They are his, because unless he acquires the right to publish them, he acquires nothing, but his labour is wholly unproductive. They are his, because civil society grows out of the natural wants of men, and its object is by every possible means, to enforce, aid, and extend those natural laws which the wants of man have ordained. They are his, because they may by law be secured to him, and be protected without difficulty, and because he may possess and enjoy them, without mischief to society, and without any possible injury to another. But above all, they are his, because the labour which produces them is meritorious, and while it secures a subsistence for himself, promotes directly and inconceivably the happiness and good of mankind.

As will be seen in this chapter, Daniel Webster expressed skepticism of the idea of a perpetual common law copyright in his capacity as a congressmen. His role as a legal advocate and duty to his client in *Wheaton v. Peters* best accounts for his association with the perpetual copyright claims advanced by Paine. Regardless of his mixed views on the matter of a perpetual federal common law copyright, throughout his careers as both a statesman and as a lawyer, Webster consistently traced copyright back to its source in a person's natural right to the proceeds of their intellectual labor. And Webster consistently linked Congress's constitutional power to secure copyright to natural right. As he argued to the Court in *Wheaton v. Peters*, "[t]he right of an author to the production of his mind is acknowledged every where. It is a prevailing feeling, and none can doubt that a man's book is his book—is his property. It may be true that it is property which requires extraordinary legislative protection, and also limitation. Be it so."

The justices were unanimous in concluding that Supreme Court opinions were not private property and therefore not copyrightable—although the reporter's case notes could be copyrighted. But *Wheaton v. Peters* was significantly complicated by the fact that Wheaton did not follow the strictures of the statute regarding copyright registration. Instead, Wheaton asserted a perpetual *federal* common law copyright. As a result, *Wheaton v. Peters* raised issues involving ambiguities about British common law copyright, the reception of British common law in the law of American colonies-turned-states, and federalism principles. In addressing those issues, the Court split 4–2 in reaching its decision. The precise holding and meaning of the decision has been debated by scholars ever since.

The complicating issues present in *Wheaton v. Peters* make it easy to overlook the justices shared recognition of a fundamental premise: that copyright is a property right rooted in a person's right to the fruits of his or her labor and protected by the constitutionally sanctioned laws. Writing for the majority, Justice John McLean readily acknowledged that "[t]he argument that a literary man is as much entitled to the product of his labor as any other member of society cannot be controverted." Of course, recognition of that natural rights premise did not provide an automatic result in the case. The result would hinge upon societal laws regarding property. As McLean explained: "That every man is entitled to the fruits of his own labor must be admitted, but he can enjoy them only, except by statutory provision, under the rules of property, which regulate society and which define the rights of things in general."

Based on his review of British common law precedents, McLean wrote: "[t]hat an author at common law has a property in his manuscript, and may obtain redress against anyone who deprives him of it or by improperly obtaining a copy endeavors to realize a profit by its publication cannot be doubted." McLean thus rejected the idea that an author enjoyed any *perpetual* common law copyright in published materials. However, the scope of any common law right was ultimately beside the point for Justice McLean because:

> It is clear there can be no common law of the United States. The federal government is composed of twenty-four sovereign and independent states, each of which may have its local usages, customs, and common law. There is no principle which pervades the union and has the authority of law that is not embodied in the Constitution or laws of the Union. The common law could be made a part of our federal system only by legislative adoption.
>
> When, therefore, a common law right is asserted, we must look to the state in which the controversy originated ...

Accordingly, Justice McLean left the door open to *state* common law copyright claims. But no reported cases involving common law copyright claims existed in Pennsylvania. McLean thus concluded that Pennsylvania never adopted British common law copyright. For the Court's majority, McLean ruled that it was the laws passed by Congress pursuant to the IP Clause that created a federally protected copyright.

The Court in *Wheaton v. Peters* rejected Justice Smith Thompson's contentions that authors possessed a perpetual federal common law copyright in their publications, and that a remedy for injunction based on that same perpetual right was not superseded by congressional legislation. But the Court's majority shared the dissent's basic recognition of the natural rights' basis of copyright. Justice Thompson's dissent declared:

> The great principle on which the author's right rests is that it is the fruit or production of his own labor, and which may, by the labor of the faculties of the mind, establish a right of property as well as by the faculties of the body, and it is difficult to perceive any well founded objection to such a claim of right. It is founded upon the soundest principles of justice, equity, and public policy.

Thompson elaborated on how copyright is to be understood as a right a person possesses by nature. Thompson proceeded to cite notes made by Edward Christian in his edition of Blackstone's *Commentaries on the Laws of England*:

> Nothing, says he, is more erroneous than the practice of referring the origin of moral rights and the system of natural equity to the savage state which is supposed to have preceded civilized establishments, in which literary composition, and, of consequence, the right to it, could have no existence. But the true mode of ascertaining a moral right is to inquire whether it is such as the reason, the cultivated reason, of mankind must necessarily assent to. No proposition seems more conformable to that criterion than that everyone should enjoy the reward of his labor, the harvest where he has sown, or the fruit of the tree which he has planted. Whether literary property is *sui generis* or under whatever denomination of rights it may be classed, it seems founded upon the same principle of general utility to society, which is the basis of all other moral rights and obligations. Thus considered, an author's copyright ought to be esteemed an invaluable right, established in sound reason and abstract morality.

> It is unnecessary, for the purpose of showing my views upon this branch of the case, to add anything more. In my judgment, every principle of justice, equity, morality, fitness, and sound policy concurs in protecting the literary labors of men to the same extent that property acquired by manual labor is protected.

In sum, while *Wheaton v. Peters* rejected the idea of a perpetual federal common law copyright, it did so principally on the basis of an anti-federal common law rationale rather than any anti-copyright rationale. Indeed, the majority's conclusion in *Wheaton v. Peters* appears to be the most straightforward way of understanding the operation of the IP Clause's grant to Congress of power to secure to authors the exclusive rights to their proceeds "for limited Times." While rejecting a perpetual federal common law copyright, the majority nonetheless regarded a natural rights understanding as the point of reference for the Constitutional Convention and First Congress in establishing federal copyright protection. The majority agreed with the dissent regarding the natural rights basis for federal copyright protection under law as directed by the terms of the IP Clause.

For his part, Justice Story made an enduring contribution to American copyright law in this same era. Story's circuit court opinion in *Burton v. Folsom* (1841) set the groundwork for what is today known as the "fair use" doctrine.

At issue in *Burton* was Charles Wentworth Upham's publication of papers of George Washington. Harvard historian Jared Sparks had been given exclusive authorization to access and publish George Washington's papers by Justice Bushrod Washington, nephew of the first President, and by Chief Justice John Marshall, author of the first major biography of the President. Sparks subsequently published his own biography of Washington and likewise edited and published *The Writings of George Washington* (1839), consisting of twelve volumes of Washington's papers. But Upham relied on Sparks' organization and publication of Washington's previously unpublished papers and essentially repackaged and republished 319 of Washington's letters in his own book, *Life of Washington* (1841). Story ultimately decided with Sparks in the case.

In addressing the question of whether that republication constituted copyright infringement, Story described a basic analytical framework for ascertaining whether an abridgement or citation of an original work was legitimately designed for purposes of fair and reasonable criticism on a matter of public importance. As Story stated in *Burton*, a court must "look to the nature and objects of the selections made, the quantity and value of the materials used, and the degree in which the use may prejudice the sale, or diminish the profits, or supersede the objects of the original work."

As Story's judicial biographer Kent Newmyer summed up the competing interests confronting Story in *Burton*:

> In copyright law Story ... confronted the tension among private property, public interest, and republican values. No one seriously doubted that literary production was property worthy of protection and encouragement of the law. But republican society, with its goal of an active and informed citizenry, put a premium on the dissemination of ideas. Story fully agreed but as an author also knew firsthand the beneficial effect of private property in literary production.

Story's framework would endure in copyright jurisprudence until Congress codified it in the Copyright Act of 1976.

Antebellum Patent Jurisprudence Reinforces the Property Rights Understanding of IP

The nature and scope of patent protection accorded to inventors pursuant to the IP Clause was also the subject of many Supreme Court and lower federal court decisions in the Antebellum Era. Based on his scholarly review of the era's jurisprudence, Professor Adam Mossoff has concluded that "nineteenth-century case law dating back to the antebellum period unequivocally classified patents as property rights." In particular, early Congresses and courts "invoked natural-rights justifications for property in defining and adjudicating patent rights." They also "explicitly relied on *real property* case law, and often invoked property concepts, such as trespass and the inchoate-choate right distinction, in adjudicating patent cases."

Early circuit court opinions by Chief Justice Marshall and Justice Washington identify patents as vested property rights. Further, as Professor Mossoff has explained:

> In 1843 in *McClurg v. Kingsland*, the Supreme Court began laying the groundwork for applying the Takings Clause to the property rights secured in patents, as distinguished from monopoly franchises and other similarly limited property rights. Although not a takings case, the *McClurg* Court held that Congress could not *retroactively* limit property rights that had been secured in now-repealed patent statutes. Justice Baldwin's opinion for the unanimous Court acknowledged that "the powers of Congress to legislate upon the subject of patents is plenary by the terms of the Constitution." Nonetheless, he concluded that a "repeal [of a patent statute] can have no effect to impair the *right of property* then existing in a patentee, or his assignee, according to the well-established principles of this court." In sum, a patent issued under now repealed statutes vested property rights in an inventor, so that "the patent must therefore stand as if the [now-repealed] acts ... remained in force."

Patent jurisprudence was to a significant degree shaped by Justice Story. This was a result of the depth of legal insight that Story brought to bear in cases heard before him amidst a career on the Supreme Court and riding circuit judge that spanned from 1811 to 1845. As Newmyer has written:

> Story grappled with patent law in some forty opinions rendered throughout his long tenure on the Court. Neither in these opinions nor in his anonymous note on patents, which appeared in Wheaton's reports in 1818, nor in his *Commentaries on the Constitution* did he deal theoretically or comprehensively with the subject. He had no doubt, however, that the law should serve the public by encouraging invention. He also accepted without question the notion that invention and writing were species of property. The need was clear. The problem was, given the sporadic and fragmentary format of case law, to fashion a body of rules that was clear enough for judges to follow and that

also recognized both property rights (themselves conflicting) and community interest—all without the guidance of settled precedent.

According to Newmyer, in *Ames v. Howard* (1833), *Blanchard v. Sprague* (1839), *Wyeth v. Stone* (1840), and other cases, "Story did what Webster suggested in 1829" and "moved away from undue reliance on English law in the direction of an American patent law that would favor inventors and, following the spirit of the Constitution, serve the national interest by promoting technical progress." In the end, "Story's authority (along with his copious exposition of doctrine) was of immense importance in giving legitimacy to the new position. Fairly or not, he was identified by contemporaries as the pioneer in the liberalization of American patent law."

In *Ames v. Howard*, Story explained his liberalized outlook toward patents as a protected form of constitutional property:

Patents for inventions are not to be treated as mere monopolies, odious to the eyes of the law, and therefore not to be favored, but on the contrary to be construed with the utmost rigor as *strictissmi juris*. The Constitution of the United States, in giving authority to Congress to grant such patents for a limited period, declares the object to be to promote the progress of science and the useful arts, an object as truly national and meritorious, and well founded in public policy, as any that can possibly be the object of national protection. Hence it has always been the course of the American courts (as it has latterly been that of the English courts also) to construe these patents fairly and liberally, and not to subject them to any over-nice and critical refinements. The object is to ascertain what, from the fair scope of the words, is the nature and extent of the invention claimed by the party, and when the nature and extent of the claim is apparent, not to fritter away his rights upon formal and subtle objections of a purely technical character.

Story's zeal for the rights of inventors was perhaps matched by Daniel Webster. At the outset, it bears mention that Webster's advocacy for discoveries and useful inventions extended beyond the courtroom or to the halls of Congress. Webster extolled the force-multiplier effects of inventions as laboring devices for the improvement of society and its economic wellbeing. He expressed such views in his *Lecture Read Before the Boston Mechanics Institution* (1828). And in Webster's *Lecture Before the Society for the Useful Diffusion of Knowledge* (1836), he declared:

If these, and other considerations may suffice to satisfy us that the application of science to art is the main cause of the sudden augmentation of wealth and comfort in modern times, a truth remains to be stated of the greatest magnitude, and the highest practical importance, and that is, that his augmentation of wealth and comfort is general and diffusive, reaching to all classes, embracing all interests, and benefitting, not a part of society, but the whole. There is no monopoly in science. There are no exclusive privileges in the working of automatic machinery, or the powers of natural bodies. The poorest, as well as the richest man in society, has a direct interest, and generally the poor a far greater interest than the rich, in the successful operation of these arts, which make the means of living, clothing especially, abundant and cheap. The advantages conferred by knowledge in increasing our physical resources, from their very nature, cannot be enjoyed by only a few. They are all open to the many, and to be profitable, the many must enjoy it.

The products of science applied to art in mechanical inventions are made, not to be hoarded, but to be sold.

Webster's concern for the societal improvements resulting from useful inventions, translated into forceful courtroom advocacy for patent rights. Contrasting English decisions with American law, Webster argued before the Supreme Court in *Pennock v. Dialogue* (1829) that:

In the courts of the United States, a more just view has been taken of the rights of inventors. The laws of the United States were intended to protect those rights, and to confer benefits; while the provisions in the statue of England, under which patents are issued, are exceptions to the law prohibiting monopolies. Hence, the construction of the British statute has been exceedingly straight and narrow, and different from the more liberal interpretation of our laws.

Webster made his final oral argument before a court of law in a patent case presided over by Justice Robert Grier. In *Goodyear v. Day* (1852), also known as the "India Rubber Case," Webster declared:

Invention, as a right of property, stands higher than inheritance or devise, because it is a personal earning. It is more like acquisitions by the original right of nature. In all these there is an effort of mind as well as muscular strength. Upon acknowledged principles, rights acquired by invention stand on plainer principles of natural law than most other rights of property. Blackstone, and every other able writer on public law, thus regards this natural right and asserts man's title to his own invention or earnings. The right of an inventor to his invention is no monopoly. It is no monopoly in any other sense than as a man's own house is a monopoly. A monopoly, as it was understood in the ancient law, was a grant of the right to buy, sell, or carry on some particular trade, conferred on one of the king's subjects, to the exclusion of all the rest. Such a monopoly is unjust. But a man's right to his own invention is a very different matter. It is no more a monopoly for him to possess that, than to possess his own homestead.

James Kent also offered Story reinforcement on the matter of patents. Scholarship by Camilla A. Hrdy has shown that Kent recognized the power of states to grant patent rights to importers of foreign inventions. Hrdy has outlined Kent's concurrent state powers rationale regarding patents, based on a reading of *Federalist No. 32*. And Hrdy has likewise observed that Story favorably cited Kent's views in his *Commentaries on the Constitution* and in his judicial opinions.

On the other hand, some evidence exists that Chief Justice Roger Taney did not share the enthusiasm of Story, Webster, and Kent for patents as constitutionally protected property rights. In *Gayler v. Wilder* (1850), Taney reaffirmed that "the discovery of a new and useful improvement is vested by law with an inchoate right to its exclusive use, which he may perfect and make absolute by proceeding in the manner which the law requires." Yet in some later opinions Taney strayed from the prevalent property rights understanding of patents. According to Professor Mossoff, on occasion Taney ignored express patent statutes and sought to limit patent protections according to Jacksonian political concerns about monopoly franchises. For instance, in *Bloomer v. McQuewan* (1852), Taney regarded patents as government-granted franchises that secure only "a right to exclude." And in *O'Reilley v. Morse* (1854), Taney's opinion for a divided court invalidated part of Samuel Morse's patent for the electromagnetic telegraph. As Professor Mossoff reminds us, Taney achieved infamy for his willingness to bring his political preferences to bear in deciding legal claims in *Dred Scott v. Sanford* (1857).

Taney's occasional aberrations aside, Antebellum era jurisprudence overwhelmingly retained and reinforced the understanding that patents are constitutional property rooted in an inventor's natural right to the fruits of his or her mental labors.

Antebellum Legislation Bolsters Copyright Protections

Regard for property rights rooted in natural rights also supplied the crucial context in which Antebellum statesmen passed legislation that extended protections for IP and improved administrative processes for securing IP rights. The intellectual context for the First Congress's passage of the Copyright and Patent Acts of 1790 was the subject of Chapter 6. The first major revisions to those early federal legislative precedents took place during the Antebellum era. In 1831, Congress made its first major revision to U.S. copyright laws since the First Congress. Passage of the Copyright Act of 1831 was a result of the persistence of author and lexicographer Noah Webster, often regarded as "the Father of Copyright" in America.

The efforts of Noah Webster to advance copyright protection in state legislatures, in the Confederation Congress, and in the Philadelphia Convention of 1787 were recounted in Chapter 3. In particular, Webster lobbied George Washington, James Madison, and others to include a provision for securing copyright in the proposed U.S. Constitution.

Webster made use of the provisions of the copyright protections enacted by Congress, registering his own works. This includes Webster's cultural achievement and greatest life's work, *The American Dictionary of the English Language* (1828). Yet Webster pursued his literary efforts with trepidation. He feared competitors would republish or otherwise plagiarize his efforts and thereby reap the proceeds of his labors. He regarded the existing law's fourteen year copyright protection term insufficient for recouping the costs of his intensive labors. As Webster explained in an 1829 letter to James Madison, his dictionary was:

> [A] work which has cost me twenty years of labor, & from twenty five to thirty thousand dollars. Whether my fellow citizens are to be benefited to that amount or to any amount, I cannot determine; but certain I am, that I can never be reimbursed by the sales during my life; though possibly a <u>more liberal copy-right law</u> might bring to my heirs something like an equivalent.

By the time of his letter to Madison, Webster had already urged legislative revision to American copyright law. In an 1826 letter to his cousin, Daniel Webster, Noah wrote: "I sincerely desire that, while you are a member of the House of Representatives in Congress, your talents may be exercised in placing this species of property on the same footing as all other property as to exclusive right and permanence of possession." In his letter, Noah deemed "contrary to all our best established principles of right and property," the British House of Lords' closely divided decision in 1774 that authors possessed a common law right only in their unpublished manuscripts or first print. Yet Noah also called attention to the fact that the British Parliament had since extended copyright to authors for twenty-eight years. Noah went so far as to insist that authors enjoyed a perpetual copyright in their works. Accordingly, Noah closed his letter by expressing his wish that Congress would "pass a new act, the preamble to which shall admit the principle that an author has, by common law or natural justice, the sole and *permanent* right to make profits by his own labor, and that his heirs and assigns shall enjoy the right, unclogged with conditions."

In his reply, Congressman Daniel Webster pointed out the House Judiciary Committee was considering important changes to the copyright law. Regarding his elder cousin's expressed views about the grounds for copyright in the right that a person by nature possesses to their own acts of intellect and creating, Congressman Webster responded, "Your opinion, in the abstract, is certainly right and incontrovertible. Authorship is, in its nature, ground of property." Still, Daniel acknowledged that British common law precedent suggesting copyright is not perpetual was persuasive to many. To this, he added:

> But after all, property, in the social state, must be the creature of law; and it is a question of expediency, high and general, not particular expediency, how and how far, the rights of authorship should be protected. I confess frannkly [sic], that I see, or think I see, objections to make it perpetual. At the same time I am willing to extend it further than at present, and am fully persuaded that it ought to be relieved from all charges, such as depositing copies, &c.

For the most obvious objections to perpetual copyright that Congressman Webster referred, one need look no further than the text of the Constitution's IP Clause, which only guarantees to authors and inventors exclusive rights to proceeds "for limited Times." Ultimately, no copyright revision would pass Congress that term. But according to David Micklethwait in *Noah Webster and the American Dictionary* (2005), "for more than four years, following his exchange of letters with Daniel Webster, he was an active and persistent lobbyist for improved statutory protection."

In 1829, Noah Webster's son-in-law William Ellsworth was elected to Congress and appointed to the House Judiciary Committee. The son of Oliver Ellsworth—Senator in the First Congress and former Chief Justice—Congressman Ellsworth referred to the Committee a petition by Webster seeking an extension of the terms of copyrights for Webster's *American Spelling Book*.

Webster travelled to Washington, D.C. in December 1830. On December 17, Ellsworth's bill to extend copyright protection to twenty-eight years with an extension available for living authors or their heirs for fourteen more years, was sent to the full House. The bill's report tracked with Webster's own thinking about the principled basis for "literary property":

Upon the first principles of proprietorship in property, an author has an exclusive and perpetual right, in preference to any other, to the fruits of his labor. Though the nature of literary property is peculiar, it is not the less real and valuable. If labor and effort in producing what before was not possessed or known, will give title, then the literary man has title, perfect and absolute, and should have his reward: he writes and he labors as assiduously as does the mechanic or husbandman. The scholar, who secludes himself, and wastes his life, and often his property, to enlighten the world, has the best right to the profits of those labors.

By this time, Webster's spelling books were well known to many and his dictionary had been published. During his stay in Washington, Webster was celebrated at the White House where he dined at the right hand of President Andrew Jackson. On January 3, 1831, Webster delivered a lecture in the Hall of the Representatives promoting copyright. And on January 7, the House passed Congressman Ellsworth's copyright bill without a division. By month's end, Ellsworth's bill passed the Senate, whose membership then included Daniel Webster. And in February President Jackson signed the Copyright Act of 1831 into law.

Noah Webster later penned an essay "Origin of Copy-Right Laws in the United States," published in 1843. There Webster recounted both his Confederation-era efforts on behalf of securing copyrights, as well as his lobbying of Congress in 1830–31. Webster's short account acknowledged the roles that Ellsworth played in the House and Daniel Webster played in the Senate in securing the Act's passage.

For his part, Ellsworth would later be elected governor of Connecticut and serve as a judge. In 1843, he would become executor of Webster's estate, which included a vested right in Webster's surviving children for the renewal term of Webster's *American Dictionary*. Ellsworth would also write a short work, *Copy-Right Manual: Designed for Men of Business, Authors, and Members of the Legal Profession* (1862). In that brief writing, Ellsworth described copyright as a form of literary property as "the result of labor, invention and study." Ellsworth defended the "exclusive right to publish for sale his thoughts and sentiments, peculiarly arranged and clothed in his own language."

In his *Copy-Right Manual*, Ellsworth credited the persistence of Noah Webster, more than anyone in or out of Congress, for securing passage of the Copyright Act of 1831. He also referenced subsequent copyright legislation passed by Congress in 1834 and 1846, which involved minor amendments regarding processes for recordation of copyright assignments and for copyright registration and deposit requirements, respectively.

Indeed, several minor amendments were made to American copyright law by Congress in the Antebellum era. Those revisions spanned nearly the entire period between the War of 1812's conclusion and the Civil War's onset:

- 1819 — provided federal circuit courts with original jurisdiction in copyright cases;
- 1834 — required recordation of assignments of copyrights;
- 1846 — required authors and proprietors of copyrighted works to deposit copies with the Smithsonian Institution and the Library of Congress in addition to the Secretary of State;
- 1855 — provided free mailing privileges for all copyright deposits;
- 1856 — granted to copyright holders of dramatic compositions the sole right of public performance;
- 1859 — provided for removal of copyright deposits from the State Department to the Department of the Interior;
- 1861 — provided for appeals to the Supreme Court in copyright cases regardless of the amount in controversy.

Taken together, these legislative enactments strongly evidence Congress's regard for protecting authors' property rights and for promoting the nation's social and economic welfare.

Antebellum Legislation Bolsters Patent Rights Protections

The first half of the 19th century likewise saw the first major revisions to federal patent law since the First Congress. IP rights in patents were granted expanded protection terms. Administrative requirements and processing for patent applications were also improved.

The Patent Act of 1836 erected the basic apparatus upon which today's patent system operates. Under the Act, the U.S. Patent Office was officially established within the State Department. The office of the Commissioner was established to head the Patent Office and to hire and train examiners for patent application examination and processing. Thus, the Act revived the concept of a reviewing process for patent applications that first appeared in the Patent Act of 1790 but was removed in 1793. But the 1836 law would establish a more administratively manageable process. Among other provisions, the Patent Act of 1836 provided that the existing fourteen year patent term could be extended for seven years upon application to the Commissioner of the Patent Office.

Henry Ellsworth, son of Oliver Ellsworth and twin brother of William, is generally credited for helping to draft the Patent Act of 1836. Ellsworth previously served in administrative posts in the Jackson administration. The legislation was passed by the 24th Congress, which included Senators Daniel Webster and Henry Clay. Upon President Jackson's signing the Patent Act into law on July 4, 1836, Ellsworth was appointed as first Commissioner of the Patent Office.

Historian Daniel Walker Howe offers a succinct summary of the Act in operation:

> Starting in 1836, a reorganized federal Patent Office carefully vetted every application before granting a patent. Despite its increasing strictness, the office got busier and busier. Where the government had granted 23 patents a year per million residents during the decade after the War of 1812, the number rose to 42 a year in the 1830s. The statistic at that time for southern New England stood at 106. All across the country, patenting activity flowed along the waterways that sustained commerce and provided power for industry.

Minor amendments were also made to American patent law by Congress in the Antebellum era. The many revisions made during this period included the following:

- 1837—provided for re-collection of patent records after the Patent Office Building burned down; for issuance of a patent to the assignee of the inventor; and for validity of patent to the extent of actual invention where patentee innocently overstated extent of invention;
- 1839—provided patents would not be debarred because invention had been patented in foreign countries where certain circumstances existed; two years public use of invention prior to application was allowable without invalidating patent; and provision for bills of equity in all cases where patents were administratively denied;
- 1842—expressly provided for design patents; required patented articles be marked with the date of the patent;
- 1848—reassigned patent extension power from a board that included the Secretary of State, Solicitor of the Treasury, and the Commissioner of Patents to the Commissioner alone; reset patent recording fees;
- 1849—transferred the Patent Office from under the Secretary of State to under the Secretary of the Interior;
- 1851—revised provisions regarding appeals from decisions of the Commissioner of Patents to judicial officers;
- February 1861—permitted appeals of all federal circuit court judgments under copyright and patent laws to the U.S. Supreme Court, regardless of the amount in controversy;

- March 1861—granted patent terms of seventeen years with no extensions; reset fees; required independent patents for specifications of improvements to existing patents; established Board of Examiners-in-Chief to hear appeals from primary examiners and for appeals from the Board to the Commissioner; prevented recovering of damages for infringement where patentee failed to mark patented articles; and repealed penalties for failure to mark patented articles.

Thus, from the passage of the Patent Act of 1836 to the dawn of the Civil War, Congress took care to extend patent protection and sought to improve patent application processing. The final two Patent Acts listed above were signed just days prior to the inauguration of President Abraham Lincoln on March 4, 1861.

Jacksonians Recognized the Constitution's Distinction Between Monopolies and IP Rights

In understanding the thinking of the Antebellum era, it is also critical to consider the era's prevailing solicitude for property rights in light of its frequent aversion to monopolies. Sharp differences of opinion existed during the period regarding precisely what types of monopolies were harmful and should be prohibited. Nonetheless, the era reflects a common commitment to private property rights undeterred by varying opposition to government grants of special privileges. More particularly, Antebellum era thinking embodied a shared understanding that copyrights and patents were constitutionally legitimate and economically beneficial types of limited monopolies that deserved the basic legal protections accorded to private property.

Opposition to government-conferred monopolies and special privileges was a hallmark of Jacksonian ideology that influenced politics and law during the Antebellum era. But it would be decidedly wrong-headed to read into Jacksonian anti-monopolistic sentiment any broad-based attack on copyrights or patents that dominated public thinking.

According to historian Daniel Walker Howe, "[t]he 'age of Jackson' was not a time of consensus." In his writings on the period, Howe has avoided the term "Jacksonian America," because "it suggests that Jacksonianism describes Americans as a whole, whereas in fact Andrew Jackson was a controversial figure and his political movement bitterly divided the American people." It would therefore be a mistake to simply claim that Jacksonian aversion to monopolies and special privileges was, in principle or in practice, contrary to IP rights. It would likewise be a mistake to simply take a single speech or letter by any one figure of the period about monopolies and to either treat it as an embodiment of general public thinking about monopolies in that era or to read it into the Constitution.

Corporations charted by special legislation drew Jacksonian ire. As Howe recounted, "the corporate form of organization remained a privilege conferred by the state in return for what were considered services to the public interest." Discontent with special treatment by government eventually led to legislative reform efforts in the states. Thus, "[i]n an effort to avoid favoritism while also allowing the multitude of small investors their chance, various states enacted general laws of incorporation that conferred corporate status upon any business applicant(s) who complied with certain rules."

"Mixed corporations," consisting of both public and private ownership interests pursuant to government charter, were the paradigmatic monopoly opposed by Jacksonians. And opposition to the Second Bank of the United States was a defining aspect of Andrew Jackson's presidency. Howe has explained that:

> The Bank of the United States was the largest example in the country of a mixed public-private corporation, and Jackson criticized both its public and private aspects. Sometimes he waged his war on the Bank as an agency of overcentralized government, but more often he attacked it as a private enterprise that had received unjust privileges, an artificial monopoly unresponsive to government or public ... Jackson himself habitually referred to the Bank as 'the Monster,' a word that implied unnatural and enormous power.

Jackson's "war" against the Bank and his favoring of state banks and hard money policies embroiled him in controversy over the meaning of the Constitution and over matters of fiscal and economic policy. Written with the assistance of cabinet members that included future Chief Justice Roger Taney, Jackson's *Veto Message Regarding the Bank of the United States* (1832), is replete with references to the Bank as a monopoly and an exclusive privilege. However controversial Jackson's characterization of the Bank or his proffered interpretation of the Constitution, his veto statement made clear the Constitution's distinction between illegitimate monopolies and legitimate IP rights:

> On two subjects only does the Constitution recognize in Congress the power to grant exclusive privileges or monopolies. It declares that "Congress shall have power to promote the progress of science and useful arts by securing for limited times to authors and inventors the exclusive right to their respective writings and discoveries." Out of this express delegation of power have grown our laws of patents and copy-

rights. As the Constitution expressly delegates to Congress the power to grant exclusive privileges in these cases as the means of executing the substantive power "to promote the progress of science and useful arts," it is consistent with the fair rules of construction to conclude that such a power was not intended to be granted as a means of accomplishing any other end. On every other subject which comes within the scope of Congressional power there is an ever-living discretion in the use of proper means, which can not be restricted or abolished without an amendment of the Constitution. Every act of Congress, therefore, which attempts by grants of monopolies or sale of exclusive privileges for a limited time, or a time without limit, to restrict or extinguish its own discretion in the choice of means to execute its delegated powers is equivalent to a legislative amendment of the Constitution, and palpably unconstitutional.

For all the divisiveness that characterized so-called Jacksonian America and which surrounded monopolies and special privileges, the distinction between illegitimate monopolies and IP rights was widely understood and accepted by ideological rivals. Historical evidence reflects they perceived the principled difference between the two concepts and recognized the Constitution's protection of copyrights and patents in the IP Clause. For that matter, several of the pro-IP Antebellum era laws passed by Congress were signed into law by anti-monopolist Presidents, namely Andrew Jackson, Martin Van Buren, and James K. Polk.

Conclusion

Antebellum era legal treatises, Supreme Court and federal circuit court jurisprudence, and adoption and implementation of congressional legislation all evidence a shared conceptual understanding about copyright and patent rooted in natural rights. In this respect, Antebellum era thinking marked the continuation of a consistent line of thought about the basic nature of intellectual property in the American constitutional order. Recognizing the principled understanding about copyright and patent that permeated this important period of history should lead us to consider anew how those enduring principles remain true today.

Sources

William Ellsworth, *Copy-Right Manual: Designed for Men of Business, Authors, and Members of the Legal Profession* (1862).

Andrew Jackson, "Veto Message Regarding the Bank of the United States" (1832).

James Kent, *Commentaries on American Law* (1826–1830).

Publius (Alexander Hamilton), *Federalist No. 12* (1788).

Publius (Alexander Hamilton), *Federalist No. 32* (1788).

Publius (James Madison), *Federalist No. 43* (1788).

Joseph Story, *A Familiar Exposition of the Constitution of the United States* (1840).

Joseph Story, *Commentaries on the Constitution of the United States* (1833).

Daniel Webster, Letter to Noah Webster (1826).

Daniel Webster, *Lecture Read Before the Boston Mechanics Institution* (1828).

Daniel Webster, *Lecture Before the Society for the Useful Diffusion of Knowledge* (1836).

Noah Webster, Letter to Daniel Webster (1826).

Noah Webster, Letter to James Madison (1829).

Noah Webster, "Origin of Copy-Right Laws in the United States" (1843).

* * *

Ames v. Howard (1833).

Bloomer v. McQuewan (1852).

Burton v. Fulsom (1841).

Dred Scott v. Sanford (1957).

Gayler v. Wilder (1850).

McClurg v. Kingsland (1843).

O'Reilley v. Morse (1854).

Wheaton v. Peters (1834).

Copyright Act of 1831.

Patent Act of 1836.

* * *

Maurice Baxter, *Daniel Webster and the Supreme Court* (1966).

James W. Ely, Jr., *The Guardian of Every Other Right: A Constitutional History of Property Rights* (3d ed.) (2008).

Daniel Walker Howe, *What Hath God Wrought: The Transformation of America, 1815–1848* (2007).

Camilla A. Hrdy, "State Patent Laws in the Age of Laissez Faire," 28 *Berkeley Tech. L. J.* 45 (2013).

David Micklethwait, *Noah Webster and the American Dictionary* (2005).

Adam Mossoff, "Patents as Constitutional Private Property: The Historical Protection of Patents Under the Takings Clause," 689 *Boston University Law Review* (2007).

Adam Mossoff, "O'Reilly v. Morse," *George Mason Law & Economics Research Paper No. 14–22* (August 18, 2014).

Kent Newmyer, *Supreme Court Justice Joseph Story* (1985).

Chapter 10

Adding Fuel to the Fire of Genius: Abraham Lincoln, Free Labor, and the Logic of Intellectual Property

At Gettysburg, President Abraham Lincoln called for a "new birth of freedom." It was a call for both successful completion of the Civil War and for advancement of the propositions of liberty and equality set out in the Declaration of Independence. The significance and permanency of change to the nation's fundamental law formally achieved in the 1860s make it an essential reference point for any analysis of constitutional powers and rights. Analysis of the constitutional foundations of intellectual property rights likewise should be informed by the new birth of freedom.

The political philosophy and constitutional thought of Abraham Lincoln are central to understanding Civil War constitutionalism. Lincoln held to what has been termed a "two-track" view of the Constitution. One track involved "the written instrument of government adopted at the nation's Founding and intended to function as a supreme legal code." The other track consisted of "the principles, ideals, institutions, laws, and procedures tending toward the maintenance of republican liberty by which the American people agreed to order their political existence."

Applying this two-track framework to the subject of intellectual property yields important insights regarding the place of IP in our constitutional order. Antislavery thought concerning "free labor" offers a logical and compelling account for IP rights. The philosophical precept of "free labor" was placed in the context of an expanding and enterprising society. And it regarded hard work in useful vocations and social mobility as the means for obtaining economic independence.

Lincoln himself linked the concept of free labor to intellectual property rights. His thought concerning free labor was grounded in the Founders' understanding, and most particularly in the Declaration of Independence's affirmation of the natural right to life, liberty, and the pursuit of happiness. "[E]ach individual is naturally entitled to do as he pleases with himself and the fruit of his labor," Lincoln wrote in 1847. Or, as he put it, to the same effect, in a more colloquial Lincolnism: "I always thought the man that made the corn should eat the corn."

Civil War constitutionalism should also be considered in light of Lincoln's actions. During his single term in Congress in the 1840s, Lincoln applied for a patent for his invention of "a device to buoy vessels over shoals." Lincoln assisted constituents with their own patent applications. And he voted for legislation modestly amending administration of patent laws in 1848 and 1849, thereby evidencing solicitude for securing IP rights. Moreover, Lincoln the lawyer was involved in at least five patent cases between 1850 and 1860.

Lincoln made the case for IP protections most emphatically in public lectures and speeches he delivered between 1858 and 1860. He delivered his *Lecture on Discoveries and Inventions* (1858) in essentially the same form a half-dozen times. In it, Lincoln juxtaposed Western civilization's 15th century achievements in writing and printing press technology with the regrettable rise of human slavery. He concluded his lecture by extolling patent laws that "added the fuel of *interest* to the *fire* of genius, in the discovery and production of new and useful things."

Further, in his *Address to the Wisconsin State Agricultural Society* (1859), Lincoln expressed regard "for the profitable and agreeable combination of labor with cultivated thought" that captures the essence of intellectual property. By securing a return to free laboring authors and inventors for their pursuit of ideas and discoveries, copyrights and patents stimulated the drive for further self-improvement and achievement of personal independence.

In *Dred Scott v. Sanford* (1857), Chief Justice Roger Taney insisted "the right of property in a slave is distinctly and expressly affirmed in the Constitution." Through several speeches, Lincoln criticized Chief Justice Taney's opinion. Other Republican and antislavery proponents pointed to the lack of any expression of the words "slave" or "slavery" or the term "property in men" in the Constitution. They cited writings from the framers of the Constitution of 1787 for the proposition that the word "slavery" was kept out of the Constitution's text in order to avoid conferring legitimacy on the institution.

The Lockean concept that the core of property consists of self-ownership and the closely related free labor concept that a person has a natural right to the fruits of his or her own labor—both of which are reflected in the Declaration of Independence—formed the principled basis for concluding, as Lincoln and other antislavery thinkers did, that slavery is wrong. The imperative of protecting intellectual property rights followed from this idea of self-ownership, as an author or inventor owned the productions of his or her mental labors and the returns those labors generated. The prevailing understanding during Lincoln's day, as it had been at the time of the Founding and the Constitution's ratification, was that copyrights and patents were the property of authors and inventors.

Antislavery thinkers countered the idea of property in men with what came to be known as "Freedom National"—the perspective that a person's inalienable right to liberty was the prevailing or default position embedded in the U.S. Constitution and that slavery existed only where the blackletter law of a state expressly provided for it. Military matters dominated political and administrative business during Civil War years that followed. However, the influence of the "Freedom National" policy had at least one important impact on IP rights during the Lincoln administration.

In 1857, future Confederate President Jefferson Davis was summarily denied a patent for a riverboat propeller invention that was the idea of a slave on the plantation of his brother Joseph. Consistent with the *Dred Scott* decision, the U.S. Patent Office denied the patent on account of the fact that the slave inventor was not a "citizen" of the United States and therefore not legally competent to obtain a patent. Likewise, the slaveowners were not the genuine inventors so they were ruled ineligible.

In 1861, Senator Charles Sumner learned a patent application by a free black inventor had been denied based on the *Dred Scott* decision. Sumner introduced and the wartime Senate approved by unanimous consent a resolution directing the Patent Office to consider if further legislation was "necessary to secure to persons of African descent, in our own country, the right to take out patents for useful inventions, under the Constitution." Attorney General Edward Bates's *Opinion on Citizenship* (1862), determining that free persons of color born in the United States were citizens, ultimately settled that free blacks would be issued copyrights and patents according to the terms of the applicable federal laws.

During Reconstruction, Congress had occasion to pass legislation that made minor adjustments to patent and copyright laws, including the Appropriations Act of 1868 and Copyright Acts of 1867 and 1868. Congress also passed and President Ulysses S. Grant signed the Copyright and Patent Acts of 1870. The Copyright Act transferred registration functions from federal district courts to the Library of Congress, centralizing and streamlining the process and thereby expanding the resources and resourcefulness of the Library. The Patent Act was a comprehensive measure gathering together the substance of preceding legislation and legal decisions. Among other things, it clearly established a first-to-file system for patent claims. Minor legislative amendments to the patent laws were also adopted in 1871 and 1874.

That pro-IP rights legislation was adopted contemporaneously with the Reconstruction Amendments gives rise to the inference that IP rights were consistent with the antislavery principles and views of property vindicated by the Civil War and that influenced the framing of those amendments. Accordingly, property is rooted in a natural right of liberty and self-ownership, and that all persons are equally entitled to the fruits of his or her own labors, protected by the rule of law.

It does not appear that Reconstruction Amendments to the Constitution impose any express limitation on the scope of copyright or patent protections under the IP Clause. The clause's grant of power to Congress "To promote the Progress of Science and useful Arts, by securing for limited Times to Authors and Inventors the exclusive Right to their respective Writings and Discoveries" leaves little role for states. However, to the extent any state laws offer supplemental or tangential protections to authors or inventors, the Fourteenth Amendment's Equal Protection Clause at least requires that any such protections be extended to all state citizens on an equal basis. Similarly, any rights of authors or inventors recognized under state law would be protected by the Fourteenth Amendment's Due Process Clause.

In sum, an examination of intellectual property in light of free labor thought, political action tied to the Civil War, and the Reconstruction Amendments bolsters the logical case for protection of IP rights and for recognition of IP's connection to the underlying principles of the American constitutional order.

The Importance of the Civil War and Reconstruction to an Understanding of America's Constitutional Order

In his *Gettysburg Address* (1863), President Abraham Lincoln called for a "new birth of freedom." It was a call for the Union to bring the Civil War to a successful completion and to advance the causes of liberty and equality set out in the Declaration of Independence. This new birth of freedom envisioned by Lincoln required a constitutional settlement following the Civil War. That settlement was informed by antislavery arguments about the ideals of the Declaration and meaning of the Constitution. It was formalized in the adoption of the Thirteenth, Fourteenth, and Fifteenth Amendments to the Constitution. The so-called Civil War or Reconstruction Amendments eliminated slavery, established citizenship for former slaves, and guaranteed basic social, legal, and political rights for all persons.

Exploration of constitutional meaning undoubtedly requires reference to the original meaning of the Constitution of 1787 and of the Bill of Rights.

But any such exploration should not end there. The significance and permanency of change to the nation's fundamental law formally achieved in the 1860s make the sectional crisis, Civil War, and Reconstruction essential reference points for any analysis of constitutional powers and rights. Indeed, on account of remediating the Constitution's accommodation to sectional chattel slavery, both contemporaries and later thinkers have viewed the Reconstruction Amendments as the completion of the Constitution of 1787. Accordingly, an analysis of the constitutional foundations of intellectual property rights should be informed by Lincoln's call for a "new birth of freedom" and the political and legal measures which embodied that call in more concrete constitutional terms.

The political and constitutional thought and actions of Abraham Lincoln are central to Civil War constitutionalism. Through his speeches and debates with Senator Stephen Douglas, Lincoln was a nationally recognized expositor of the logic of antislavery constitutionalism in the years before the War. As President, Lincoln's public pronouncements and executive actions helped ensure the survival of the Constitution. He was proactive in securing congressional adoption of the proposed Thirteenth Amendment and his actions set the stage for adoption of the Fourteenth and Fifteenth Amendments.

Scholars have widely credited the influence of Sir William Blackstone on Lincoln's self-education in law. As a practicing lawyer, Lincoln also frequently relied upon the common law insights of Joseph Story and James Kent. The legalistic aspects of Lincoln's thought pervaded his statesmanship. The connection between Lincoln's political philosophy and the principles of the Declaration of Independence has also been expounded by scholars—most notably, Harry V. Jaffa in his book *The Crisis of the House Divided* (1959).

Constitutional historian Herman Belz encapsulates both the legalistic and philosophical dimensions of Lincoln's thought in describing his "two-track" view of the Constitution. One track involved "the written instrument of government adopted at the nation's Founding and intended to function as a supreme legal code." The other track consisted of "the principles, ideals, institutions, laws, and procedures tending toward the maintenance of republican liberty by which the American people agreed to order their political existence." On the one hand, Lincoln viewed the checks and balances expressed in the text of the Constitution as binding and regarded the original understanding of the text as authoritative. And on the other hand, Lincoln resorted to the constitutional background ideals and principles as a guide for wise policymaking. As Belz described it: "Lincoln adhered to the written Constitution of the framers—its forms, procedures, principles, and spirit—and was guided by it in political action aimed at achieving the ideals asserted in the Declaration of Independence."

This two-track framework is particularly useful for understanding core constitutional concepts. In the sections below, this framework will be applied to the subject of intellectual property. First, certain principles, ideals, and logic of antislavery thought will be examined for the light they can shed on our understanding of copyrights and patents in the American constitutional order. Second, certain implications of the texts of the Reconstruction Amendments regarding the scope of copyright and patent protections provided for under the Article I, Section 8 IP Clause will be briefly considered. As will be seen, IP rights readily conform to, and are in important respects linked to, the logic of antislavery concepts and actions that were to a significant extent formalized in the Reconstruction Amendments.

The Free Labor Logic
of Intellectual Property Rights

Antislavery thought concerning the role of "free labor" offers a logical and compelling account relevant to an understanding of IP rights. Antecedents to the Republican free labor outlook include the thought of the Founders and their understanding and acceptance of the political writings of John Locke and British common law. In his famous *Second Treatise of Government* (1689), Locke linked an individual's own labor to his property interest:

> [E]very man has a property in his own person: this no body has any right to but himself. The labour of his body, and the work of his hands, we may say, are properly his. Whatsoever then he removes out of the state that nature hath provided, and left it in, he hath mixed his labour with, and joined to it something that is his own, and thereby makes it his property.

Following Locke, James Madison, the principal drafter of our Constitution, declared that individuals possess property rights "in their actual possessions, in the labor that acquires their daily subsistence, and in the hallowed remnant of time which ought to relieve their Fatigues and soothe their cares."

Historian Eric Foner explored the basic contours of antislavery thinking in *Free Soil, Free Labor, Free Men: The Ideology of the Republican Party Before the Civil War*. According to Foner:

> For the concept of 'free labor' lay at the heart of the Republican ideology, and expressed a coherent social outlook, a model of the good society. Political anti-slavery was not merely a negative doctrine, an attack on southern slavery and the society built upon it; it was an af-

firmation of the superiority of the social system of the North—a dynamic, expanding capitalist society, whose achievements and destiny were almost wholly the result of the dignity and opportunities which it offered the average laboring man.

The concept of free labor was placed in the context of America's expanding and enterprising society. This view regarded hard work in useful vocations and social mobility as the means for obtaining economic independence. Observed Foner, "[t]he aspirations of the free labor ideology were thus thoroughly middle-class, for the successful laborer was one who achieved self-employment, and owned his own capital—a business, farm, or shop ... The key figure in the Republicans' social outlook was thus the small independent entrepreneur."

The flip side to the concept of free labor was its critique of slave labor and the ethic of a slaveholding society. The new Republican party in the late 1850s and 1860s made criticisms of slave labor part of its appeal to voters in Northern states. As encapsulated by Eric Foner:

> The Republican critique of southern society thus focused upon the degradation of labor—the slave's ignorance and lack of incentive, and the laboring white's poverty, degradation, and lack of social mobility. The result was not only regional economic stagnation, but a system of social ethics entirely different from that of the North.

Lincoln and Free Labor

Abraham Lincoln's thought concerning "free labor" was grounded in the Founders' understanding, and most particularly in the Declaration's affirmation, of the natural right to life, liberty, and the pursuit of happiness. In his opposition to slavery, but also in a more universal sense, Lincoln repeatedly articulated the Lockean view that all individuals, of whatever race or creed, possess a natural right to enjoy the fruits of their own labor, to make those fruits their own property. "[E]ach individual is naturally entitled to do as he pleases with himself and the fruit of his labor," Lincoln wrote in 1847. Or, as he put it in his own inimitable way: "I always thought the man that made the corn should eat the corn."

In Lincoln's understanding, the Constitution safeguarded a person's unalienable right to the fruits of their labor—to their private property. Of course, the Constitution's concessions to the institution of slavery formed an unmistakable exception. Lincoln maintained that the Founding Fathers hoped that slavery would be extinguished over the course of time. He regarded free labor, individual initiative, and property rights as essential elements of the American free enterprise system.

Finally, in extolling the virtue of labor and property, Lincoln frequently admonished those who would set one man or class against another. As he put it in 1847:

> [I]t has so happened in all ages of the world, that some have laboured, and others have without labour, enjoyed a large proportion of the fruits. This is wrong and should not continue. To [secure] each labourer the whole product of his labour, or as nearly as possible, is a most worthy object of any good government.

Lincoln echoed those sentiments as President in his *Reply to the New York Workingmen's Democratic Republican Association* (1864):

> Property is the fruit of labor ... property is desirable ... is a positive good in the world. That some should be rich shows that others may become rich, and hence is just encouragement to industry and enterprise. Let not him who is houseless pull down the house of another; but let him labor diligently and build one for himself....

Lincoln the Pro-Entrepreneur, Pro-IP Whig

It should come as no surprise that, as an enthusiast for free labor, Lincoln was also an enthusiast for securing the rights of intellectual labor. Securing copyrights for authors and patents for inventors fits squarely within the political and social outlook of the Whig party in which Lincoln the politician emerged. Daniel Walker Howe, the leading contemporary scholar of the Whig party, has shed important light on Whig thought that emphasized economic and social progress. The Whigs' regard for progress—or "improvements"—included enthusiasm for manufactures and technological achievements in particular. Along with Whig luminaries such as Henry Clay and Daniel Webster, Lincoln promoted intellectual property rights in law and policy.

During his single term as a Whig member of the House of Representatives (1847–1849), Congressman Lincoln applied for a patent for his invention of "a device to buoy vessels over shoals." As recounted by Jason Emerson in his monograph *Lincoln the Inventor* (2009), Lincoln's idea for the device came after a flatboat on which he was a hired hand became stuck on the Rutledge milldam near New Salem, Illinois, in 1831. Congressman Lincoln toured the U.S. Patent Office with his son Robert, examining some of the approximately 200,000 invention models then on display in the office building's third floor. According to Emerson, the tradition that Senator Daniel Webster assisted Lincoln in getting the patent office to approve of Lincoln's application is bolstered by a February 1849 letter from Webster to Lincoln. Ultimately, on May 22, 1849, Lincoln's application was approved and assigned as patent #6469. While most scholars have concluded that Lincoln's device did not meaningfully contribute to riverboat navigation, Lincoln's patent award exemplifies the Whig promotion of self-improvement. Further, Emerson astutely observed that "[w]hile a Congressman, Lincoln assisted at least two of his constituents with applying for their own patents." Lincoln's votes in favor of legislation modestly amending administration of patent laws in 1848 and 1849 similarly evidence his solicitude for securing IP rights.

Following his service in Congress, Lincoln the lawyer also encountered IP rights. Emerson concludes that Lincoln was involved as a lawyer in at least five patent cases between 1850 and 1860. Acquaintance's recollections indicate that Lincoln took deep interest in the inventions and legal merits of his patent cases.

Lincoln the Pro-IP Republican

It was during the 1850s that the Whig party ultimately dissolved. As Howe has written of Lincoln, "[h]e remained an active and loyal Whig until the newly organized Republican party absorbed most northern Whigs in the mid-1850s. This new party represented for Lincoln a continuation of the same aspirations as the Whigs, for the modernization of American society and the creation of new opportunities for self-fulfillment."

Lincoln the Republican made the case for IP protections most emphatically in a handful of public lectures and speeches he delivered between 1858 and 1860. In the interval between his loss to Senator Douglas and his nomination for president by the Republican party, Lincoln would deliver a half-dozen times, in essentially the same form, his *Lecture on Discoveries and Inventions* (1858). His lecture offered a cursory overview of the discoveries and inventions of human civilization, providing insights about the economic and social progress they facilitated. In the course of his lecture, Lincoln contrasted Western Civilization's 15th century achievements in writing and printing press technology with the coinciding rise of human slavery. And his high regard for inventions and writings in advancing the social and economic progress of mankind could hardly be missed. Observed Lincoln: "[I]n the world's history, certain inventions and discoveries occurred, of peculiar value, on account of their great efficiency in facilitating all other inventions and discoveries. Of these were the arts of writing and printing—the discovery of America, and the introduction of Patent laws."

Lincoln regarded the discovery of America as "an event greatly favoring and facilitating useful discoveries and inventions." And he concluded his lecture by extolling patent laws:

> Before then these, any man might instantly use what another had invented; so that the inventor had no special advantage from his own invention. The patent system changed this; secured to the inventor, for a limited time, the exclusive use of his invention; and thereby added the fuel of *interest* to the *fire* of genius, in the discovery and production of new and useful things.

In general, Lincoln's *Lecture on Discoveries and Inventions* has received mixed reviews from scholars. More recent scholarship, however, has at last treated Lincoln's lecture more seriously. According to Emerson, "Lincoln's lecture on discoveries and inventions was not a passing whim or a half-hearted composition. It was something to which he gave long and deliberate attention and that he delivered at least six times." Lincoln's own abiding interest in his *Discoveries* lecture and the underlying ideas it contained is also reflected at a January 1865 meeting he had with Harvard professor Louis Agassiz. Wrote Emerson, in that meeting Lincoln "talked about his lecture on discoveries and inventions, saying it was not quite perfected and that after his presidency he planned to work on it some more and perhaps have it published."

Lincoln made his most direct connection between free labor and patent rights of inventors in his *Address to the Wisconsin State Agricultural Society* (1859). In the address, Lincoln gave a brief exposition of the free labor outlook, with its emphasis on self-improvement, upward mobility, and independence. He criticized the "mud-sill" theory of labor—the notion that "labor is available only in connection with capital," that "all laborers are necessarily either hired laborers, or slaves" and that "whoever is once a hired laborer, is fatally fixed in that condition for life." Lincoln answered that it was in error to assume that all labor must be either hired labor or slave labor and also in error that education and labor were incompatible. In further answer, Lincoln set out the more dynamic perspective of free labor advocates:

> The prudent, penniless beginner in the world, labors for wages awhile, saves a surplus with which to buy tools or land, for himself; then labors on his own account another while, and at length hires another new beginner to help him. This, say its advocates, is *free* labor—the just and generous, and prosperous system, which opens the way for all—gives hope to all, and energy, and progress, and improvement of condition to all. If any continue through life in the condition of the hired laborer,

it is not the fault of the system, but because of either a dependent nature which prefers it, or improvidence, folly, or singular misfortune.

Moreover, as Lincoln memorably put it:

> Free Labor argues that, as the Author of man makes every individual with one head and one pair of hands, it was probably intended that heads and hands should cooperate as friends; and that that particular head, should direct and control that particular pair of hands. As each man has one mouth to be fed, and one pair of hands to furnish food, it was probably intended that that particular pair of hands should feed that particular mouth—that each head is the natural guardian, director, and protector of the hands and mouth inseparably connected with it; and that being so, every head should be cultivated, and improved, by whatever will add to its capacity for performing its charge. In one word Free Labor insists on universal education.

In his *Agricultural Society Address*, Lincoln praised agricultural fairs for "improving the great calling of agriculture" through "mutual exchange of agricultural discovery, information, and knowledge." According to Lincoln, agricultural fairs serve a vital purpose:

> [N]ot only to bring together, and to impart all which has been *accidentally* discovered or invented upon ordinary motive; but, by exciting emulation, for premiums, and for the pride and honor of success—of triumph, in some sort—to stimulate that discovery and invention into extraordinary activity. In this, these Fairs are kindred to the patent clause in the Constitution of the United States; and to the department, and practical system, based upon that clause.

Further, in the *Agricultural Society Address*, Lincoln's regard "for the profitable and agreeable combination of labor with cultivated thought" captures the essence of the meaning of intellectual property. By securing a return to free laboring authors and inventors for their pursuit of ideas and discoveries, copyrights and patents stimulated the drive for further self-improvement and achievement of independence. And society also stood to benefit from the intellectual and material progress advanced by authors and inventors.

As illustrated by his experiences as a lecturer and inventor as well as his career as a legislator, candidate, and lawyer, Lincoln appreciated the conceptual foundations of intellectual property and the rationale for protecting IP rights. His respect for IP rights in securing the benefits of free labor constituted just one facet of the antislavery ideology that influenced Lincoln in his understanding of the U.S. Constitution and the laws of property. Of course, antislavery views about the Constitution and property were at the very heart of an unresolved dispute that divided the nation and that led to Civil War.

Property in Men as an Inversion of Liberty and Self-Ownership

Related to antislavery ideology's espousal of free labor were the sharp attacks it leveled upon the ethical and constitutional propriety of property rights in human beings. As will be seen, the idea of property rights existing in men runs contrary to the Lockean natural rights understanding of the Founders and of antislavery thought that property consists principally in self-ownership. Indeed, IP rights had historically been premised on the self-ownership principle.

Historian James Oakes has brought renewed attention to divisiveness of the "chattel principle"—treating slaves as commodified property—in the ideological clash that precipitated the Civil War. As Oakes explained in *The Scorpion's Sting: Antislavery and the Coming of the Civil War*:

> What tore the nation apart was a dispute over two very different labor systems, and the crucial difference between them was, once again, the chattel principle. Here was the issue debated everywhere during the sectional crisis. To fight over slavery was to disagree about the moral, political, economic, and constitutional legitimacy of what Americans at the time called "property in man."

Writing about the conflict over "the right versus the wrong of 'property in man,'" Oakes recounted that "[i]n every major dispute over the appropriate relationship between slavery and the federal government, the debate was framed in these broader philosophical terms."

That debate began with at least one generally acknowledged principle. According to Oakes, "[i]t was a standard precept of Anglo-American political philosophy that the protection of property was a primary reason—arguably *the* primary reason—for establishing *any* form of government." Beginning in the 1830s, however, conflicting views emerged regarding the proper implications of that fundamental premise of the purpose of government. Pro-slavery ideology rejected the natural equality of all persons, claimed that a natural right of white men to own property in slaves preceded government, and claimed that the Constitution thereby implicitly protected that property. In *Dred Scott v. Sanford* (1857), Chief Justice Roger Taney insisted "the right of property in a slave is distinctly and expressly affirmed in the Constitution." Other pro-slavery voices insisted a right of property in slaves was implicitly protected by the Constitution.

"But for slavery's opponents the concept of 'human property' was a self-contradiction," wrote Oakes. Moreover, "[l]ike nearly all Republicans, Lincoln believed that the conflict over slavery was, at bottom, a fundamental disagreement over property rights in human beings."

Lincoln expressed the underlying terms of the conflict in his *Speech at New Haven* (1860):

> Whenever this question shall be settled, it must be settled on some philosophical basis. No policy that does not rest upon some philosophical public opinion can be permanently maintained. And hence, there are but two policies in regard to Slavery that can be at all maintained. The first, based on the property view that Slavery is right, conforms to that idea throughout, and demands that we shall do everything for it that we ought to do if it were right ... The other policy is one that squares with the idea that Slavery is wrong, and it consists in doing everything that we ought to do if it is wrong.

In several speeches, including his *Speech on the Dred Scott Decision* (1857) and his *Cooper Union Address* (1860), Lincoln criticized Chief Justice Taney's opinion. His criticism included the obvious fact that "neither the word 'slave' nor 'slavery' is to be found in the Constitution, nor the word 'property' even, in any connection with the language alluding to the thing slave, or slavery, and that whenever in the instrument the slave is alluded to, he is called a 'person';— and wherever his master's legal right in relation to him is alluded to, it is spoken of as 'service or labor which may be due,'—as a debt payable in service or Labor." Lincoln also insisted that "contemporaneous history" established "that this mode of alluding to slaves and slavery, instead of speaking of them was employed on purpose to exclude from the Constitution the idea that there could be property in man." To Lincoln, the omission of the word was made intentionally by the Constitution's framers to accommodate the eventual extinction of slavery.

Other Republicans and antislavery proponents pointed to the lack of any expression of the words "slave" or "slavery" or the term "property in men" in the Constitution. They cited writings from the framers of the Constitution of 1787 for the proposition that the word "slavery" was kept out of the Constitution's text in order to avoid conferring legitimacy on the institution. For instance, in an article published in the *New York Times* titled "Property in Men" (1860), James A. Hamilton, son of Alexander Hamilton, summarized the "contemporaneous history" evidencing the Founders earnest intent to keep the written

Constitution free from any express endorsement of slavery. Among the references cited, Hamilton quoted from the posthumously published *Notes of Debates in the Federal Convention of 1787* (1840) that James Madison "thought it wrong; to admit in the Constitution the idea that there could be property in man. We intend this Constitution to be the great charter of human liberty to the unborn millions who may enjoy its protection, and who shall never see that such an institution was ever known in their midst." Summarizing Madison's *Notes*, Hamilton continued: "The Convention concurring in these opinions without debate, unanimously resolved that the words, 'Slave' and 'Slavery' should be stricken out; and the words 'such person' and 'other persons' should be substituted wherever they occurred." Hamilton would later enclose his article in a letter to Lincoln, explaining it was inspired by the *Cooper Union Address* that he so much admired.

The Lockean concept that the core of property consists of self-ownership and the closely-related free labor concept that a person has a natural right to the fruits of his or her own labor are both reflected in the Declaration of Independence. Those natural rights concepts informed the principled view of Lincoln and other antislavery thinkers that slavery is inherently wrong. IP rights fit squarely within this idea of self-ownership, as an author or inventor owned the productions of their mental labors and the returns those labors generated. The prevailing understanding during Lincoln's day, as it had been at the time of the Constitution's ratification, was that copyrights and patents were the property of authors and inventors. The revenues and profits generated by written works and inventions were the fruits of their intellectual labors and thereby rightfully owned by the respective authors and inventors so long as the earnings were generated during the terms provided by law. Slavery inverted the concept of property and was self-contradictory.

"Freedom National" as a Policy Program for Liberty and Property

Antislavery thinkers such as Lincoln recognized that the Constitution's accommodation to slavery limited the ability of the federal government to interfere with that institution in the states where it existed. Nonetheless, as a matter of constitutional politics, antislavery thinkers countered the idea of property in men with the position that a person's unalienable right to liberty was the prevailing or default position and that slavery existed only where the blackletter law of a state expressly provided for it.

James Oakes traced the origin and eventual success of the antislavery movement's program for "denationalizing" the idea of property in men in *Freedom*

National: The Destruction of Slavery in the United States, 1861–1865. Oakes recounted the contributions of Theodore Weld, Joshua Giddings, Salmon P. Chase, Charles Sumner, and William Seward to the antislavery legal and constitutional arguments for cordoning slavery off with free states and restricting it to those states where it already existed.

In Eric Foner's estimation, credit is primarily due to Salmon P. Chase in leading the transformation of the antislavery movement from a social cause to a political and legal cause. As an antislavery lawyer representing a fugitive slave in the *Matilda* case (1838), Chase explained: "The right to hold a man as a slave is a naked legal right. It is [a] right which, in its own nature, can have no existence beyond the territorial limits of the state which sanctions it, except in other states whose positive law recognizes it and protects it."

Chase would serve as Ohio's Governor and a U.S. Senator prior to serving as Lincoln's first-term Treasury Secretary. Lincoln later nominated Chase to serve as Chief Justice of the Supreme Court. As Foner summarized Chase's basic position, "the founders deplored the institution and hoped for its early abolition. They regarded freedom and equality as the natural condition of men, and viewed slavery as a temporary and abnormal state." On account of Chase's efforts, the "Freedom National" banner eventually formed "the constitutional basis of the Republican party program." Sumner would memorably appropriate Chase's arguments from the *Matilda* case and use them in his first major antislavery speech in the Senate, titled *Freedom National; Slavery Sectional* (1852). As Oakes summarized:

> For Republicans, freedom was the natural, default condition, the presumed status of everyone living under the protection of the Constitution, unless expressly overruled by a positive law enacted by a sovereign state. The doctrine was enshrined in the Republican party's 1860 platform resolution … declaring that 'the normal condition of all the territory of the United States is that of freedom.'

Following the 1860 election, "Freedom National" effectively became the policy program of the administration of President Abraham Lincoln. To that end, Congress addressed the divisive issue of property in men. With Lincoln's signature, in the early 1860s Congress abolished slavery in the District of Columbia and banned slavery in all federal territories. And through a combination of legislative and executive action, military emancipation formed a critical component of the implementation of Freedom National.

Emancipation by military means, as Oakes has written, "had never been central to the abolitionist agenda, much less to the Republican party platform." Of course, Lincoln's *Emancipation Proclamation* (1863) ultimately became the chief antislavery measure of the administration.

Rolling Back *Dred Scott*'s Rule on Intellectual Property Rights

Military matters dominated political and administrative business during the Civil War years. However, the influence of the "Freedom National" program had at least one important impact on IP rights during the Lincoln administration.

In 1857, U.S. Senator and future Confederate President Jefferson Davis summarily was denied a patent for a riverboat propeller. The invention was the idea of a slave on the plantation of his brother Joseph. As retold in a 2013 article by Sean Vanatta, the novel propeller was designed by Benjamin Butler. Davis's brother sought a patent on a more specific part of the invention but was similarly denied. Consistent with *Dred Scott*'s holding that only whites could become citizens of the United States, U.S. Patent Office Commissioner Joseph Holt denied the patent on account of the fact that the slave inventor was not a "citizen" of the United States and therefore not legally competent to obtain a patent. Likewise, the slaveowners were not the genuine inventors and ruled ineligible.

Lincoln denied that the decision in *Dred Scott* would extend beyond the parties to the lawsuit and bind the policy for his administration. But the mere fact of Lincoln's inauguration did not automatically eliminate the court decision's impact. On December 16, 1861, Senator Charles Sumner reported that the federal district court in Boston had denied a patent application by an inventor who was a free black. The denial was apparently based on the *Dred Scott* decision that blacks were not citizens under the Constitution and therefore not entitled to patents. Sumner introduced and the Senate approved by unanimous consent a resolution declaring: "Resolved, That the Committee on Patents and the Patent Office be directed to consider if any further legislation is necessary to secure to persons of African descent, in our own country, the right to take out patents for useful inventions, under the Constitution of the United States."

Sumner later remarked in his collected *Works*:

> The Committee made no report on the resolution. It was a case for interpretation rather than legislation, and the question, like that of passports, was practically settled not long afterwards by the opinion of the Attorney-General, that a free man of color, born in the United States, is a citizen. Since then patents have been issued to colored Inventors.

Although conduct of the Union war effort undoubtedly preoccupied Congress from 1861 to 1865, during that same timeframe, Congress did adopt— and President Lincoln signed—modest revisions to federal laws regarding copyrights and patents. Copyright amendments made in 1865 were significant for extending protection to photographs and to photo negatives. Further technical amendments were made to copyright law in 1867. And amendments were made to patent laws in 1863 and 1865. Attorney General Edward Bates's *Opinion on Citizenship* (1862) settled that free blacks would be issued copyrights and patents according to the terms of those federal laws.

Intellectual Property Rights Under Reconstruction

Reconstruction is generally regarded as time between the surrender at Appomattox Court House in 1865 and the hotly disputed Hayes-Tilden election of 1876. During this difficult period the antislavery aims only partially achieved under the policy of "Freedom National" were precariously maintained under military emancipation and occupation. Though not fully realized in practice, those aims were made permanent by three crucial amendments to the Constitution.

During the final weeks of his life, President Lincoln urged Congress to pass the proposed Thirteenth Amendment. Incorporating language nearly identical to Article 6 of the Northwest Ordinance, the Amendment declared: "Neither slavery nor involuntary servitude, except as a punishment for crime whereof the party shall have been duly convicted, shall exist within the United States, or any place subject to their jurisdiction." The Senate's final vote of approval for the proposed Amendment barring property in men and effectively constitutionalizing the reversal of *Dred Scott* was held on April 8, 1865. Lincoln was assassinated just six days later.

President Andrew Johnson's plans for rapid and easy Executive Reconstruction fizzled as his relations broke down with Congress. As Johnson became the first President ever impeached, only barely avoiding conviction and removal, Congress took an especially active role in reaching a constitutional and legal settlement to the recently concluded Civil War. In the face of Johnson's opposition, Congress proposed the Fourteenth Amendment for ratification in 1865. Section 1 of the Amendment contained four critical clauses:

All persons born or naturalized in the United States, and subject to the jurisdiction thereof, are citizens of the United States and of the state wherein they reside. No state shall make or enforce any law which shall abridge the privileges or immunities of citizens of the United States; nor shall any state deprive any person of life, liberty, or property, without due process of law; nor deny to any person within its jurisdiction the equal protection of the laws.

According to Professor Michael Kent Curtis, the views of Republican Congressmen during this time "were shaped by their experience of the assault on civil liberties that occurred during the crusade against slavery and by a political ideology that emphasized the Declaration of Independence and the rights of the Individual." More particularly:

> Republicans accepted the following tenets of antislavery constitutional thought. First, after the passage of the Thirteenth Amendment abolishing slavery, blacks were citizens of the United States. Republicans held this view even though the Dred Scott decision was to the contrary. Second, the guaranties of the Bill of Rights applied to the states even prior to the passage of the Fourteenth Amendment. Most Republicans held this view even though the Supreme Court had ruled to the contrary in the case of *Barron v. Baltimore*, decided in 1833. Third, the privileges and immunities clause of the original Constitution protected the fundamental rights of American citizens against state action. Fourth, the due process clause of the Fifth Amendment protected all persons from enslavement in the District of Columbia and in the federal territories.

The Fourteenth Amendment and related civil rights legislation were the critical campaign issues of the 1866 congressional elections. The electorate resoundingly endorsed the actions of the 39th Congress, and the next Congress proposed the Fifteenth Amendment for ratification. It provided "[t]he right of citizens of the United States to vote shall not be denied or abridged by the United States or by any state on account of race, color, or previous condition of servitude."

Amidst the conflict with Johnson over Reconstruction and related matters, the 40th Congress had occasion to pass legislation that made minor adjustments to patent and copyright laws: the Appropriations Act of 1868 and Copyright Acts of 1867 and 1868. That pro-IP legislation was adopted contemporaneously with the Fourteenth and Fifteenth Amendments gives rise to the inference that the IP rights were fully consistent with the antislavery principles and views of property vindicated by the War and that influenced the framing of those amendments—namely, that property is rooted in a natural right of liberty and self-ownership, and that all persons are equally entitled to the fruits of their own labors, protected by the rule of law. It also gives rise to the inference that the 40th Congress viewed its IP legislation as consistent with the textual provisions of the amendments as the specifically enforceable supreme law designed to protect rights informed by those principles. Had there been something illegitimate about IP rights or some sort of conflict between IP rights and antislavery principles, they almost certainly would have surfaced during those debates. Any perceived conflict would have at least made IP rights a candidate for curtailment or caused pro-IP legislation to be discarded.

The Fifteenth Amendment was passed by Congress just prior to the inauguration of Ulysses S. Grant. Grant deserves credit alongside Lincoln for preserving the Constitution and thereby enabling the new birth of freedom. Historian and biographer H.W. Brands offered a valid point in writing:

> The Union victory wasn't simply or even chiefly an intellectual victory; it was a military victory. Southerners were no less certain than Northerners of the legitimacy of their interpretation of the principles of self-government; the South lost from lack not of conviction but ammunition. Grant didn't convince the South; he conquered the South.

As Josiah Bunting put it in his brief book about Grant's presidency, Grant had "a commitment to uphold what he understood to be the legacy of victory in the Civil War: not [with] the aggressive zeal of the reformer but an implacable commitment to a principle already established." Moreover, Bunting added that:

> [T]he depth of Grant's commitment to Reconstruction seemed to grow stronger as resistance to the realization of what he believed itself became more determined. The identification of the Democratic party with the positions that seemed aimed on destroying the hard-won gains of black Americans seemed to the president a betrayal of all they had gained by the war and a betrayal of those who had labored to make its results permanent.

In his *First Annual Message* (1869), Grant identified "where all labor rightfully belongs—in the keeping of the laborer," and commended Congress for giving ample attention to "protecting and fostering free labor." Grant also described it essential to the nation's peace, prosperity, and fullest development "to secure protection to the person and property of the citizen of the United States in each and every portion of our common country." During his presidency, Grant accordingly advanced the "new birth of freedom" by requesting from Congress legislation to enforce the Reconstruction Amendments.

Historians acknowledge the civil rights laws as enforced by Grant were not particularly successful at the time in achieving their intended purpose. And subsequent rulings of the Supreme Court would unfortunately limit or strike down some of those laws for enforcing the Reconstruction Amendments. Still, it is important to recognize that Grant's commitment to civil rights legislation also coincided with modest pro-IP legislation. Here again, a reasonable inference can be made that the contemporaneous adoption and enforcement of Reconstruction rights legislation and pro-IP rights legislation. The two types of measures were on some level consistent, or at least there certainly was nothing inconsistent between them.

In his *First Annual Message*, Grant praised manufactures for their role in furthering national economic independence and in providing employment opportunities. More importantly, Congress passed and Grant signed the Copyright and Patent Acts of 1870. The Copyright Act transferred registration functions from federal district courts to the Library of Congress, centralizing and streamlining the process and thereby expanding the resources and resourcefulness of the Library. Some slight amendments to copyright laws followed in 1874.

The Patent Act of 1870 was a comprehensive measure gathering together the substance of preceding legislation and legal decisions. Among other things, it clearly established a first-to-file system for patent claims. Minor legislative amendments to the patent laws were also adopted in 1871 and 1874.

On January 11, 1870, Grant did veto a bill that would have specifically extended a patent for the inventor of improvements in repeat-fire pistols. The inventor had obtained a patent in 1855 but wanted patent protection beyond the initial 14-year term provided by law. Congress passed a bill authorizing its extension. That Grant issued the veto can be explained by his perception that justification was lacking for affording special treatment to one particular inventor. Grant's record in signing general laws favoring IP rights suggests that veto was a special case.

Grant's favorable disposition toward IP rights is also evidenced by his role with respect to the Centennial Exhibition held in Philadelphia in 1876. In 1871, Grant signed legislation creating the Centennial Commission. The purpose of the legislation was to support an exhibition to be hosted for the 100th anniversary of American Independence that would celebrate and showcase the nation's progress in manufactures and the arts. On May 10, 1876, Grant delivered the opening address at the event, formally known as the "International Exhibition of Arts, Manufactures, and products of the Soil and Mine." In his *Eighth Annual Message* (1876), Grant declared the event "has proven a great success," and that "[i]t has shown the great progress in the arts, sciences, and mechanical skill made in a single century."

Finally, during the last year of his life, Grant would seek the potential financial rewards ensured by copyright protection. Though cancer-stricken, Grant labored to write an autobiographical account in order to save his wife Julia from the financial woes the couple encountered after leaving the White House. Grant pressed on until his final days of life to complete his *Personal Memoirs of U.S. Grant*, published in two volumes in 1885 and 1886. Samuel Clemens—perhaps better known by his pen name, "Mark Twain"—assisted

Grant with the publishing arrangements, editing, and marketing. Grant's *Memoirs* generated approximately $450,000 for the benefit of Julia, and has been hailed as a classic.

Implications of the Civil War Amendments for Intellectual Property Rights

While the sectional conflict over slavery that led to the Civil War and the constitutional amendments ratified during Reconstruction involved critical matters regarding the basic principles, ideals, and institutions of the Constitution, the formal adoption of those amendments included specific textual additions to the nation's supreme legal code.

It does not appear that Civil War Amendments to the Constitution impose any express limitation on the scope of copyright or patent protections under the IP Clause. The clause's grant of power to Congress "to promote the Progress of Science and useful Arts, by securing for limited Times to Authors and Inventors the exclusive Right to their respective Writings and Discoveries" leaves little role for states. However, to the extent any state laws offer supplemental or tangential protections to authors or inventors, the Fourteenth Amendment's Equal Protection Clause at least requires that any such protections be extended to all state citizens on an equal basis. Similarly, any rights of authors or inventors recognized under state law would be protected by the Fourteenth Amendment's Due Process Clause.

Conclusion

Significant and permanent of change to the nation's fundamental law followed the Civil War. The formal changes to the U.S. Constitution obtained in the Thirteenth, Fourteenth, and Fifteenth Amendments are essential reference points for any analysis of constitutional powers and rights. Such analysis should necessarily include consideration of the intellectual building blocks for those constitutional amendments. No analysis of the constitutional foundations of intellectual property rights is complete without at least considering the possible implications of those amendments and the ideas upon which they were premised.

The political philosophy, constitutional thought, and actions of Abraham Lincoln are central to Civil War constitutionalism. Antislavery thought about free labor offers a logical and compelling account for IP rights. The Lockean concept that the core of property consists of self-ownership and the closely-related free labor concept that a person has a natural right to the fruits of his or her own labor are reflected in the Declaration of Independence. Those concepts formed the principled basis for concluding that slavery is wrong in principle. Intellectual property rights fit squarely within this idea of self-ownership, as an author or inventor owned the productions of their mental labors and the returns those labors generated. The prevailing understanding during Lincoln's day was that copyrights and patents were the property of authors and inventors, respectively. Not surprisingly, Lincoln himself linked the concept of free labor with protection of IP rights.

The influence of the "Freedom National" program had at least one important impact on IP rights during the Lincoln administration. Attorney General Edward Bates's *Opinion on Citizenship* effectively settled that free blacks would be issued copyrights and patents according to the terms of those federal laws.

The fact that pro-IP legislation was adopted contemporaneously with the Reconstruction Amendments gives rise to the inference that the IP rights were consistent with the antislavery principles and views of property vindicated by the Civil War and that influenced the framing of those amendments.

Further, it does not appear that the Reconstruction Amendments to the Constitution impose any express limitation on the scope of copyright or patent protections under the Intellectual Property Clause.

In all, examination of intellectual property in light of antislavery thought, political action tied to the Civil War, and the Reconstruction Amendments, bolsters the logical case for protection of intellectual property rights and its connection to the underlying principles of the American constitutional order.

Sources

Declaration of Independence (1776).

Dred Scott v. Sanford (1857).

Northwest Ordinance (1789).

Edward Bates, *Opinion on Citizenship* (1862).

Ulysses S. Grant, *First Annual Message* (1869).

Ulysses S. Grant, *Veto Message* ("An act for the relief of Rollin White") (Jan. 11, 1780).

Ulysses S. Grant, *Eighth Annual Message* (1876).

Ulysses S. Grant, *Personal Memoirs of U.S. Grant* (1885–1886).

James A. Hamilton, "Property in Men," *New York Times* (1860).

Abraham Lincoln, *Lecture on Discoveries and Inventions* (1858–1860).

Abraham Lincoln, *Speech on the Dred Scott Decision* (1857).

Abraham Lincoln, *Address to the Wisconsin State Agricultural Society* (1859).

Abraham Lincoln, *Cooper Union Address* (1860).

Abraham Lincoln, *Speech at New Haven* (1860).
Abraham Lincoln, *Emancipation Proclamation* (1863).
Abraham Lincoln, *Gettysburg Address* (1863).
Abraham Lincoln, *Reply to the New York Workingmen's Democratic Republican Association* (1864).
John Locke, *Second Treatise of Government* (1689).
James Madison, *Notes of Debates in the Federal Convention of 1787* (1840).
Charles Sumner, *Freedom National; Slavery Sectional* (1852).
Charles Sumner, *Resolution and Remarks in the Senate* (1861).

* * *

Herman Belz, *Abraham Lincoln, Constitutionalism, and Equal Protection in the Civil War Era* (1998).
H.W. Brands, *The Man Who Saved the Union: Ulysses Grant in War and Peace* (2012).
Josiah Bunting III, *Ulysses S. Grant* (2004).
Walter Brown, *A Brief History of Patent Legislation in the United States* (1889).
Michael Kent Curtis, *No State Shall Abridge: The Fourteenth Amendment and the Bill of Rights* (1986).
Jason Emerson, *Lincoln the Inventor* (2009).
Eric Foner, *Free Soil, Free Labor, Free Men: The Ideology of the Republican Party Before the Civil War* (2d ed.) (1995).
Daniel Walker Howe, *The Political Culture of the American Whigs* (1979).
Daniel Walker Howe, *What Hath God Wrought: The Transformation of America, 1815–1848* (2007).
Harry V. Jaffa, *Crisis of the House Divided: An Interpretation of the Issues in the Lincoln-Douglas Debates* (50th Anniv. ed.) (2009).
James Oakes, *Freedom National: The Destruction of Slavery in the United States, 1861–1865* (2013).
James Oakes, *Scorpion's Sting: Antislavery and the Coming of the Civil War* (2014).
U.S. Copyright Office, "Copyright Enactments: Laws Passed in the United States Since 1783 Relating to Copyright," *Bulletin No. 3* (Rev. ed.) (1973).
Sean Vanatta, "How the Patent Office Helped to End Slavery," *Bloomberg* (February 8, 2013).

Bibliographical Essay

Original sources and numerous scholarly works have informed this book's exploration of the constitutional foundations of intellectual property rights and its natural rights perspective. What follows is an overview of select scholarly resources that primarily address critical concepts, important philosophical ideas, influential thinkers, and historical developments in American constitutionalism. While many of the works cited address American constitutionalism in a broad, more encompassing way, select scholarly resources that examine intellectual property concepts in greater detail are likewise included.

Those persons interested in learning more about the subjects covered in this book may benefit from consulting these further readings—and, indeed, hopefully will find the learning experience enjoyable.

* * *

Edward S. Corwin, *The "Higher Law" Background of American Constitutional Law* (Cornell University Press, 1955), surveys the development of natural justice and higher law concepts from classical antiquity through Medieval times and up to sixteenth and seventeenth century Great Britain. Corwin credits the influence of higher law doctrine associated with British philosophers, John Locke, for example, and common law jurists such as Sir Edward Coke, on Colonial America from the time of settlement up to the time of the American Revolution. Richard Tuck, *Natural Rights Theories: Their Origin and Development* (Cambridge University Press, 1979), offers a succinct but slightly more detailed account of the development of natural rights theories. Tuck begins with Medieval and Renaissance thinkers' rediscovery and expansion on classical Roman ideas. He examines the contributions of Enlightenment philosophers Hugo Grotius, John Selden, and Thomas Hobbes, and he traces influential interpretations of those philosophers by their respective followers.

A primer of the context of Locke's writings and the unifying elements of his life's work is offered by John Dunn, *Locke: A Very Short Introduction* (Oxford University Press, 2003). Steven M. Dworetz, *The Unvarnished Doctrine: Locke, Liberalism, and the American Revolution* (2d. ed.) (Duke University Press, 1994), considers the relevance of Locke to the American Revolutionary era. Dworetz places Lockean liberalism at the center of Revolutionary ideology and connects it to the outlook of New England clergy, with an analysis that differs in key respects from Corwin's. He pays close attention to the theory of natural rights presented in the text of Locke's primary works and to the understanding and application of Lockean concepts of natural rights in America leading up to the Revolution. In persuasive manner, Dworetz criticizes the historiographies that treat Locke as a proponent of unbounded acquisitiveness or as an anti-revolutionary whose ideas played no part in American Revolutionary philosophy. Edward J. Erler, *The American Polity: Essays on the Theory and Practice of Constitutional Government* (Routledge, 1991), treats the influence of natural rights in the American Founding and in concise fashion relates it to issues at the heart of the Civil War in his inaugural chapter.

Tom Bethell, *The Noblest Triumph: Property and Prosperity Throughout the Ages* (St. Martin's Press, 1998), offers a defense of private property that is rich with reflections drawn from social, economic, political, ethical, and theological sources that have shaped property's course in Western Civilization. Bethell forthrightly acknowledges the importance of John Locke's justification of private property rights, if not Locke's epistemology. Ultimately, Bethell defends Locke's case for property rights as perceptively rooted in human nature, not owing to historical contingences of seventeenth century philosophy. In a short chapter, Bethell ruminates on unique aspects of intellectual property, though without reaching any definitive conclusions about the institution save perhaps for his recognitions of its incentive to creators and the challenges posed to its existence by advances in digitization, reproduction technologies, and mass communications. James V. DeLong, *Property Matters: How Property Rights are Under Assault—and Why You Should Care* (The Free Press, 1997), presents a short primer on property rights principles and argues for the need to defend property rights in land from various kinds of modern-day regulatory incursions. DeLong also dedicates a chapter to the articulation and defense of intellectual property rights.

Thomas G. West, *Vindicating the Founders, Race, Sex, Class, and Justice in the Origins of America* (Rowman & Littlefield Publishers, 1997), includes an ardent defense of the Founding Fathers' understanding of private property as intimately connected to liberty. West's chapter on property rights draws the connection between Locke and the Founders' understanding of the equal right of individuals to acquire property. He spotlights Founding-era reforms that eliminated feudalistic controls over property ownership and transfer, including primogeniture and entail. West also defends the Founders' understanding of property as an institution promoting efficiency over waste, virtue instead of vice, and advancement of the poor rather than indifference to their plight. James W. Ely, Jr., *The Guardian of Every Other Right: A Constitutional History of Property Rights* (3d ed.) (Oxford University Press, 2008), is a concise study of the constitutional status of property rights and economic liberty in American history. Ely pays particularly close attention to the treatment of property rights by the U.S. Supreme Court and other judicial authorities. Intellectual property receives only passing mention by Ely, with slight reference to it as a limited grant of monopoly that the U.S. Supreme Court has construed narrowly.

Thomas W. Merrill and Henry E. Smith, *The Oxford Introductions to U.S. Law: Property* (Oxford University Press, 2010), lives up to its title, sketching out basic theoretical justifications for property rights and summarizing key property concepts such as origin and acquisition, enjoyment and use, ownership and title, transfer and sale, as well as government powers and rule of law protections. Intellectual property is briefly treated by Merrill and Smith.

Ronald A. Cass and Keith N. Hylton, *Laws of Creation: Property Rights in the World of Ideas* (Harvard University Press, 2013), makes a thorough case for intellectual property rights from a utilitarian framework that deems most answers to practical issues regarding such rights as answerable by rudimentary cost-benefit analysis. Cass and Hylton ably trace the contours of patent law, trade secrets, copyright law, and trademark law, and address unique issues raised by those different types of intellectual property. The authors reject the Lockean "labor-mixing" theory and natural rights perspective as implausible in most practical circumstances. For more in depth scholarly analysis of intellectual property principles and law, we commend the following excellent papers: Richard A. Epstein, "The Disintegration of Intellectual Property? A Classical Liberal Response to Premature Obituary," 62 *Stanford Law Review* 455 (2010); Richard A. Epstein, "Liberty versus Property? Cracks in the Foundation of Copyright Law," 42 *San Diego Law Review* 1 (2005); Richard A. Epstein, "Intellectual Property: Old Boundaries and New Frontiers," 76 *Indiana Law Journal* 803 (2001); Adam Mossoff, "Saving Locke from Marx: The Labor Theory of Value in Intellectual Property Theory," 29 *Social Philosophy and Policy* 283 (2012); Adam Mossoff, "Locke's Labor Lost," 9 *University of Chicago Law School Roundtable* 155 (2002); Adam Mossoff, "Exclusion and Exclusive Use in Patent Law," 22 *Harvard Journal of Law and Technology* 1 (2009); Adam Mossoff, "Patents as Constitutional Private Property: The Historical Protection of Patents Under the Takings Clause," 689 *Boston University Law Review* (2007); Adam Mossoff, "Is Copyright Property?" 42 *San Diego Law Review* 29 (2005); Mark F. Schultz, "Reconciling Social Norms and Copyright Law: Strategies for Persuading People to Pay for Recorded Music," 17 *Journal of Intellectual Property Law* 59 (2009); Mark F. Schultz, "Live Performance, Copyright, and the Future of the Music Business," 43 *Richmond Law Review* 685 (2008); Mark F. Schultz, "Copynorms: Copyright and Social Norms," in Peter K. Yu (ed.), *Intellectual Property and Information Wealth: Issues and Practices in the Digital Age,* Vol. 1 (Praeger Publishers, 2007); and Mark F. Schultz and David Walker "The New International Intellectual Property Agenda," *Are Intellectual Property Rights Human Rights?* 7–31 (Federalist Society, 2006).

James R. Stoner, Jr., *Common Law and Liberal Theory: Coke, Hobbes and the Origins of American Constitutionalism* (University Press of Kansas, 1992), offers an introduction to British Common Law's method of reasoning through case-by-case adjudication, its intellectual sources, jurisprudential content, and its influence on American constitutionalism. Stoner contrasts the legal thought of Sir Edward Coke and Thomas Hobbes, and also traces the common law elements in the works of Sir William Blackstone, the Baron de Montesquieu, John Locke, and *The Federalist Papers.* Daniel J. Boorstin, *The Mysterious Science of the Law: An Essay on Blackstone's Commentaries* (Beacon Press, 1958), describes key features of that common law jurist's magnum opus. Boorstin credits Locke's influence on Blackstone's treatment of natural rights, including property rights. Boorstin also considers Blackstone's view of property as a dynamic social institution that should expand beyond the forms found in nature to encompass new objects as society develops. As Boorstin recounts, Blackstone grounded copyright in the natural claim of a person to the product of his or her labor. Albert Alschuler, "Rediscovering Blackstone," 145 *University of Pennsylvania Law Review* 1 (1996), describes the reception of Blackstone in early America. While Blackstone's *Commentaries* were heavily influential in America, Alschuler nonetheless maintains that Americans proved willing to modify or reject aspects of Blackstone that were incompatible with America's constitutional republicanism. Alschuler also considers Blackstone's understanding of the relationship between the law of nature and common law as well as his conceptual understanding of private property rights. James R. Stoner, Jr., *Common-Law Liberty: Rethinking American Constitutionalism* (University Press of Kansas, 2003), considers common law concepts largely in an American context. While primarily devoted to examining contemporary constitutional doctrines and issues from a historical common law perspective, along the way Stoner offers insights and useful introductions to jurists such as Justice Joseph Story and Chancellor James Kent.

Ronald M. Peters, Jr., *The Massachusetts Constitution of 1780: A Social Compact* (University of Massachusetts Press, 1978), analyzes the historical backdrop and text of the fundamental law of Massachusetts. Peters examines the underlying political philosophy of the Massachusetts Constitution of 1780, and necessarily includes the thoughts of its principal drafter, John Adams. Forrest McDonald, *Novus Ordo Seclorum: The Intellectual Origins of the Constitution* (1985), is the third volume of a trilogy, the first two of which focused on political economy and economic interests relating to the Constitution. This work broadens the horizon by examining intellectual, political, economic, and social origins of the Constitution. McDonald's volume is rich with insights, and as usual, the analysis he brings to bear from the perspective of political economy is particularly astute. McDonald rightfully acknowledges the congeniality of Lockean principles to the American Revolution. However, Madison scholars have maintained that McDonald underestimated the originality and underlying consistency of Madison's constitutional statesmanship. Catherine Drinker Bowen, *Miracle at Philadelphia: The Story of the Constitutional Convention, May to September 1787* (Little, Brown and Company, 1966), is a classic retelling of the story of the work of the federal Constitutional Convention. Richard Beeman, *Plain, Honest Men: The Making of the American Constitution* (Random House, 2009), is a more recent historical account of the Convention. Both works on the Constitutional Convention are accessible to general readers.

Steven G. Calabresi & Larissa C. Liebowitz, "Monopolies and the Constitution: A History of Crony Capitalism," 36 *Harvard Journal of Law & Public Policy* 983 (2013), explores the right of the people to be free from government-granted monopolies. The authors supply a useful summary of British parliamentary and common law responses to royal monopolistic practices in Tudor England. Calabresi and Liebowitz's article similarly contains a helpful overview of the anti-monopolistic thinking in Revolutionary, Jacksonian, and Reconstruction America before taking aim at modern-day monopolistic practices, such as restrictions such as occupational licensing requirements, tax benefits for privileged industries, and price controls.

Brian Z. Tamanaha, *On the Rule of Law: History, Politics, Theory* (Cambridge University Press, 2004), explores the rule of law as an ideal through the lenses of history, politics, and theory. Tamanaha credits Locke, Montesquieu, and *The Federalist Papers* as having cemented the rule of law's place within classical liberalism and shaped its modern form in Western liberal democracies. In addition to considering different formal and substantive theoretical formulations on the rule of law, Tamanaha thematically characterizes the rule of law as involving limits on government by legal formalities rather than merely personal will or caprice. Herman Belz, *Constitutionalism and the Rule of Law in America* (Heritage Foundation, 2009), summarizes the origin and development of the rule of law as it is uniquely conceived within American constitutionalism. Belz explores the Founding Fathers' legacy of establishing limited

constitutional government under a fundamental written law based on principles of reason and justice, intended to secure national independence, preserve
individual liberty, and ensure social freedom. In summarizing the rule of law
in American constitutionalism, Belz touches upon the nature of the American
Union and the role of the government's branches, including the judiciary's role
in judicial review. The significance of Lincoln and Reconstruction to the restoration and advancement of America's rule of law is duly recognized, though Belz
also challenges 20th century progressive criticisms of constitutionally limited
government and individual natural rights of liberty. Ronald A. Cass, *The Rule
of Law in America* (John Hopkins University Press, 2001), presents essential
elements of the rule of law and sketches out how the rule of law is applied in
the context of American constitutionalism. Cass emphasizes the role of the judiciary and its relationship to the rule of law in America. And he considers
various complaints raised against the rule of law, minimizing the weight of
those complaints while also calling attention for the need to secure the rule of
law in response. Ronald A. Cass, "Property Rights Systems and the Rule of
Law," *The Elgar Companion to Property Right Economics* (Enrico Colombatto,
ed., 2003), considers the implications of the rule of law elements—or their
absence—for the security and value of private property rights.

Nathan S. Chapman and Michael W. McConnell, "Due Process As Separation of Powers," 121 *Yale Law Journal* 1672 (2012), looks at how lawyers
and jurists from the Revolution to the Civil War viewed due process of law
as forbidding direct legislative deprivation of individual rights, particularly
vested property rights. Chapman and McConnell emphasize the necessary
role of the judiciary, acting in accord with established general rules, in that
process of law which involves protecting individual rights. The authors accordingly cast due process as a particular instantiation of the separation of
powers.

Richard A. Epstein, *Takings: Private Property and the Power of Eminent Domain* (Harvard University Press, 1985), presents a compelling, if controversial, conceptual understanding of private property, government takings, and
just compensation principles. To be sure, Epstein's approach does not ap-
proximate prevailing eminent domain jurisprudence, which is exceedingly def-
erential to government power claims. Nonetheless, his book has succeeded in
spurring renewed attention and vigorous debate over principles of private property rights and limited government. Richard A. Epstein, *Supreme Neglect: How
to Revive Constitutional Protection for Private Property* (Oxford University Press,
2008), critiques modern-day eminent domain jurisprudence for lacking clear
limiting principles and failing to secure rights and value in private property, including intellectual property.

Daniel E. Troy, *Retroactive Legislation* (AEI Press, 1998), addresses moral and economic arguments against retroactive laws and emphasizes American constitutional constraints on civil laws with illegitimately retroactive effects. Troy concludes that most modern retroactive laws are unjustifiable and that greater legal protections—including specifically judicial protections—against illegitimate retroactive laws are needed.

William Lee Miller, *The Business of May Next: James Madison and the Founding* (University of Virginia Press, 1992), looks at how the younger Madison brought his extensive studies in 1786 and 1787 on the defects of ancient confederations to bear on the Articles of Confederation. Miller follows the development of Madison's thinking as well as his contributions to the U.S. Constitution's drafting and ratification. Lance Banning, *Sacred Fire of Liberty: James Madison and the Founding of the Federal Republic* (Cornell University, 1995), examines Madison's role in shaping the U.S. Constitution with an eye toward the development of Madison's own constitutional understanding between the years of 1780 and 1800. While Madison's *National Gazette* newspaper essays had long been overlooked by historians as mere partisan opposition writing, Banning deems them critical to grasping Madison's systematic understanding of the Constitution's objects and principles. Banning relates Madison's *National Gazette* essays to *The Federalist* and to the Constitutional Convention. Gary Rosen, *American Compact: James Madison and the Problem of Founding* (University of Kansas Press, 1999), takes seriously Madison's originality as a political theorist who refined pre-existing social compact concepts rooted in natural rights and developed practical applications of those concepts in the American constitutional context. Rosen presents the social compact as the fundamental idea of Madison's political thought, relating it to the problem of factions and the protection of property rights. He emphasizes Madison's plea for the republican form of government as expressed in Madison's defense of the Federal Convention in *Federalist Papers* 37 through 40. Garrett Ward Sheldon, *The Political Philosophy of James Madison* (John Hopkins University Press, 2001), examines Madison's political and constitutional thought as a changing but coherent appropriation of contrasting natural rights and classical liberal influences. Sheldon credits Protestant-influenced visions of imperfect human nature and volatile political society as Madison's reference point for mediating those contrasting thought traditions and applying them to social and political circumstances confronting the American nation.

Richard Labunski, *James Madison and the Struggle for the Bill of Rights* (Oxford University Press, 2006), spotlights Madison's crucial efforts in ensuring the First Federal Congress's passage of the Bill of Rights. Labunski provides an accessible narrative that encompasses Madison's expanded role as a Constitutional Framer, Ratifier, and *Federalist* essayist, reluctant election campaigner for a Bill of Rights, and persevering parliamentarian in the First Congress. Robert A. Goldwin, *From Parchment to Power: How James Madison Used the Bill of Rights to Save the Constitution* (AEI Press, 1998), looks at Madison's deft maneuvering of the proposed Bill of Rights through the House of Representatives during the First Federal Congress. Goldwin credits Madison with helping ensure passage of a set of protections for individual rights that would solidify popular support for the Constitution while preserving the forms and powers newly-bestowed on the federal government. Madison thereby appropriated the constitutional amendment process to thwart the aims of anti-Federalists who sought to significantly restrict the new government's powers.

Harlow Giles Unger, *Noah Webster: The Life and Times of an American Patriot* (Wiley, 1998), provides a thoroughly readable and sympathetic biographical account of the life, character, thought, and achievements of its subject. Unger recounts aspects of Webster's copyright lobbying and book tour in the early 1780s. Joshua Kendall, *The Forgotten Founding Father: Noah Webster's Obsession and the Creation of an American Culture* (Putnam, 2010), is a balanced and accessible biographical account that places greater emphasis on Webster's interest in and influence on a distinct American culture united through a common usage of words. Much of Kendall's narrative is written with an eye toward Webster's "Blue Back Speller" and his dictionary. Kendall follows Webster's connection to George Washington and also recounts aspects of Webster's lobbying for copyright and his book tour in the early 1780s. David Micklethwait, *Noah Webster and the American Dictionary* (McFarland & Company, 1999), focuses on Webster's magnum opus, including its intellectual influences and literary characteristics. Micklethwait also recounts the role of Webster's life and times in shaping his *American Dictionary*. Micklethwait's admitted dislike of Webster as a man is reflected in his oft-unsympathetic account of Webster, despite Micklethwait's admiration for his subject's accomplishments. Webster's lobbying trip to Washington, D.C., in late 1830 to obtain congressional extension of copyright terms is also covered.

The last half-century has seen substantial scholarly commentary on *The Federalist*. Gottfried Dietze: *The Federalist: A Classic on Federalism and Free Government* (Johns Hopkins Press, 1961), is a widely-respected study of its subject. Dietze analyzes how *The Federalist* advanced beyond the orthodox conceptions of federation prevalent during its day, articulating a form of constitutionalism to serve as a means of maintaining security from foreign powers while preserving peace among the federation's own members. He also analyzes *The Federalist*'s constitutional ideal of free government, which implied a popular government restricted by law in furtherance of the classic liberal principle of protection of individual rights. Dietze's study includes the historical setting in which *The Federalist* was written, as well as its philosophical precursors. He expressly recognizes the indebtedness of the *Federalist's* constitutionalism to John Locke. Michael I. Meyerson, *Liberty's Blueprint: How Madison and Hamilton Wrote The Federalist, Defined the Constitution, and Made Democracy Safe for the World* (Basic Books, 2008), is a recent work that chronicles the writing and publication history of the *The Federalist* and also analyzes its key features and lasting impact on constitutional discourse. Meyerson demonstrates a familiarity with an extensive body of *Federalist Papers* scholarship. Aspects of *The Federalist* are also addressed in numerous biographies and treatments of the constitutional and political thought of its two principal authors. In addition to the scholarly assessments of Madison described earlier, perhaps the most in-depth and well-written look at political thought of his main *Federalist Papers* co-author may be found in Gerald Strouzh's, *Alexander Hamilton and the Idea of Republican Self-Government* (Stanford University Press, 1970). Strouzh's study pays close attention to Hamilton's essays in *The Federalist Papers*. John D. Gordan, III, "*Morse v. Reid*: The First Reported Federal Copyright Case," 11 *Law and History Review* 21 (1993), tells the story of a nearly forgotten copyright infringement case from the mid-1790s in which Alexander Hamilton and James Kent successfully served as plaintiff's co-counsel for author Jedidiah Morse. Chief Justice Oliver Ellsworth served as a circuit judge during an early stage of the case.

Glenn A. Phelps, *George Washington and American Constitutionalism* (University Press of Kansas, 1993), takes Washington seriously as a constitutional statesman. Phelps examines key themes of Washington's constitutional thinking, developed over the course of his generalship of the Continental Army and in retirement. He credits Washington's involvement in constitution-making and attentiveness to constitutional issues in his roles both as President and as a voting Virginia delegate at the 1787 Philadelphia Convention. As Phelps acknowledges, Washington closely followed the ratification debate and read *The Federalist* in its entirety. And Phelps addresses Washington's sensitivity to constitutional requirements and their proper application in presidential decision-making. Edward J. Larson, *The Return of George Washington: 1783–1789* (HarperCollins, 2014), examines the oft-overlooked activities of Washington during the period between his retirement from the Continental Army and his Inauguration as the first President of the United States. Washington's interactions with Noah Webster during this span are not touched upon, but Larson does reference Washington's assistance to Virginia inventor James Rumsey. Larson also references Washington's discarded draft for his inauguration, which included calls for Congress to enact copyright and patent protections. Without attribution, his epilogue credits Thomas Jefferson with establishing a set of national intellectual property rights during his service as Secretary of State in the Washington administration. Forrest McDonald, *The Presidency of George Washington* (University Press of Kansas, 1974), provides an overview of Washington's presidency that is at once accessible and learned. With verve and command of ideas, events, and personalities, McDonald analyzes key policy themes and initiatives of the Washington administration, both on the domestic and international front. Conceding the extraordinary ability of many of Washington's subordinates and the indispensableness of Washington himself to establishing the office of President, McDonald credits the Washington administration for its accomplishments and for the institutional precedents it set. Leonard D. White, *The Federalists: A Study in Administrative History* (Macmillan Company, 1948), comprehensively analyzes government processes, offices, and personalities of the Federalist administrations that operated during the first dozen years under the Constitution. In the course of his study, White credits Washington's ability as an administrator and emphasizes the importance of Washington's character in shaping the presidency. Matthew Spalding and Patrick J. Garrity, *A Sacred Union of Citizens: Washington's Farewell Address and the American Character* (Rowman & Littlefield Publishers, 1996), expounds upon the text and context of what was once widely regarded as one of the premier state documents in American history, alongside the Declaration of Independence, the Constitution, and *The Federalist*. Spalding and Garrity analyze key themes of union and independence in Washington's Farewell Address (1796), both of which form an essential part of the national character Washington sought to impart. Extending the scope of their study beyond the text to include the trajectory of Washington's career and to future interpreters, Spalding and Garrity present a character-driven portrait of Washington's constitutional statesmanship.

Charlene Banks Bickford and Kenneth R. Bowling, *Birth of the Nation: The First Federal Congress, 1789–1791* (Rowman & Littlefield Publishers, 1989), ably summarizes the legislative accomplishments, political controversies, and key figures of the First Congress. With much justification, the authors deem the First Congress the most important in American history. David P. Currie, *The Constitution in Congress: The Federalist Period, 1789–1801* (University of Chicago Press, 1997), surveys congressional interpretation of constitutional matters during the first dozen years under the Constitution. The First Federal Congress's initial interpretation of a number of Constitutional provisions is the focus of the first part of Currie's work.

William C. diGiacomantonio, "To Form the Character of the American People: Public Support for the Arts, Sciences, and Morality in the First Congress," in Kenneth R. Bowling and Donald R. Kennon (eds.), *Inventing Congress: Origins and Establishment of the First Federal Congress* (Ohio University Press, 1999), offers insightful context to the First Congress's adoption of the first copyright and patent acts. Analysis of the first Copyright Act is supplied by Edward C. Walterscheid, *Understanding the Copyright Act of 1790: The Issue of Common Law Copyright in America and the Modern Interpretation of the Copyright Power*, 53 J. Copyright Soc. USA 313 (2006), and Oren Bracha, "Commentary on the Copyright Act of 1790," in *Primary Sources on Copyright* (1450–1900) (L. Bently & M. Kretschmer, eds.) (2008).

Leonard W. Levy, "Property as a Human Right," 5 *Constitutional Commentary* 169 (1988), persuasively argues that the Declaration of Independence's recognition of the "pursuit of happiness" as an inalienable right rather than "property" or "estate" constituted no break with the property-conscious classical liberalism of Locke. Levy's argument involves a close reading of how Locke, Jefferson, and Jefferson's contemporaries understood "property" in a broad sense, as a human right without which no one could enjoy life or liberty as a free and independent person. More particularly, Levy argues that Jefferson used the term "pursuit of happiness" to mean property in its broadest, Lockean sense, and that Jefferson did believe possessions were unalienable rights— as distinct from indispensable natural rights. Douglas Scott Gerber, *To Secure These Rights: The Declaration of Independence and Constitutional Interpretation* (NYU Press, 1995), offers a theory of constitutional interpretation based on the interplay of the principles and ideals embodied in the two documents named in the title. While not endorsing the particular approach to constitutional interpretation presented, Gerber makes a persuasive case about the significance of Lockean liberalism to the character of the American Revolution and to a proper understanding of the Declaration of Independence. Consistent with Levy, whom he cites favorably, Gerber also argues why the Declaration's substitution of "the pursuit of happiness" for "property" or "estate" does not involve any principled rejection of Lockean respect for private property rights.

Garrett Ward Sheldon, *The Political Philosophy of Thomas Jefferson* (John Hopkins University, 1991), regards Jefferson's contribution to the Declaration of Independence as embodying a modified form of Lockean liberalism, but he insists Jefferson's post-revolutionary development of classical republican theory provided a means for preserving individual natural rights. Forrest McDonald, *The Presidency of Thomas Jefferson* (University Press of Kansas, 1976), focuses on Jefferson's activities as President, acknowledging his skills as an administrator who masterfully handled subordinates. But McDonald recognizes that Jefferson's abilities in this regard owed more to personality traits—traits that masked his administrative shortcomings—than to principles or policy

programs, deeming Jefferson Republicanism's system of national policy bank-
rupt by 1807. In McDonald's estimation, when his administration concluded
Jefferson was embittered and exhausted, with government nearly ceasing to
function. Lynton K. Caldwell, *The Administrative Theories of Jefferson and
Hamilton* (1964), emphasizes the principles of Thomas Jefferson as a public
administrator. Caldwell highlights the importance of Jefferson's personality
and political ideology in defining his thought on administration. Jefferson's
natural law grounding for limited constitutional government is duly recognized, as that grounding influenced guiding Jeffersonian administrative principles, such as preserving harmony among the branches, maintaining simplicity
in governmental operations, and concern for control of power. Caldwell also
contrasts the administrative emphasis of Jefferson in preserving liberty and
decentralized control in the electorate with the emphasis of Alexander Hamilton in preserving responsibility and national unity. However, Caldwell concludes that differences over their political and administrative principles received
greater attention than similarities, heightened by sharp personality contrasts.

The "Jeffersonian mythology" by which Jefferson's role in shaping the Con-
stitution's Intellectual Property Clause is unjustifiably elevated is effectively
dismantled by Adam Mossoff, "Who Cares What Thomas Jefferson Thought
About Patents? Reevaluating the Patent 'Privilege' in Historical Context," 92
Cornell Law Review 953 (2007), and Justin Hughes, "Copyright and Incomplete Historiographies: Of Piracy, Propertization, and Thomas Jefferson," 79
Southern California Law Review (2006). Edward C. Walterscheid, "Thomas
Jefferson and the Patent Act of 1793," *Essays in History* 40 (1998), weighs evidence of Jefferson's role in drafting and encouraging amendments by Congress
to the first Patent Act that would make the patent application and review process
less administratively burdensome.

Daniel Walker Howe, *What Hath God Wrought: The Transformation of America, 1815–1848* (Oxford University Press, 2007), is a magisterial treatment of
the social history of the Antebellum era. Howe is acutely attentive to religious,
political, economic, and other ideological currents prevalent during the time period covered. His work presents vivid character portraits of influential figures
from a cross-section of American life and takes stock of critical events that
shaped the march of American life from the conclusion of the War of 1812 to
the end of the Mexican War. Howe acknowledges the emergence of general cor-
poration laws and expansion of intellectual property for their importance to
American economic and technological progress. Daniel Walker Howe, *The Political Culture of the American Whigs* (University of Chicago Press, 1979), is a rich
study of intellectual character and outlook of American Whiggery. Howe deftly
examines Whig ideas, including Whig preoccupation with social and personal

improvements through respect for law and property, enterprise, and self-discipline. And significant historical figures, such as John Quincy Adams, Henry Clay, Daniel Webster, William Seward, and Abraham Lincoln receive biographical treatments that connect them to the currents of American Whiggery.

Charles F. Hobson, *The Great Chief Justice: John Marshall and the Rule of Law* (University of Kansas, 1996), successfully explicates Marshall's jurisprudence in one short volume. Hobson surveys the common law background in which Marshall was steeped as a law student and practicing attorney in Virginia. The strong constitutional protection accorded to property and contract rights in Marshall's jurisprudence is also examined. The account offered of Marshall's conception of the role of the judicial branch and of its duty of judicial review under a written constitution is informative, as is its overview of Marshall's jurisprudential approach to legal principles, judicial precedents, and interpretative issues. R. Kent Newmyer, *John Marshall and the Heroic Age of the Supreme Court* (Louisiana State University Press, 2001), is an excellent intellectual biography of Marshall, charting the development of his jurisprudential outlook and placing it in the context of his life and times.

John Theodore Horton, *James Kent: A Study in Conservatism*, 1763–1847 (D. Appleton-Century Company, 1939), is the last biographical treatment of Kent. More recently, G. Edward White, "The Chancellor's Ghost," 74 *Chicago-Kent Law Review* 229 (1998), has insisted on the need for an updated and improved biographical account. His article offers additional insights on Kent's jurisprudence, legal scholarship, and impact on American law. John H. Langbein, "Chancellor Kent and the History of Legal Literature," *Faculty Scholarship Series*, Paper 549 (1993), reviews Kent's judicial career, his influence on American reporting, and the influence of Kent's *Commentaries on American Law*. On account of its breadth and conscious attempt to sort out the relationship between the American republic, American law, and the British common law that preceded it, Langbein regards Kent's Commentaries as perhaps the last of a long tradition of great institutionalist works of law that stretches from the second century Roman Institutes of Gaius through later European writers and up through Blackstone. Langbein thereby distinguishes Kent's *Commentaries* from subsequently published American legal treatises.

Camilla A. Hrdy, "State Patent Laws in the Age of Laissez Faire," 28 *Berkeley Tech. L. J.* 45 (2013), is an extensively researched article examining long-forgotten facets of state law patent protection and promotion. Hrdy's thorough acquaintance with the jurisprudence of Chancellor James Kent and related source materials deserve appreciation apart from policy considerations of state promotion of patents. R. Kent Newmyer, *Supreme Court Justice Joseph Story: Statesman of the Old Republic* (University of North Carolina Press, 1985), is the definitive biography of the life and times of the high court's greatest legal scholar. Newmyer takes stock of Story's early political career, his work as a Harvard Law Professor and treatise writer, as well as his service as a judicial circuit rider and Associate Justice during the heyday of the Marshall Court and the early years of the Taney Court. Story's national conservatism, respect for enterprise and property rights, as well as his regard for patent rights are all appreciated in Newmyer's biography. Maurice Baxter, *Daniel Webster and the Supreme Court* (University of Massachusetts Press, 1966), analyzes the lengthy and influential legal practice of Daniel Webster before the bar of the U.S. Supreme Court. Baxter highlights landmark constitutional cases in which Webster served as counsel before the Court and explores themes of Webster's constitutional advocacy, including national federal power and interstate commercial matters, as well as vested rights in contracts and private property. Webster's role as a legal advocate in intellectual property cases is also observed.

Eric Foner, *Free Soil, Free Labor, Free Men: The Ideology of the Republican Party Before the Civil War* (2d ed.) (Oxford University Press, 1995), explores the ideas, values, and commitments around which the nascent Republican party of the 1860s coalesced and acted on the political stage. Foner's study includes Republican concepts of "free labor" and its attack on the Southern aristocratic system built on slave labor, as well as Salmon Chase's constitutionalism and attack on the slave power. James Oakes, *Freedom National: The Destruction of Slavery in the United States, 1861–1865* (W.W. Norton & Company, 2013), masterfully examines the background and implementation of "Freedom Nation" as an anti-slavery policy principle. Oakes traces the origins of the Republican party's twin goals of achieving liberty and preserving the Union and follows the course of emancipation during the Civil War. James Oakes, *Scorpion's Sting: Antislavery and the Coming of the Civil War* (W.W. Norton & Company, 2014), is the published form of a short series of lectures focused on the Republican program for gradually bringing about the elimination of slavery by cordoning slave states with free states, but which was all but abandoned in favor of an unexpected and accelerated process of wartime emancipation. Oakes analyzes the Civil War in terms of a war over the idea of property in men and also as a war about race. Justin Buckley Dyer, *Natural Law and the Antislavery Constitutional Tradition* (Cambridge University Press, 2012), traces the history of antislavery constitutionalism's roots in natural law principles, running through British common law, the Declaration of Independence, Antebellum era controversies, the debate over *Dred Scott v. Sanford* (1857), and Lincoln's constitutional thought.

Mark E. Steiner, "Abraham Lincoln and the Rule of Law Books," 93 *Marquette Law Review* 1283 (2010), focuses on how Lincoln was influenced by legal scholars and jurists such as Blackstone, Kent, and Story through his self-study in law and in his private practice as an Illinois lawyer. Harry V. Jaffa, *Crisis of the House Divided: An Interpretation of the Issues in the Lincoln-Douglas Debates* (50th Anniversary ed.) (University of Chicago Press, 2009), recovers the vital connection between the political philosophy of Abraham Lincoln and the principles of the Declaration of Independence. Jaffa analyses the Illinois 1858 U.S. Senate race as a clash over principles of natural right and over the meaning of the Declaration. Chris DeRose, *Congressman Lincoln: The Making of America's Greatest President* (Threshold Editions, 2013), takes seriously Lincoln's single term as a member of the U.S. Congress. Whereas many scholars have denigrated Lincoln's congressional service, DeRose rescues Congressman Lincoln from charges that he was an imprudent and ineffectual member. DeRose's analyzes the logical rigor of Lincoln's congressional floor speeches and resolutions and argues that both the man and his political views commanded underappreciated respect and influence. In addition to narrating Lincoln's Whig party activism and his sole argument as a lawyer before the U.S. Supreme Court, DeRose chronicles the efforts made by Lincoln to obtain patent #6469 while serving as a member of Congress.

Jason Emerson, *Lincoln the Inventor* (Southern Illinois University Press, 2009), is a monograph dedicated to Lincoln's interest in mechanical inventions and improvements. Emerson recounts the story of how Lincoln conceived his idea for improving riverboat navigation and obtained patent #6469 in the course of his term as a member of Congress. The contextual backdrop of Lincoln's lecture on patents is also provided. Emerson helpfully explains how Lincoln's so-called "First Lecture on Discoveries and Inventions" and his "Second Lecture on Discoveries and Inventions" are most likely the same lecture. Lincoln's lecture is conveniently included as an appendix in the volume. Harold Holzer, *Lincoln at Cooper Union: The Speech that Made Abraham Lincoln President* (Simon & Schuster, 2004), examines themes and purposes of Lincoln's speech at New York's Cooper Union in February 1860. Holzer presents the most thorough account written of events culminating in Lincoln's *Cooper Union Address* (1860), and the overwhelmingly positive reaction it received from its audience and in the press, as well as its prominent role in securing Lincoln's nomination for President. Holzer characterizes the *Cooper Union Address* as Lincoln's first and last campaign speech for the presidency.

Herman Belz, *Abraham Lincoln, Constitutionalism, and Equal Protection in the Civil War Era* (Fordham University Press, 1997), regards the Civil War and Reconstruction as constitutive national experiences that profoundly shaped modern American politics. Belz analyzes Lincoln's political thought and constitutionalism and also explores Civil War and Reconstruction emancipation and equal rights policies and their underlying principles. Later chapters offer the author's perspective on the meaning of equality under the Fourteenth Amendment as well as his assessment of the impact of Reconstruction and subsequent developments on the Constitution. Herman Belz, *A New Birth of Freedom: The Republican Party and the Freedmen's Rights, 1861–1866* (2d ed.) (Fordham University Press, 2000), discusses Attorney General Edward Bates' 1862 opinion on citizenship in the context of the Lincoln administration's use of measures involving military service in furtherance of a Republican theory of national citizenship that was contrary to Chief Justice Taney's holding in *Dred Scott*.

Michael Kent Curtis, *No State Shall Abridge: The Fourteenth Amendment and the Bill of Rights* (Duke University Press, 1986), examines the historical background, framing by Congress, and state ratification process for the Fourteenth Amendment, as well as subsequent interpretations of the Amendment by Congress and the Courts. Curtis argues that the Fourteenth Amendment was intended to provide full incorporation of the Bill of Rights' protections from state interference. Akhil Reed Amar, *The Bill of Rights: Creation and Reconstruction* (Yale University Press, 1998), emphasizes the original Bill of Rights' integration within the structure of the original Constitution. Upon examining antebellum ideas as well as the Fourteenth Amendment's text and history, Amar argues that the Amendment transforms the nature of the Bill of Rights and offers a "refined incorporation" perspective on how the Bill of Rights should apply to the states in light of the Amendment. While this book's analysis of the constitutional foundations of intellectual property is neither staked upon, nor especially relevant to, any particular theory of incorporation, the scholarship of Curtis and Amar nonetheless offers an important emphasis on the critical role of the Fourteenth Amendment to American Constitutionalism and sheds light on the Amendment's early history. Robert J. Reinstein, *Completing the Constitution: The Declaration of Independence, Bill of Rights and Fourteenth Amendment*, 66 Temple L. Rev. 361 (1991), regards the Fourteenth Amendment as a constitutional fulfillment of the principles of the Declaration.

Although we are not aware of any definitive modern study of Ulysses S. Grant's constitutionalism, H.W. Brands, *The Man Who Saved the Union: Ulysses Grant in War and Peace* (Doubleday, 2012), and Josiah Bunting III, *Ulysses S. Grant* (Times Books, 2004), are part of a continuing trend of positive assessments of Grant's presidency, pushing back against the decidedly negative—and arguably shallow and off-base—assessments from earlier generations of scholars. Neither of these works address Grant's signing of legislation expanding intellectual property rights protections. Charles Bracelen Flood, *Grant's Final Victory: Ulysses S. Grant* (Da Capo Press, 2011) tells the story of the retired, indebted, and cancer-stricken hero's valiant effort to write a memoir of his military experiences before his death in the hopes that its publication and marketing campaign by Samuel Clemens would secure the financial future of his wife Julia.

About the Authors

RANDOLPH J. MAY is founder and President of The Free State Foundation. The Free State Foundation is an independent, non-profit free market-oriented think tank founded in 2006.

From October 1999–May 2006, Mr. May was a Senior Fellow and Director of Communications Policy Studies at The Progress & Freedom Foundation, a Washington, D.C.-based think tank. Prior to joining PFF, he practiced communications, administrative, and regulatory law as a partner at major national law firms. From 1978 to 1981, Mr. May served as Assistant General Counsel and Associate General Counsel at the Federal Communication Commission.

Mr. May has held numerous leadership positions in bar associations. He is a past Chair of the American Bar Association's Section of Administrative Law and Regulatory Practice. He is a Fellow of the National Academy of Public Administration. Mr. May also serves as Public Member of the Administrative Conference of the United States.

Mr. May has published more than 180 articles and essays on communications, administrative, and constitutional law topics. He is author of *A Call for a Radical New Communications Policy: Proposals for Free Market Reform*, published in 2011. Mr. May is editor of two books, *Communications Law and Policy in the Digital Age: The Next Five Years*, published in 2012, and *New Directions in Communications Policy*, published in 2009. In addition, he is the co-editor of two other books, *Net Neutrality or Net Neutering: Should Broadband Internet Services Be Regulated?* and *Communications Deregulation and FCC Reform*. Mr. May has written regular columns on legal and regulatory affairs for *Legal Times* and the *National Law Journal*, leading national legal periodicals.

He received his A.B. from Duke University and his J.D. from Duke Law School, where he serves as a member of the Board of Visitors.

SETH L. COOPER is a Senior Fellow at The Free State Foundation. His work on federal communications and technology policy at the Free State Foundation began in 2009. Mr. Cooper previously served as Director to the Telecommunications and Information Technology Task Force at the American Legislative Exchange Council (ALEC).

Mr. Cooper served as judicial clerk to the Honorable James Johnson at the Washington State Supreme Court. He has worked in law and policy staff positions at the Washington State Senate and at the Discovery Institute. Mr. Cooper is a 2009 Lincoln Fellow at the Claremont Institute.

Mr. Cooper previously contributed to two chapters in *Communications Law and Policy in the Digital Age* (2012), published by Carolina Academic Press. His work has also appeared in such publications as *CommLaw Conspectus*, the *Gonzaga Law Review*, the *San Jose Mercury News*, *Forbes.com*, the *Des Moines Register*, the *Baltimore Sun*, the *Washington Examiner*, and the *Washington Times*.

Mr. Cooper earned his B.A. degree in Political Science from Pacific Lutheran University and received his J.D. from Seattle University School of Law.

Index

A

Abraham Lincoln, Constitutionalism, and Equal Protection in the Civil War Era (Belz), 201–02

"Abraham Lincoln and the Rule of Law Books" (Steiner), 200–01

Adams, John, 110, 125

Address to the Wisconsin State Agricultural Society (Lincoln), 164, 172–73

The Administrative Theories of Jefferson and Hamilton (Caldwell), 198

Agassiz, Louis, 172

Alexander Hamilton and the Idea of Republican Self-Government (Strouzh), 195

Alien and Sedition Acts, 116–17

Allen, Darcy v., 57

Alschuler, Albert, "Rediscovering Blackstone," 190

Amar, Akhil Reed, *The Bill of Rights*, 202

American Compact (Rosen), 193

The American Dictionary of the English Language (Webster), 60, 77, 154, 156

The American Polity (Erler), 188

American Revolution: and monopolies, 58–59; and rule of law, 120, 124

American Spelling Book (Webster), 45, 155

Ames, Fisher, 89

Ames v. Howard, 151

Annapolis Convention, 48

Answers to Mr. Mason's Objections to the New Constitution (Iredell), 61–62

Antebellum era: about, 135; Constitution in, 137; copyright jurisprudence during, 145–49; copyright legislation during, 153–57; copyright/patent protections during, 137; Due Process Clause during, 142; government and property rights in, 138–39; IP rights in, 13, 135–36, 161; monopolies in, 137, 159–61; natural rights during, 136, 137–43, 161; patent legislation during, 157–59; patents jurisprudence during, 149–53; private property and natural rights during, 137–43; property rights

understanding of IP in, 143–53;
property rights vs. monopolies
in, 159–61; Supreme Court in,
139–41; Takings Clause in, 141
anti-IP views, 8, 54–55; Jefferson
and, 103, 106, 107
antislavery principles: and
Constitution, 173–74; and free
labor, 13–14, 163, 168–69,
183; and human property, 175;
and IP rights, 14, 166, 168, 180,
184; Lincoln and, 164, 173–74;
natural right to fruits of own
labor and, 164; and property,
174; property as self-ownership
and, 164; and property in men,
165, 174–77; Republicans and,
180; as social vs. political/legal
cause, 177. *See also* slavery
Appeal to the Inhabitants of Quebec
(First Continental Congress),
58–59
Appropriations Act of 1868, 165,
180
Articles of Confederation: and
copyright, 43, 48–49; in *The
Federalist*, 70; N. Webster and,
43. *See also* Confederation
Congress
Ashcroft v. Eldred, 94
Ashley-Cooper, Anthony, 18

B
Baldwin, Henry, in *McClurg v.
Kingsland*, 150
Baltimore, Barron v., 141, 142, 180
Bank of the United States, 160
Banning, Lance, *Sacred Fire of
Liberty*, 193

Barbier v. Connolly, 130
Barron v. Baltimore, 141, 142, 180
Bates, Edward, *Opinion on
Citizenship*, 165, 179, 184
Baxter, Maurice, 140, 142; *Daniel
Webster and the Supreme Court*,
200
Beckett, Donaldson v., 73, 74, 75
Beeman, Richard, *Plain, Honest
Men*, 191
Belz, Herman, 122–23, 167;
*Abraham Lincoln,
Constitutionalism, and Equal
Protection in the Civil War Era*,
201–02; *Constitutionalism and
the Rule of Law in America*,
191–92; *A New Birth of
Freedom*, 202
Bethell, Tom, *The Noblest Triumph*,
40, 188
Bickford, Charlene Bangs, 88, 89,
90; *Birth of the Nation*, 196
Bill of Rights: and Constitution, 99;
and Copyright/Patent Acts, 87;
Declaration of Independence
and, 112; First Congress and,
12, 87, 88, 91, 92, 97–98,
99–100, 126–27; and
government-conferred
monopolies, 54; Hamilton and,
62; Jefferson and, 103, 107,
109–10; limitation on federal
power, 141; Madison and, 63,
98–99, 126–27; states and, 180
The Bill of Rights (Amar), 202
Birth of the Nation (Bickford;
Bowling), 196
blacks: citizenship and, 165, 180;
copyrights/patents issued to,

179; IP rights for, 184; and patents, 165, 178

Blackstone, Sir William: *Commentaries on the Laws of England*, 32, 34, 74, 75–76, 148; on common law copyright, 72; on IP rights, 76–77; Lincoln and, 167; and natural rights, 36; and patents, 152; and property as originating in nature vs. society, 36–37; as replacing Coke in common law, 75; and rule of law, 119

Blanchard v. Sprague, 151

Bloomer v. McQuewan, 153

Boorstin, Daniel, *The Mysterious Science of Law*, 36, 190

Boston Tea Party, 58, 75

Boudinot, Elias, 89, 93

Bowen, Catherine Drinker, *Miracle at Philadelphia*, 191

Bowling, Kenneth R., 88, 89, 90, 98; *Birth of the Nation*, 196

Brands, H.W., 181; *The Man Who Saved the Union*, 202

Bunting, Josiah, 181

Burlamaqui, Jean Jacques, 22, 113

Burton v. Folsom, 148–49

The Business of May Next (Miller), 193

C

Calabresi, Steven G., "Monopolies and the Constitution," 191

Caldwell, Lynton K., 115–16; *The Administrative Theories of Jefferson and Hamilton*, 198

Cass, Ronald A., 8; *Laws of Creation*, 189; "Property Rights

Systems and the Rule of Law," 192; *The Rule of Law in America*, 122, 192

Centennial Exhibition, Philadelphia, 1876, 182

"Chancellor Kent and the History of Legal Literature" (Langbein), 199

"The Chancellor's Ghost" (White), 199

Chapman, Nathan S., 128; "Due Process As Separation of Powers," 192

Chase, Salmon P., 177; *Freedom National; Slavery Sectional*, 177

Christian, Edward, 148

Cicero, 18

citizenship: of blacks, 180; in Fourteenth Amendment, 179; of slaves, 165; whites and, 178

civil laws: and different types of property, 32–33, 41; and natural rights basis for IP rights, 35–36, 37; and natural rights of property, 32–33; and property rights, 10, 82; two-track understanding of property and, 32

Civil Rights Act of 1866 (U.S.), 129

civil society: and copyright, 5; and patent rights, 5; self interest within, 68; two-track understanding of property and, 32

Civil War: Amendments (*See* Reconstruction Amendments); antislavery views about Constitution/property leading to, 174; chattel principle of labor and, 174; constitutionalism, 163; and IP rights, 13, 14; IP rights legislation during, 178–79; Lincoln's *Gettysburg Address* and, 166; and property rights, 13–14; views on property during, 166

classical liberalism: and Constitution, 10, 15, 110; and copyright, 16; definition of property, 15, 113; framework of government and IP rights protection, 94; and individual property rights, 86; Jefferson and, 103; and natural rights, 76; and natural rights perspective on intellectual property, 6; and patent, 16; and purpose of government, 120; and rule of law, 86, 119; understanding of property, 10, 33, 34–35

Clay, Henry, 137, 158, 170

Clemens, Samuel ("Mark Twain"), 182–83

Cohens v. State of Virginia, 90

Coke, Sir Edward, 75, 119; *Institutes of the Law of England*, 57, 129

Commentaries on American Law (Kent), 138–39, 144

Commentaries on the Constitution of the United States (Story), 72, 130–31, 143, 150, 153

Commentaries on the Laws of England (Blackstone), 32, 34, 74, 75–76, 148

Commerce Department, 2012 report, 31, 40

common law: Colonists' entitlement to protections of, 57; Constitutional Convention and, 75; and copyright, 72–74, 136–37, 147, 148, 154–55; fruits of one's labor and copyright under, 77; House of Lords' dismissal of, 75; and independent judiciary, 124; Madison on IP rights in, 72, 73–76; and monopolies, 53–54; and natural rights, 6, 76–77; and perpetual copyright, 147, 148; and protection of individual rights, 123–24; and rule of law, 124; states and, 74–75, 147; in *Wheaton v. Peters*, 146

Common Law and Liberal Theory (Stoner), 190

Common Sense (Paine), 58

Common-Law Liberty (Stoner), 190

Completing the Constitution (Reinstein), 202

Confederation Congress: and copyright, 43, 48–49, 92–93; and IP rights, 78–79; Madison and, 93; and security of literary property, 86; N. Webster and, 93. *See also* Articles of Confederation

Congress: abolition of slavery, 177; and due process of law, 128–29; IP Clause and, 27, 95–96, 103–04, 136–37, 183; and IP rights, 86, 93, 107, 120, 127; Johnson and, 179; and patent rights, 158–59; and rule of law, 120, 127; and securing of copyright to natural right, 146

Congressman Lincoln (DeRose), 201
Connecticut, copyright law, 44–45
Connolly, Barbier v., 130
Constitution: in Antebellum era,
    137; antislavery ideology and,
    173–74; Bill of Rights and, 99;
    classical liberalism and, 10, 15,
    110; and copyright, 43;
    Declaration of Independence
    and, 16–17, 112; *The Federalist
    Papers* and, 69–71; First
    Congress and, 86–87, 89–91;
    and Freedom National
    program, 165; and freedom of
    the press, 62, 63; and fruits of
    one's labor, 169–70; and
    government, 16, 80–81,
    115–17; Grant and, 181; and IP,
    119; and IP rights, 64, 106–07,
    127; Jefferson and, 104, 105,
    107, 109–10, 115–17; limits on
    federal power, 60–61; Lincoln's
    two-track view of, 163, 167–68;
    Locke and, 24; Madison and,
    49, 88; and monopolies,
    60–61, 63, 64; natural rights
    and, 23–24; and natural rights
    perspective on IP, 6–7; original
    understanding of, 7; and
    preservation of Union, 70; and
    property rights, 139–41;
    Reconstruction Amendments,
    166; Reconstruction
    Amendments as completion of,
    167; republican nature of
    government under, 62; and rule
    of law, 122–23, 126, 132–33;
    and slavery, 167, 169–70,
    174–76; states and, 63, 138;

Takings Clause, 121; and vested
    rights, 131; Washington and,
    97; workable government in, 88
The Constitution in Congress
    (Currie), 196
Constitutional Congress. *See* First
    Congress
Constitutional Convention:
    Annapolis Convention as
    precursor to, 48; and common
    law, 75; and copyright, 44,
    49–50, 59; Jefferson and, 103,
    107; membership of First
    Congress and, 89, 90; as
    political compromise, 107; N.
    Webster and, 50, 93
constitutionalism: Civil War, 163;
    Declaration of Indepence and,
    111–12; *The Federalist Papers*
    and, 67; government-conferred
    monopolies and, 11; of IP
    rights, 93–94, 121–22, 133; IP
    theft and, xv–xvi; Jefferson and,
    110; key components of, 120,
    127; and patent rights, 6–7;
    and protection of individual
    rights, 127; and rule of law,
    119, 120, 122–27, 132–33;
    thought systems underlying, 6
*Constitutionalism and the Rule of
    Law in America* (Belz), 191–92
Continental Congress, First: *Appeal
    to the Inhabitants of Quebec*,
    58–59; Boston Tea Party and, 75
Continental Congress, Second, and
    Declaration of Independence,
    110–12
Cooper Union Address (Lincoln),
    90–91, 99, 175, 176

Copyright Act: of 1790, 12, 93, 95, 97, 109, 135, 154; of 1793, 135; of 1802, 105, 117, 135; of 1831, 137, 154, 156; of 1867, 165, 180; of 1868, 165, 180; of 1870, 87, 92, 165, 182; of 1976, 149; amendments during Civil War, 179; amendments of 1834 and 1846, 156–57; amendments of 1867, 179; First Congress and, 85–86, 91–92, 100

Copy-Right Manual (Ellsworth), 156

Copyright Term Extension Act of 1998 (CTEA), 94–95

copyright(s): during Articles of Confederation, 48–49; civil society and, 5; classical liberalism and, 16; common law and, 72–74, 136–37, 147, 148, 154–55; Confederation Congress and, 48–49, 92–93; and Constitution, 43; at Constitutional Convention, 49–50; constitutionalism and, 6–7; defined, 3; fair use doctrine, 100, 148–49; and First Amendment, 98, 99; First Congress and, 97–98; foundations of protection of, 43; free speech vs., 97–100; fruits of one's labor(s) and, 43, 46, 49, 59, 77, 146–47; government and, 4; Grant and, 182–83; included in IP rights, 3–4; IP Clause and normativity of, 44; Jefferson and, 106; jurisprudence during Antebellum era, 145–49; Kent on, 144; legislation during

Antebellum era, 153–57; as literary property, 11, 43, 44, 49, 51, 59, 99; Madison and, 43, 44, 49, 51, 99; natural rights and, 3–5, 45–46, 76, 147–48; perpetual, 136–37, 147, 148, 155; republication and, 149; and rule of law, 44; states and, 43, 44–48, 49, 154; and Stationers' Company, 57; time periods for, 94–95, 154–56; as type of property, 49; N. Webster and, 43, 44–47, 51, 60, 97, 154–56; in *Wheaton v. Peters,* 145–49. *See also* intellectual property (IP)

corporations, 160

Corwin, Edwin S., 20; *The Higher Law Background of American Constitutional Law,* 18, 187

Crisis of the House Divided (Jaffa), 201

The Crisis of the House Divided (Jaffa), 167

Currie, David P., 93; *The Constitution in Congress,* 196

Curtis, Benjamin, in *Murray's Lessee v. Hoboken Land & Improvement Co.,* 128–29

Curtis, Michael Kent, 180; *No State Shall Abridge,* 202

D

Daniel Webster and the Supreme Court (Baxter), 200

Darcy v. Allen, 57

Dartmouth College v. Woodward, 141

Davis, Jefferson, 165, 178

Davis, Joseph, 165, 178

Day, Goodyear v., 152–53

Declaration of Independence: and
 Bill of Rights, 112; and
 Constitution, 16–17, 112; and
 constitutionalism, 111–12; and
 free labor, 169, 183; and fruits
 of one's labor, 138, 183; and
 government, 103, 116; Jefferson
 and, 23, 103, 104–05, 110–13,
 117; Lincoln and, 17, 163–64,
 167; Lockean definition of
 property and, 33; Locke's
 Second Treatise on Government
 and, 112; and natural rights, 3,
 6, 28, 183; and purpose of
 government, 112; and rule of
 law, 124

*Declaration of the Causes and
 Necessity of Taking Up Arms*
 (Jefferson), 110, 112

Defoe, Daniel, *Robinson Crusoe*, 23

Delaware, copyright in, 46–47

DeLong, James V., *Property Matters*,
 188

DeRose, Chris, *Congressman
 Lincoln*, 201

Detached Memoranda (Madison), 60

Dickinson, John, 110, 112

Dietze, Gottfried, *The Federalist*,
 194–95

diGiacomantonio, William C., "To
 Form the Character of the
 American People," 196–97

digital revolution/technologies: and
 intellectual vs. physical
 property, 38–39; IP protection
 and, 15, 31; IP rights in, 40;
 and piracy of intellectual
 property, xv–xvi

Discourses Concerning Government
 (Sidney), 21–22

Dix, West River Bridge Company v.,
 141

Donaldson v. Beckett, 73, 74, 75

Douglas, Stephen, 167, 171

Dred Scott v. Sanford, 153, 164, 165,
 174, 175, 178, 179, 180

"Due Process As Separation of
 Powers" (Chapman;
 McConnell), 192

Due Process Clause, 141, 142, 166,
 180, 183

due process of law: Congress and,
 128–29; and IP rights, 121,
 128–29; and separation of
 powers, 128–29

Dunn, John, *Locke: A Very Short
 Introduction*, 187–88

Dworetz, Steven M., 23; *The
 Unvarnished Doctrine*, 20, 188

Dyer, Justin Buckley, *Natural Law
 and the Antislavery
 Constitutional Tradition*, 200

E

economy, IP and, 31, 40, 55

Eldred, Ashcroft v., 94

Ellsworth, Henry, 157–58

Ellsworth, Oliver, 89, 155, 157

Ellsworth, William, 155, 156, 157;
 Copy-Right Manual, 156

Ely, James W., Jr., 113, 140, 141,
 142; *The Guardian of Every
 Other Right*, 138–39, 189

Emancipation Proclamation
 (Lincoln), 177

Emerson, Jason, 172; *Lincoln the
 Inventor*, 170–71, 201

eminent domain, 141, 142
Epstein, Richard A., 8, 122;
  Supreme Neglect, 192; *Takings,*
  192
Equal Protection Clause, 166, 183
equal protection of laws, 129–30
Erler, Edward J., *The American
  Polity,* 188
Evans, Oliver, 117
Evans v. Jordan, 132
*An Examination into the Leading
  Principles of the New Federal
  Constitution* (Webster), 51
exclusion: IP rights and, 56;
  property rights and, 56
Exclusion Crisis (U.K.), 18

F
fair use doctrine, 100, 148–49
Fairfax County Resolves
  (Washington), 58
*A Familiar Exposition of the
  Constitution of the United States*
  (Story), 143
The Federalist (Dietze), 194–95
The Federalist Papers: Constitution
  and, 69–71; and
  constitutionalism, 67; federal
  government powers in, 78; IP
  in, 67–69; legacy/importance
  of, 67, 71; Madison and,
  50–51, 69–70; public good in,
  68–69, 79–80; "Publius," 50,
  70–71; republican government
  in, 70; and rule of law, 120,
  126; utility to the union in, 68,
  70, 77–81; Washington and,
  70–71, 97; *No. 1* (Hamilton),
  70; *No. 10* (Madison), 68,

79–80; *No. 12* (Hamilton), 126;
  No. 37 (Madison), 68, 69,
  73–74; *No. 39* (Madison), 16,
  61; *No. 40* (Madison), 77; *No.
  41* (Madison), 77; *No. 43*
  (Madison), 11, 16, 50, 61,
  67–68, 69, 71–79, 82–83, 143;
  No. 49 (Madison), 109; *No. 51*
  (Madison), 68, 80; *No. 62*
  (Madison), 126; *No. 78*
  (Hamilton), 69, 75, 126; *No. 84*
  (Hamilton), 62, 126; *Nos.
  37–40* (Madison), 24
The Federalists (White), 196
Field, Stephen, in *Barbier v.
  Connolly,* 130
Fifteenth Amendment, 166, 180,
  181, 183
Fifth Amendment: Due Process
  Clause, 141, 142; and due
  process of law, 138; equal
  protection of laws in, 129; and
  just compensation, 138;
  restriction of federal
  government vs. states, 141;
  Takings Clause, 130–31
Filmer, Sir Robert, *Patriarcha,* 18
First Amendment: copyright and,
  98, 99; Free Press Clause, 61;
  and freedom of the press, 54,
  63; and harmony between IP
  rights, 87; and IP Clause, 99
First Congress: about, 85; as
  authority on constitutional
  meaning, 89–91; and Bill of
  Rights, 12, 87, 88, 91, 97–98,
  99–100, 126–27; and
  Compromise of 1790, 92;
  consitutional precedent-setting

by, 87–89; and Constitution,
86–87; and copyright, 97–98;
and copyright vs. free speech,
97–100; and Copyright/Patent
Acts, 91–92, 100; and freedom
of the press, 61; importance of,
87–89; and IP Clause, 93,
94–95; and IP rights, 12,
85–87; and Judiciary Act, 90,
92, 96; legislative agenda,
91–92; Lincoln on, 90–91, 99;
Madison and, 93; membership
of, 89, 90; precedential value,
95–96; and restriction of
slavery, 90; Supreme Court and,
94–95; twelve proposed
amendments, 88; and workable
government, 88
First Inaugural Address (Jefferson),
104–05, 116
First Treatise of Government (Locke),
18–19
Fletcher v. Peck, 141
Flood, Charles Bracelen, *Grant's
Final Victory,* 202–03
Folsom, Burton v., 148–49
Foner, Eric, 177; *Free Soil, Free
Labor, Free Men,* 168–69, 200
The Forgotten Founding Father
(Kendall), 194
Fourteenth Amendment, 127, 166,
179–80, 183; Due Process
Clause, 166; Equal Protection
Clause, 129–30, 166
free blacks. *See* blacks
free government(s). *See*
government(s)
free labor: antecedents to concept
of, 168–69; antislavery

principles and, 13–14, 163,
168–69, 183; Declaration of
Independence and, 169;
definition of, 172; and
entrepreneurship, 169; fruits of
own labors and, 13, 176; Grant
and, 181; and IP rights,
168–69, 173–74, 184; Lincoln
and, 169–70, 172, 173; and
natural right to fruits of labor,
164, 183; and patent rights,
172–73
Free Soil, Free Labor, Free Men
(Foner), 168–69, 200
Freedom National (Oakes), 176–77,
200
Freedom National program, 14,
165, 177, 178, 179, 184
Freedom National; Slavery Sectional
(Chase), 177
freedom of speech: copyright vs.,
97–100; First Amendment and,
63; First Congress and, 87; IP
rights and, 5, 87, 100
freedom of the press: Alien and
Sedition Acts and, 116–17; in
Colonial period, 58–59;
Constitution and, 62, 63;
federal government and, 61–62;
First Amendment and, 54, 63;
government and, 54; Hamilton
on, 62; republican government
and, 62; states and, 63; N.
Webster on, 62
From Parchment to Paper
(Goldwin), 194
fruits of one's labor(s): Constitution
and, 169–70; and copyright,
11, 43, 44, 46, 49, 51, 59, 77,

146–47; Declaration of
Independence and, 138;
equality of entitlement to, 180;
expropriations of, 40; free labor
and, 13, 164, 176, 183;
government protection of, 4,
41; IP and, 26–27; IP Clause
and, 27; and IP rights, 41, 53,
55, 64, 68, 76–77, 114–15;
Jeffersonian principle of
administration and IP rights,
117; Lincoln on, 164, 169, 170;
Madison and, 25; natural
right(s) to, 4, 32, 35, 164, 176,
183; others reaping, 4–5;
private property protection laws
and, 4; as property, 169, 170,
180; and property rights, 38,
82; rights to, 4–5; unalienable
rights to, 104; understanding of
property and right to, 32

G
Gardner v. Village of Newburgh, 142
Garrity, Patrick J., A Sacred Union
of Citizens, 196
Gayler v. Wilder, 132, 153
generational theory, 104, 108–09
George Washington and American
Constitutionalism (Phelps), 195
Georgia, copyright in, 46
Gerber, Douglas Scott, To Secure
These Rights, 197
Gettysburg Address (Lincoln), 166
Giddings, Joshua, 177
Golan v. Holder, 94–95
Goldwin, Robert A., From
Parchment to Paper, 194
Goodyear v. Day, 152–53

Gordan, John D., III, "Morse v.
Reid," 195
government(s): classical liberalism
and purpose of, 120; conferring
of monopolies, 59, 60–61, 64;
Constitution and, 16, 60–61,
88; and copyright, 4;
Declaration of Independence
and, 103, 112, 116; and dispute
resolution, 123; in The
Federalist Papers, 78; First
Congress and, 88; and freedom
of the press, 54, 61–62; and
fruits of personal labors, 4, 41;
and individual rights, 123; IP
Clause and, 6–7, 33; and IP
rights, 37; Jefferson and
administration of, 104–05,
115–17; Madison on powers of,
78; and monopolies, 11, 53, 55,
107–08; natural law and, 18,
19; and natural rights, 15,
16–17, 27, 28; and patent
rights, 4; and personal rights vs.
property rights, 34; and private
property rights, 24–25;
property protection and power
of, 37–38; and property rights,
10, 17, 25, 51, 80, 81, 125, 136,
138–39; purpose of, 15; and
records system, 37; and rule of
law, 37–38, 119, 122; and
slavery, 176–77; social
compacts establishing, 17, 28,
82
Grant, Julia, 182, 183
Grant, Ulysses S., 165, 181–83;
Personal Memoirs of U.S. Grant,
182–83

Grant's Final Victory (Flood), 202–03

The Great Chief Justice: John Marshall and the Rule of Law (Hobson), 199

Grier, Robert, 152

Grotius, Hugo, 18, 22

The Guardian of Every Other Right (Ely), 138–39, 189

H

Hamilton, Alexander, 63, 69, 70–71; *Federalist No. 1*, 70; *Federalist No. 78*, 69, 75, 126; *Federalist No. 84*, 62, 126; *Report on Public Credit*, 92

Hamilton, James A., "Property in Men," 175–76

The Higher Law Background of American Constitutional Law (Corwin), 18, 187

"The Historical Protection of Patents Under the Takings Clause" (Mossoff), 131

The History of the American Revolution (Ramsay), 91

Hoboken Land & Improvement Co., Murray's Lessee v., 128–29, 142

Hobson, Charles F., *The Great Chief Justice: John Marshall and the Rule of Law*, 199

Holder, Golan v., 94–95

Holt, Joseph, 178

Holzer, Harold, *Lincoln at Cooper Union*, 201

Hooker, Joseph, 18

Horton, John Theodore, *James Kent*, 199

Howard, Ames v., 151

Howe, Daniel Walker, 144, 158, 159–60, 170, 171; *The Political Culture of the American Whigs*, 198–99; *What God Hath Wrought*, 198

Hrdy, Camilla A., 153; "State Patent Laws in the Age of Laissez Faire," 199

Hunter's Lessee, Martin v., 90

Hylton, Keith, 8; *Laws of Creation*, 189

I

India Rubber Case. *See Goodyear v. Day*

Information Rules (Shapiro; Varian), 40

Institutes of the Law of England (Coke), 57, 129

intellectual property (IP): Constitution and, 119; as constitutional law, 27–28; criticisms of, 26–27 (*see also* anti-IP views); defined, 3–4; and economy, 31, 40; and employment, 55; in *Federalist Papers*, 67–69; as form of property, 68; and fruits of one's labor, 26; Jefferson and, 103; as kind of property, 81; Lincoln's two-track view of Constitution and, 163; in Lockean conception of property, 26–27; as non-exhaustible, 38, 39; as non-rivalrous, 38, 39; physical property compared, 31, 38–39; piracy of, xv–xvi; policy, 39–40; as property, 26–27, 39, 41, 46–47; rule of law and, 119,

132–33; vested rights in, 131–32. *See also* copyright(s); natural rights perspective for IP; patent(s)

Intellectual Property (IP) Clause: about, 6–7, 15; adaptation to changing circumstances, 95–96; and anti-monopolistic concerns, 59, 60; commercial trade monopolies vs. IP rights and, 110; and Congress, 27, 86, 95–96, 103–04, 136–37, 183; and federal government, 33; in *Federalist No. 43*, 50, 71–76, 78, 82–83; First Amendment and, 99; First Congress and, 93, 94–95; and IP as normative constitutional feature, 28; and IP policy, 39; Jefferson and, 12, 104; limiting principles, 120, 127; Madison and, 44, 50; and monopolies, 54, 61, 62, 63, 120, 127; natural rights and, 16; and natural rights to fruits of labor, 27; and normativity of copyright, 44; Reconstruction Amendments and, 183, 184; and states, 183; Story and, 143; and time period for rights, 82, 120, 127

intellectual property (IP) rights: during Antebellum era, 13, 135–36; antislavery principles and, 14, 163–64, 166, 168, 180, 183, 184; Bill of Rights and, 87; Blackstone on, 76–77; boundaries of, 40, 82; and branches of government, 12–13; Civil War and, 13, 14, 178–79;

classical liberal framework of government and, 94; commercial trade monopolies vs., 110; in common law, 72, 73–76; Confederation Congress and, 78–79; Congress and, 86, 93, 107, 120, 127; Constitution and, 64, 106–07, 127; constitutionalism and, 8, 93–94, 107, 121–22, 133; copyright included in, 3–4; criticisms of, 31, 53, 64, 114, 133 (*see also* anti-IP views); defined, 3–4; and digital age economy, 15; diminishment of, xv–xvi; due process of law and, 121, 128–29; enforceability of, 35–36, 37, 127; and entry into occupations, 56; equal protection of law(s) and, 121, 129–30; equal treatment of all property interests within, 121, 130; and exclusion, 56, 108; federal vs. state governments and, 6–7; in *Federalist No. 43*, 67–68; First Amendment and, 87; First Congress and, 12, 85–87, 91–92, 100; for free blacks, 184; free labor and, 163–64, 168–69, 173–74, 183, 184; fruits of one's labor and, 53, 55, 64, 68, 76–77, 114–15; Grant and, 181–83; idea/expression dichotomy in, 114; in Information Age, 40; infringement of, and court of law, 121, 127; Jefferson and, 105, 109–10, 116–17; limitations on, 55–56, 59, 60,

64, 104, 108; Lincoln and, 164, 170–71, 173–74; locus of power for protection of, 68; Madison and, 67–68, 81; and monopolies, 11, 53–56, 64, 108, 137, 159–61; patent rights included in, 3–4; property rights and, 10, 11, 12–13, 79, 108, 143–53; prudential calculations and, 5; real property applied to claims, 136; during Reconstruction, 165, 179–83; Reconstruction Amendments and, 13, 14, 166, 183, 184; and rights/freedom of others to create/invent, 56, 64; rule of law and, 12–13, 121–22, 127; self-ownership and, 164–65, 176, 184; social context of, 5; and specific literary works/inventions of authors/inventors, 55–56, 64; states and, 68, 78–79, 86, 92–93; Story on, 143; Takings Clause and, 121, 130–31; time period/terms for, 4, 5, 81, 109–10, 114; and trade competition, 56; unique features of, 5; utilitarianism of, 81–82; utility to the union and, 77–79; vested rights, 121; Washington's call for legislation securing, 96–97; N. Webster and, 93; Whigs and, 170. *See also* natural rights perspective for IP rights

Iredell, James, 63, 87–88; *Answers to Mr. Mason's Objections to the New Constitution*, 61–62

J

Jackson, Andrew, 137, 153, 156, 158, 159–61; *Veto Message Regarding the Bank of the United States*, 160–61

Jaffa, Harry V., *Crisis of the House Divided*, 167, 201

James Kent (Horton), 199

James Madison and the Struggle for the Bill of Rights (Labunski), 193–94

Jay, John, 69

Jefferson, Thomas: and administration of government, 12, 104–05, 115–17; as American revolutionary leader, 110; anti-IP views, 12, 103, 106, 107; and Bill of Rights, 107, 109–10; classical liberalism of, 103; and Constitution, 104, 105, 107, 109–10, 117; and Copyright Act of 1802, 105; and copyrights, 106; and Declaration of Independence, 17, 23, 103, 104–05, 110–13, 117; *Declaration of the Causes and Necessity of Taking Up Arms*, 110, 112; *First Inaugural Address*, 104–05, 116–17; and generational theory, 104, 108–9; on ideas, 105–06; and IP, 103; and IP Clause, 12, 104, 109–10; and IP rights, 108, 109–10; letter to McPherson, 105–06, 114; letter to Oliver Evans, 117; Locke and, 22, 23; as Lockean, 113; Madison's letters to/from, 59, 61, 63, 105,

107–08, 109–10; and
monopolies, 104, 105, 108–10;
mythology around, 12, 103;
and natural rights, 12, 22, 23,
113; *Notes on the State of
Virginia*, 109; in Paris, 12, 103,
107; and patents, 106, 114, 117;
private letters on IP, 105–06,
117; and property, 112,
113–14; and revolution of
1800, 116; *Second Inaugural
Address*, 113; as Secretary of
State, 107; *A Summary View of
the Rights of British America*, 58,
108, 110
Jefferson and the Rights of Man
(Malone), 109
The Jeffersonians (White), 115
*John Marshall and the Heroic Age of
the Supreme Court* (Newmyer),
199
Johnson, Andrew, 179, 180
Jordan, Evans v., 132
Journal of the Continental Congress,
48
Judiciary Act: of 1789, 86, 90, 92,
96; of 1800, 117

K
Kendall, Joshua, 45, 50, 51; *The
Forgotten Founding Father*, 194
Kent, James, 13, 136, 140, 153, 167;
*Commentaries on American
Law*, 138–39, 144; in *Gardner v.
Village of Newburgh*, 142
Kercheval, Samuel, 109
Ketcham, Ralph, 81
King, Rufus, 89
Kingsland, McClurg v., 132, 150

L
labor: chattel principle, 174; hired
vs. free, 172–73; mud-sill
theory of, 172; theory of value,
20–21. *See also* free labor; fruits
of one's labor(s)
Labunski, Richard, *James Madison
and the Struggle for the Bill of
Rights*, 193–94
Langbein, John H., "Chancellor
Kent and the History of Legal
Literature," 199
Larson, Edward J., *The Return of
George Washington*, 195–96
Laws of Creation (Cass; Hylton),
189
Lecture on Discoveries and Inventions
(Lincoln), 164, 171–72
*Lecture Read Before the Boston
Mechanics Institution* (Webster),
151
*Lecture Read Before the Society for
the Useful Diffusion of
Knowledge* (Webster), 151–52
Lee, Henry, 17, 111
Leland, Wilkinson v., 139
Levy, Leonard W., 113; "Property as
a Human Right," 197
Liberty's Blueprint (Meyerson), 195
Library of Congress, 165, 182
Licensing Act (U.K.), 57
Liebowitz, Larissa C., "Monopolies
and the Constitution," 191
Lincoln, Abraham: *Address to the
Wisconsin State Agricultural
Society*, 164, 172–73; and
antislavery ideology, 164,
173–74; assassination of, 179;
and Blackstone, 167; and

Chase, 177; and Civil War constitutionalism, 167, 183–84; in Congress, 164; *Cooper Union Address*, 90–91, 99, 175, 176; and Declaration of Independence, 17, 163–64, 167; and *Dred Scott v. Sanford*, 164, 175, 178; *Emancipation Proclamation*, 177; on First Congress, 90–91; and free labor, 169–70, 172, 173; and Freedom National, 177; on fruits of labor, 164, 169, 170; at Gettysburg, 163; *Gettysburg Address*, 166; and IP rights, 164, 170–71, 173–74; and labor, 13–14, 170–71; *Lecture on Discoveries and Inventions*, 164, 171–72; and link of free labor to IP rights, 163–64; and patents, 164, 170–71, 172; on personal/property rights relationship, 34–35; and Reconstruction Amendments, 167; *Reply to the New York Workingmen's Democratic Republican Association*, 170; as Republican, 171–74; *Speech at New Haven*, 175; *Speech on the Dred Scott Decision*, 175; and Thirteenth Amendment, 179; two-track view of Constitution, 163, 167–68; as Whig, 170, 171

Lincoln, Robert, 170

Lincoln at Cooper Union (Holzer), 201

Lincoln the Inventor (Emerson), 170–71, 201

literary property: Confederation Congress resolution regarding, 86; and copyright, 11, 43, 44, 49, 51, 59, 99, 155–56; natural rights and, 137, 145–46; N. Webster on, 155–56

Locke: A Very Short Introduction (Dunn), 187–88

Locke, John: Blackstone and, 36; and classical liberalism, 110; and Constitution, 24; definition of property, 10, 25, 26; *First Treatise of Government*, 18–19; on individual's labor and property interest, 168; influence of, 22–25; and Jefferson, 113; and natural rights, 18–20, 35–36; and private property rights, 77; on property, 20–21; and rule of law, 119; *Second Treatise of Government*, 18, 19–21, 33, 34, 35–36, 112, 113, 123, 168; and self-ownership, 164; *Two Treatises of Government*, 18, 22

M

Madison, James: about, 43–44; and Bill of Rights, 63, 98–99, 126–27; and Confederation Congress, 48, 93; and Constitution, 49, 88; and copyright, 44, 49, 51, 59, 99; definition of property, 26, 32, 33, 34, 41; *Detached Memoranda*, 60; *Federalist No. 10*, 79–80; *Federalist No. 37*, 69, 73–74; *Federalist No. 39*, 16, 61; *Federalist No. 41*, 77; *Federalist*

No. 43, 11, 16, 50, 61, 67–68, 69, 71–79, 82–83, 143; Federalist No. 49, 109; Federalist No. 51, 80; Federalist No. 62, 126; Federalist Nos. 37–40, 24; and Federalist Papers, 50–51, 69–70; in First Congress, 93; and fruits of personal labors, 25; and generational theory, 109; and government, 61, 80–81; on government and property rights, 37–38, 80; and government protection of property, 25; and IP Clause, 50; and IP rights, 67–68, 79, 81, 82; and IP rights in British common law, 72, 73–76; Jefferson's letters to/from, 61, 63, 105, 107–8, 109–10; as Jefferson's Secretary of State, 117; on justice and property rights, 80; and literary property, 49, 59; as member of House of Representatives, 89; and monopolies, 59–60, 61, 107–08; and natural rights, 23–24, 76–77; Notes of Debates in the Federal Convention of 1787, 50, 176; "On Property," 25, 34, 35, 113; "On Sovereignty," 24; and patent rights, 44, 76, 77; on personal vs. property rights, 34; on powers of federal government, 78; on property rights, 168; and social compact, 24; on social usefulness of IP rights, 82; on states and IP rights, 78–79; and tangible vs. intangible property,

26; and types of property, 49, 79, 81; Vices of the Political System of the United States, 49, 77, 78; and Virginia's copyright law, 79; Washington's letters to/from, 74–75, 97; N. Webster and, 43, 47, 48, 50

Malone, Dumas, 107, 113, 116; Jefferson and the Rights of Man, 109

The Man Who Saved the Union (Brands), 202

Mansfield, Lord, 72

Marshall, John: achievements of, 139–40; in Barron v. Baltimore, 141; and Burton v. Folsom, 149; in Cohens v. State of Virginia, 90; in Evans v. Jordan, 132; on Judiciary Act, 90; in McCulloch v. Maryland, 95; and patents as vested rights, 136, 150; and vested rights doctrine, 131, 141

Martin v. Hunter's Lessee, 90

Maryland, copyright in, 45

Maryland, McCulloch v., 95

Mason, George, 61–62, 74, 75

Massachusetts: Constitution, 120, 125; copyright in, 45–46

The Massachusetts Constitution of 1780 (Peters), 190–91

Matilda case, 177

McClurg v. Kingsland, 132, 150

McConnell, Michael W., 128; "Due Process As Separation of Powers," 192

McCulloch v. Maryland, 95

McCullough v. Virginia, 131–32

McDonald, Forrest, 97; Novus Ordo Seclorum, 22, 191; The

Presidency of George Washington, 196; *The Presidency of Thomas Jefferson*, 197–98
McKeever v. U.S., 131
McLean, John, 146–47
McPherson, Isaac, 105–06, 114
McQuewan, Bloomer v., 153
Merrill, Thomas W., *The Oxford Introductions to U.S. Law: Property*, 189
Meyerson, Michael I., *Liberty's Blueprint*, 195
Micklethwait, David, *Noah Webster and the American Dictionary*, 155, 194
Millar v. Taylor, 72, 74
Miller, John C., 71
Miller, William Lee, 49, 50, 81; *The Business of May Next*, 193
Milton, John, 110
Miracle at Philadelphia (Bowen), 191
monopolies: American Revolution and, 58–59; in Antebellum era, 137; Bill of Rights and, 54; in Britain, 53–54, 56–57, 108; Coke's definition, 57; commercial trade, 108, 110; common law and, 53–54, 56–57; Constitution and, 60–61, 63, 64; corporations and, 160; and freedom of the press, 58–59; government-conferred, 11, 53, 55, 59, 60–61, 64; Intellectual Property (IP) Clause and, 127; IP Clause and, 59, 60, 61, 62, 63, 120; IP rights and, 11, 53, 64, 137; IP rights vs., 53–56,

64, 159–61; Jackson and, 153; Jefferson and, 104, 105, 108–10; limited, 104, 108; Madison and, 59–60, 61, 107–08; patents as, 151; and printing press, 57; and property rights, 159–61; republican government and, 61; N. Webster on, 60
"Monopolies and the Constitution" (Calabresi; Liebowitz), 191
Montesquieu, Baron de, 119; *Spirit of the Laws*, 123–24
Morris, Robert, 89
Morse, O'Reilley v., 153
Morse, Samuel, 153
"*Morse v. Reid*" (Gordan), 195
Mossoff, Adam, 8–9, 106, 149–50, 153; "The Historical Protection of Patents Under the Takings Clause," 131
Murray's Lessee v. Hoboken Land & Improvement Co., 128–29, 142
The Mysterious Science of Law (Boorstin), 36, 190

N
Nachbar, Thomas B., 106
natural law: and civil government, 18, 19; and vested rights doctrine, 141
Natural Law and the Antislavery Constitutional Tradition (Dyer), 200
natural right(s): during Antebellum era, 136; Blackstone and, 36–37; classical liberalism and, 76; common law and, 6, 76–77; and Constitution, 23–24; and

copyright, 3–5, 45–46, 76, 147–48; Declaration of Independence and, 3, 28; defined, 3; in *Federalist No. 43*, 72–76; free labor and, 164; to fruits of own labors, 4, 32, 35, 164, 176; government and, 15, 16–17, 27, 28; and inequality, 79; and IP Clause, 16; Jefferson and, 12, 23, 113; and literary property, 137, 145–46; Locke and, 18–20, 35–36; Madison and, 23–24, 76–77; and ownership of property in slaves, 174–75; and patent rights, 3–5, 76, 150; personal vs., 35, 41; and private property during Antebellum era, 137–43; and property rights, 35, 36–37, 41, 174–75; and slavery, 176; and social utility, 82; state courts and, 142; Supreme Court and, 136–37; two-track understanding of property and, 32, 41; and vested rights for patents, 136

natural rights perspective for IP: Antebellum era and, 161; in *Federalist No. 43*, 72–76, 81; and intellectual vs. physical property rights, 32; IP Clause and, 16; Locke and, 25; Madison and, 25, 72–76, 81, 82; and rules for copyrights/patents, 39; and social utility, 82

natural rights perspective for IP rights: civil laws and, 35–36, 37; classical liberalism and, 6;

Constitution and, 6–7; Declaration of Independence and, 6; first principles vs. history and, 7; Jefferson and, 105; prudential judgments and, 5, 9; and unalienable rights to fruits of labors, 114–15; utilitarian/pragmatic defenses of IP vs., 8–9

Natural Rights Theories (Tuck), 187

Navigation Acts (U.K.), 58

A New Birth of Freedom (Belz), 202

New Hampshire, copyright in, 45–46

New Jersey, copyright in, 45–46

New York (state), copyright in, 45, 46

Newmyer, R. Kent, 139, 143, 149, 150; *John Marshall and the Heroic Age of the Supreme Court*, 199; *Supreme Court Justice Joseph Story*, 199–200

No State Shall Abridge (Curtis), 202

Noah Webster (Unger), 194

Noah Webster and the American Dictionary (Micklethwait), 155, 194

The Noblest Triumph (Bethell), 40, 188

North Carolina: copyright in, 46; refusal to ratify Constitution, 63

Northwest Ordinance of 1787, 90, 99, 179

Notes of Debates in the Federal Convention of 1787 (Madison), 50, 176

Notes on the State of Virginia (Jefferson), 109

Novus Ordo Seclorum (McDonald), 22, 191

O

Oakes, James: *Freedom National,* 176–77, 200; *The Scorpion's Sting,* 174–75, 200
"On Property" (Madison), 25, 34, 35, 113
"On Sovereignty" (Madison), 24
On the Rule of Law (Tamanaha), 191
Opinion on Citizenship (Bates), 165, 179, 184
O'Reilley v. Morse, 153
"Origin of Copy-Right Laws in the United States" (Webster), 156
Otis, James, 22, 110
The Oxford Introductions to U.S. Law: Property (Merrill; Smith), 189

P

Paine, Elijah, Jr., 145–46
Paine, Thomas, 22, 110; *Common Sense,* 58
Patent Act: of 1790, 12, 87, 92, 95–96, 97, 135, 154, 157; of 1793, 96, 137, 157; of 1836, 137, 157–58; of 1870, 165, 182; amendments during Antebellum era, 137, 158–59; amendments during Civil War, 179; First Congress and, 85–86, 91–92, 100
Patent Board, 95–96
Patent Office, 96, 137, 157, 170–71
patent rights: civil society and, 5; Congress and, 158–59; constitutionalism and, 6–7; defined, 3; free labor and, 172–73; government and, 4; included in IP rights, 3–4; Lincoln and, 164; Madison and, 44, 76, 77; natural rights and, 76, 150; natural rights principles and, 3–5; real property case law and, 150; societal improvements from inventions and, 152; states and, 153
patent(s): classical liberalism and, 16; conditions on granting of, 56; and *Dred Scott,* 178; free blacks and, 165, 178; Grant and, 182; Jefferson and, 106, 114, 117; jurisprudence during Antebellum era, 149–53; legislation during Antebellum era, 157–59; limitations on, 151; Lincoln and, 164, 170–71, 172; and monopolies, 151; as property rights, 150; Second Congress and, 96; slaves and, 165, 178; Takings Clause and, 131; Taney and, 153; terms for, 157, 182; vested rights for, 136, 150; Washington and, 97. *See also* intellectual property (IP)
Paterson, James, 89
Patriarcha (Filmer), 18
Peck, Fletcher v., 141
Pennock vs. Dialogue, 152
Pennsylvania: common law copyright in, 147; copyright in, 49
Personal Memoirs of U.S. Grant (Grant), 182–83

personal rights: natural right(s) vs., 35, 41; property rights vs., 32, 34–35, 41

Peters, Richard, 145

Peters, Ronald M., Jr., *The Massachusetts Constitution of 1780*, 190–91

Peters, Wheaton v., 136–37, 145–48

Phelps, Glenn A., *George Washington and American Constitutionalism*, 195

Philadelphia Convention of 1787. *See* Constitutional Convention

physical property: as exhaustible, 38, 39; IP vs., 31, 38–39; as rivalrous, 38, 39

Pierce, Henry L., 34–35

Plain, Honest Men (Beeman), 191

The Political Culture of the American Whigs (Howe), 198–99

The Political Philosophy of James Madison (Sheldon), 193

The Political Philosophy of Thomas Jefferson (Sheldon), 23, 113, 197

Polk, James K., 137, 161

The Presidency of George Washington (McDonald), 196

The Presidency of Thomas Jefferson (McDonald), 197–98

printing press, 57, 61, 164, 171

private property: government and rights to, 24–25; Locke and rights to, 77; and natural rights during Antebellum era, 137–43; protection laws and rights to fruits of personal labors, 4

proceeds of labor. *See* fruits of one's labors

property: alienable vs. unalienable, 113; antislavery views and, 174; Blackstone's definition, 34; civil laws and different types of, 32–33; classical liberalism and, 15, 33, 34–35, 113; Founding Fathers and, 31–32; fruits of labor as, 169, 170, 180; government protection of, 10, 25; inequality of distribution of, 79–80; intellectual vs. physical property and, 39; IP as, 26–27, 39, 41, 46–47, 68, 79, 81; Jefferson and, 112, 113–14; Locke on, 10, 20–21, 25, 26, 33; Madison's definition, 26, 32, 33, 41; in men, 14, 35, 165, 174–77, 175; natural rights of liberty/self-ownership and, 180; as originating in nature vs. society, 36–37; and pursuit of happiness, 35, 113; real, 136, 150; records system for, 37; and right to fruits of one's labors, 32; self-ownership and, 164, 174, 176, 183; tangible vs. intangible, 10, 26, 32–33, 38, 121; two-track understanding/definition of, 10, 32, 34–35, 41, 113; vested rights in, 131–32. *See also* intellectual property (IP); literary property; physical property; private property

"Property as a Human Right" (Levy), 197

"Property in Men" (Hamilton), 175–76

Property Matters (DeLong), 188

property rights: approach to intellectual property reform, 39–40; civil laws and, 10, 82; Civil War and, 13–14; classical liberalism and, 86; Constitution and, 139–41; and copyright, 146–47; defined, 3; ease of use/transfer and, 39; English constitution and, 36; and equal rights of all people, 4; and exclusion, 56; and freedom to create/invent, 11; fruits of labor(s) and, 38, 82, 146–47; government and, 17, 37–38, 51, 80, 125, 136, 138–39; in human beings, 175; IP rights as, 10, 11, 108; and IP rights during Antebellum era, 143–53; justice and, 80; labor and, 10, 168; Locke and, 168; Madison on, 168; and monopolies, 159–61; natural rights and, 10, 41, 105; patents as, 150; personal rights vs., 32, 34–35, 41; and property in personal rights, 33; prudential calculations and, 4; rule of law and, 37–38; and safeguarding of individualized decision-making, 37; slaves and, 174–75; social context of, 4–5; state courts and, 142; and time period of exclusive rights, 4. *See also* intellectual property (IP) rights
"Property Rights Systems and the Rule of Law" (Cass), 192
public good: in *Federalist Papers*, 68–69, 79–80; self interest and, 68

"Publius" *(Federalist Papers)*, 70–71
Puffendorf, Samuel von, 18, 22

R
Ramsay, David, *The History of the American Revolution*, 91
real property: applied to IP claims, 136; and patent rights, 150
Reconstruction: Grant and, 181; IP legislation during, 165; IP rights under, 179–83
Reconstruction Amendments: about, 166; as completion of Constitution of 1787, 167; Grant and, 181; and IP Clause, 184; and IP rights, 13, 14, 183, 184; IP rights legislation and, 166; Lincoln and, 167; and scope of IP protections under IP Clause, 166; Supreme Court and, 181
"Rediscovering Blackstone" (Alschuler), 190
Reinstein, Robert J., *Completing the Constitution*, 202
Remini, Robert, 88–89, 93, 98
Reply to the New York Workingmen's Democratic Republican Association (Lincoln), 170
Report on Public Credit (Hamilton), 92
Retroactive Legislation (Troy), 193
The Return of George Washington (Larson), 195–96
Rhode Island: copyright in, 45–46; refusal to ratify Constitution, 63
Roane, Spencer, 116
Robinson Crusoe (Defoe), 23

Rosen, Gary, 24; *American Compact*, 193
rule of law: about, 119–22; American Revolution and, 120, 124; basic precepts, 119, 122; classical liberalism and, 86, 119; Congress and, 120, 127; Constitution and, 122–23, 126, 132–33; constitutionalism and, 119, 120, 122–27, 132–33; copyright and, 44; Declaration of Independence and, 124; defined, 122; and equal protection of the law, 121; in *The Federalist Papers*, 126; and free/just society, 119; and government, 37–38, 119, 122; and individual property rights, 86; and individual rights protection, 119; and IP, 119, 132–33; and IP rights, 12–13, 121–22, 127; in Locke's *Second Treatise*, 19–20, 123; republican government and, 125–26; states and, 120, 124–25
The Rule of Law in America (Cass), 122, 192
Rumsey, James, 97
Rutherforth, Thomas, 22

S
Sacred Fire of Liberty (Banning), 193
A Sacred Union of Citizens (Spalding; Garrity), 196
Sanford, Dred Scott v., 153, 164, 165, 174, 175, 178, 179, 180
Schultz, Mark, 8–9
The Scorpion's Sting (Oakes), 174–75, 200
Second Congress, and patents, 96

Second Inaugural Address (Jefferson), 113
Second Treatise of Government (Locke), 18, 19–21, 33, 34, 35–36, 112, 113, 123, 168
self-ownership: and IP rights, 164–65, 176, 184; and property, 174, 176, 183
separation of powers: and due process of law, 128–29; in Locke's *Second Treatise*, 19–20; Montesquieu and, 123; vested rights and, 142
Seward, William, 177
Shapiro, Carl, *Information Rules*, 40
Sheldon, Garrett Ward: *The Political Philosophy of James Madison*, 193; *The Political Philosophy of Thomas Jefferson*, 23, 113, 197
Sherman, Roger, 89
Sidney, Algernon, 110; *Discourses Concerning Government*, 21–22
Sketches of American Policy (Webster), 47
slavery: abolition in federal territories, 177; Constitution and, 167, 169–70, 174–76; First Congress and restriction of, 90; natural rights and, 176; as property in men, 35; states vs. federal government and, 176–77. *See also* antislavery principles
slaves: and citizenship, 165; and patents, 165, 178; right of property in, 174–75. *See also* blacks
Smith, Henry E., *The Oxford Introductions to U.S. Law: Property*, 189

South Carolina, copyright in, 45
Spalding, Matthew, 97; *A Sacred Union of Citizens,* 196
Sparks, Jared, 149; *The Writings of George Washington,* 149
Speech at New Haven (Lincoln), 175
Speech on the Dred Scott Decision (Lincoln), 175
Spirit of the Laws (Montesquieu), 123–24
Sprague, Blanchard v., 151
State of Virginia, Cohens v., 90
"State Patent Laws in the Age of Laissez Faire" (Hrdy), 199
states: and Bill of Rights, 180; and common law, 74–75, 147; and Constitution, 138; and copyright, 43, 44–48, 49, 154; courts, and natural rights/property rights principles, 142; Equal Protection Clause and, 183; and freedom of the press, 61, 63; IP Clause and, 183; and IP rights, 68, 78–79, 86, 92–93; legislatures in *The Federalist,* 70; and patent rights, 153; ratification of Constitution, 63; ratification of Constitutional amendments, 88; and rule of law, 120, 124–25; and slavery, 176–77
Stationers' Company, 57
Statute of Anne (U.K.), 57, 73, 74, 93, 109
Statute of Monopolies (U.K.), 57, 73
Steiner, Mark E., "Abraham Lincoln and the Rule of Law Books," 200–01

Stone, Wyeth v., 151
Stoner, James R., Jr., 75; *Common Law and Liberal Theory,* 190; *Common-Law Liberty,* 190
Story, Joseph: in *Ames v. Howard,* 151; in *Blanchard v. Sprague,* 151; in *Burton v. Folsom,* 148–49; *Commentaries on the Constitution of the United States,* 72, 130–31, 143, 150, 153; and copyright/patents as private property, 13; *A Familiar Exposition of the Constitution of the United States,* 143; on Judiciary Act, 90; Lincoln and, 167; in *Martin v. Hunter's Lessee,* 90; and patents, 150–51, 153; and property rights protection as core function of government, 136; respect for property rights, 140; in *Terrett v. Taylor,* 139; in *Wilkinson v. Leland,* 139; in *Wyeth v. Stone,* 151
Strouzh, Gerald, *Alexander Hamilton and the Idea of Republican Self-Government,* 195
A Summary View of the Rights of British America (Jefferson), 58, 108, 110
Sumner, Charles, 165, 177, 178
Supreme Court: and *Ashcroft v. Eldred,* 94; in *Barron v. Baltimore,* 141, 180; on Bill of Rights applying to states, 180; Chase in, 177; and fair use doctrine, 100; and First Congress, 94–95; in *Gayler v. Wilder,* 132; and *Golan v.*

Holder, 94–95; Mashall as Chief Justice, 139–40; in *McClurg v. Kingsland*, 132, 150; in *McCullough v. Virginia*, 131–32; and natural rights understanding of copyright/patent, 136–37; and patent protection, 149; and property rights, 139–41; and Reconstruction Amendments, 181; reporters, 145–48; and Takings Clause, 131; in *Terrett v. Taylor*, 139; and vested rights doctrine, 131–32, 141; in *Wheaton v. Peters*, 136–37, 145–49

Supreme Court Justice Joseph Story (Newmyer), 199–200

Supreme Neglect (Epstein), 192

T

Takings (Epstein), 192

Takings Clause: federalism and, 141; and IP rights, 121, 130–31; and patents, 131

Tamanaha, Brian Z., *On the Rule of Law*, 191

Taney, Roger, 140; in *Bloomer v. McQuewan*, 153; in *Dred Scott v. Sanford*, 153, 164, 174, 175; in *Gayler v. Wilder*, 153; and Jackson's *Veto Message Regarding the Bank of the United States*, 160; in *O'Reilley v. Morse*, 153

Taylor, Millar v., 72, 74

Taylor, Terrett v., 139

Tenth Amendment, 63

Terrett v. Taylor, 139

Thirteenth Amendment, 166, 179, 180, 183

"Thomas Jefferson and the Patent Act of 1793" (Walterscheid), 198

Thompson, Smith, 147–48

Thornton, William, 117

time period(s)/terms: for copyright, 154–56, 194–95; of exclusion, 108; in IP Clause, 82, 120, 127; of IP rights, 4, 5, 81, 109–10, 114; for patents, 157, 182

"To Form the Character of the American People" (diGiacomantonio), 196–97

To Secure These Rights (Gerber), 197

Troy, Daniel E., *Retroactive Legislation*, 193

Trumbull, John, 88

Tuck, Richard, *Natural Rights Theories*, 187

Two Treatises of Government (Locke), 18, 22

U

Unger, Harlow Giles, 47; *Noah Webster*, 194

The Unvarnished Doctrine (Dworetz), 20, 188

Upham, Charles Wentworth, 149; *Life of Washington*, 149

utilitarianism: of IP rights, 81–82; natural rights and, 82

V

Van Buren, Martin, 137, 161

Vanatta, Sean, 178

Varian, Hal R., *Information Rules*, 40

Vattel, Emmerich de, 22, 113
vested rights: of intellectual
  property protection, 121;
  natural law and, 141; patents
  and, 150; in property, 131–32;
  and separation of powers, 142;
  Supreme Court and, 131–32
*Veto Message Regarding the Bank of
  the United States* (Jackson),
  160–61
*Vices of the Political System of the
  United States* (Madison), 49,
  77, 78
Village of Newburgh, Gardner v.,
  142
Vindicating the Founders (West),
  188–89
Virginia: Constitutional
  Convention, 34; copyright in,
  44, 45, 47–48, 79
Virginia, McCullough v., 131–32

W
Walterscheid, Edward C., "Thomas
  Jefferson and the Patent Act of
  1793," 198
Washington, Bushrod, 149, 150
Washington, George: *Annual
  Message to Congress* (1790), 96;
  and Constitution, 97; and
  Copyright Act, 87, 97; *Fairfax
  County Resolves,* 58; and
  Federalist Papers, 70–71, 97;
  Madison's letters to/from,
  74–75, 97; and Northwest
  Ordinance, 90; and Patent Act,
  12, 87, 97; and patents, 97; and
  Philadelphia Convention,
  96–97; publication of papers

of, 149; N. Webster and, 43,
  47–48, 50, 97
Webster, Daniel: about, 136; on
  copyright as fruits of labor, 146;
  and copyright laws, 137; and
  copyright/patents, 13; in
  *Dartmouth College v.
  Woodward,* 141; as "defender of
  the Constitution," 13, 136, 140;
  and due process in property
  rights, 142; in *Goodyear v. Day,*
  152–53; and inventions,
  151–52; and IP rights, 170;
  *Lecture Read Before the Boston
  Mechanics Institution,* 151;
  *Lecture Read Before the Society
  for the Useful Diffusion of
  Knowledge,* 151–52; and
  Lincoln's patent application,
  171; and Patent Act of 1836,
  158; and patents, 152–53; in
  Pennock vs. Dialogue, 152; and
  perpetual common law
  copyright, 146; and property
  rights, 140; in Senate, 156; N.
  Webster's letter to, 154–55; in
  *West River Bridge Company v.
  Dix,* 141; in *Wheaton v. Peters,*
  145, 146
Webster, Noah: about, 43; *The
  American Dictionary of the
  English Language,* 60, 77, 154,
  156; *American Spelling Book,* 45,
  155; and Confederation
  Congress, 48–49, 93; and
  Connecticut General Assembly,
  44–45; and Constitutional
  Convention, 50, 93; and
  copyright, 43, 44–48, 51, 60,

97, 154–56; *An Examination into the Leading Principles of the New Federal Constitution,* 51; on *The Federalist,* 50; on fruits of labors and copyright, 46; and H.R. 10, 93; on IP as property, 46–47; and IP rights, 93; on justice, 80; and Madison, 43, 47, 48, 50, 60; on monopoly, 60; and natural rights understanding of literary property, 137; "Origin of Copy-Right Laws in the United States," 156; *Sketches of American Policy,* 47; and Washington, 43, 47–48, 50, 97

Weld, Theodore, 177

West, Thomas G., 21–22; *Vindicating the Founders,* 188–89

West River Bridge Company v. Dix, 141

What God Hath Wrought (Howe), 198

Wheaton, Henry, 145, 146, 150

Wheaton v. Peters, 136–37, 145–48

Whig party, 170–71

White, G. Edward, "The Chancellor's Ghost," 199

White, Leonard D.: *The Federalists,* 196; *The Jeffersonians,* 115

Wilder, Gayler v., 132, 153

Wilkinson v. Leland, 139

Williamson, Hugh, 89

Woodward, Dartmouth College v., 141

The Writings of George Washington (Sparks), 149

Wyeth v. Stone, 151